Carry Me Home

BEN COHEN

Carry Me Home

MY AUTOBIOGRAPHY

with Sarah Edworthy

EBURY
PRESS

3 5 7 9 10 8 6 4 2

Ebury Press, an imprint of Ebury Publishing
20 Vauxhall Bridge Road
London SW1V 2SA

Ebury Press is part of the Penguin Random House group of companies
whose addresses can be found at global.penguinrandomhouse.com

Penguin
Random House
UK

First published by Ebury Press in 2015

www.eburypublishing.co.uk

A CIP catalogue record for this book is available from the British Library

ISBN 9781785031274 (hardback)
ISBN 9781785031281 (trade paperback)

Printed and bound in Great Britain by Clays Ltd, St Ives PLC

Penguin Random House is committed to a sustainable future
for our business, our readers and our planet. This book is made
from Forest Stewardship Council® certified paper.

For Isabelle and Harriette.
And for Mum and Dad.

CONTENTS

PREFACE

RESPECT THE JERSEY

You have to give your all in a game or you don't survive to play again.

Each time I won international honours – England Colts, Under 21s, Sevens, 'Clive Woodward's England' and the British Lions – I donated my shirt to the Northampton Old Scouts Rugby Football Club. I felt it was important to share those jerseys. This was the junior club that welcomed me as a thundering, unskilled, enthusiastic 13-year-old back in the early autumn of 1991 and launched the beginning of a rugby venture that I shared with my dad – who knew absolutely nothing about the game. We embarked on a journey fuelled by the tantalising mirage-cum-dream of me one day winning the right to wear an England jersey. And we got there. We had to prove a point or two, or three or four, along the way, but Dad saw me run out in all but one of those representative jerseys.

I was photographed regularly by the local paper handing over a shirt to the club president to hang on the clubhouse wall and inspire the youngsters – perhaps Northampton lads, like me, not necessarily from a 'traditional' rugby background, who might discover a similar all-consuming passion and take their game to the highest level. It must have been like Groundhog Day for the photographer: me, holding up another white shirt to display the rose badge and my initials on the front, and Keith Shurville receiving it, both of us smiling broadly. Same act, same pose. I loved the thought of my shirts hanging proudly on the wall, of giving something back and letting youngsters get a sniff of top-level rugby. Each shirt has a story; each one has memories woven into its fibres. But later, when I surveyed the display for the first time, I became upset. These shirts that I'd fought so hard for had been folded up multiple times and put in unsuitably small frames. There is an accepted way of framing shirts and this was not it. It seemed to me that there was no proper appreciation of the England badge; no respect for what each shirt represented. What kid would be inspired by a ball of material like that? So I took them back. Everyone thought it was a joke, but I was adamant.

'Do you have *any idea*,' I said, as I reclaimed them, 'how much went into these shirts?'

So much work and pain that I wouldn't want to live my life again.

PROLOGUE

13 NOVEMBER 2000

Dad was always the first person I'd call from the England camp when I heard I'd been picked to play in the starting XV. That was our custom and it was sacrosanct. He'd been my closest rugby mate ever since I was 13, a larger-than-life presence on the sidelines who never understood the rules – which was a running joke – but willed me on in the game with the 'wrong-shaped' ball that he could see I loved.

I shared my daily ups and downs with him. He wasn't a pushy dad; he didn't know enough about the game for that. It wasn't in his nature either to be one of those 'OAFS' (over-anxious fathers) that coaches dread. He was simply a proud family man who wanted me to embrace something I was good at and see where passion and effort could take me. Or take *us*, actually, as a family with a heritage. His motto was: 'Whatever you're good at, be the best at.' For Dad, it didn't seem unrealistic to encourage me to toil away in order to play at the highest level. His older brother George had gone from kicking a ball around the streets of war-damaged Fulham with his brothers to being part of the legendary football team that won the World Cup in 1966. Dad was extremely proud of his brother's honours. George, he'd tell me, had always worked hard.

For nearly three weeks now, Dad had been lying in a hospital bed in a high dependency unit on Benham Ward in Northampton General Hospital. His allotted bay was decorated with a scattering of cards and flowers, and personalised with a sign above his bed written in biro by Mum on a blue hospital-issue paper hand towel: <u>DO NOT</u> SHAVE, PETER HAS A BEARD + MOUSTACHE! Dad was wired up to monitors and machines, paralysed down his right side and prone to seizures. His attempts at speech were distorted by a tracheostomy tube that had been inserted to ease his breathing. I missed his affectionate daily growl, 'Who loves ya?' We all did. He was a good talker, a proper listener and he galvanised us all to follow our passions in life and have plenty of fun along the way. For my sister Sam, his eldest, it was horses and her kids. For my older brother Justin, motorbikes, music and Eternity, the nightclub business they ran together. For me, it was rugby, a sport which I'd discovered by pure accident. And for Mum, Dad was simply her rock. For a month now, we'd been existing in limbo, confused at seeing our indestructible family stalwart – possibly the most undentable, streetwise bloke on the planet – left so vulnerable and debilitated, suffering all sorts of physical indignities.

I'd pop in to see him every single day in my tracksuit and trainers, just like I'd pop around to Mum and Dad's for a chat after training – outwardly calm and pragmatic, trying to carry on as normal – but the news never seemed good. Dad was the glue in our family. None of us were coping well with his condition. I'd spent the last four weeks bottling up tension about how things would pan out for him, angry about why he was in this state, anxious, fearful and confused about the future, but I'd let myself relax a bit when the touch-and-go stage was over. There were signs that he was starting to improve. He'd come out of the terrifying coma where he lay motionless, as good as dead, and begun to spend a few hours a day in a wheelchair on the ward. Justin – Jay, as we call him – and I had even wheeled him outside for some fresh air. He was paralysed down one side, still wrung by seizures and reliant on tubes and the full-on care of nurses, but his condition had calmed from grave or extremely critical. Things were looking up … ish.

Eighty miles away, cocooned in the luxurious chintzy world of the England team's country-house hotel, I paced around the antique four-poster bed in my room. I couldn't wait to share my selection news. Renewing our rugby conversation would boost Dad. It'd be business as usual between us and give him something to look forward to. He'd have a game to watch on

TV on Saturday to help tolerate the hours anchored helplessly to his hospital bay. Rugby, not for the first time in his life, would help him regain some pride.

Dad, more than anyone, understood how elated I would be to hear from Clive Woodward that I'd proved myself on a tough summer 2000 tour to South Africa, and that I would be playing on the wing against Australia, the world champions, at Twickenham in the first of the Autumn Internationals. Some pundits expressed surprise that I'd been chosen ahead of the versatile and nimble Austin Healey to play in the backs alongside Mike Catt, Mike Tindall, Dan Luger and Matt Perry, and that would make telling Dad all the more satisfying. He'd be well chuffed. I'd worried my England career had only ever been as a stopgap for the often injured Dan Luger, but I'd done enough for Clive to find a way to accommodate both of us. He'd referred to the pair of us as a 'fantastic strike force' that he wanted to see play together for the first time. Dad would love that. He thrived on talk of drive and ambition.

So I phoned Mum, who was sitting with him in on the ward, and told her I'd be winning my seventh cap. She passed on the news and his eyes gleamed. Despite the physical effort it must have cost him, Dad lifted his good arm and punched his fist in the air with real pride.

That was it. Our last father–son interaction.

The next morning dawned a true blue-sky day, bright, sunny, with the rustle of excitement and anticipation that comes in the week before the Autumn Internationals. England, as Six Nations champions, were drawn against the Tri-Nations champions Australia in the first Test, followed by games against Argentina and South Africa in successive weeks. I loved the whole set-up at Pennyhill Park, the spa hotel at Bagshot in Surrey, which is the official training base for the England rugby team. Tuesdays were always full-on. Up early for breakfast, meetings or treatments from 8.30am, a strengthening session, then I'd stick with the backs and we'd walk, run, prepare attacking moves. Between unit work and lunch, those of us chosen for media duty would slip off and come back for a rigorous afternoon training session. I had just finished radio interviews. The huddle of journalists had asked after Dad, and I had spoken of his recovery, how he had come out of a coma, then been transferred out of Intensive Care and was now looking forward to watching the game on television. I said I was feeling happier about my rugby now he was improving and that I'd like to dedicate my selection and my seventh cap to him: 'Facing the world champions is the biggest game of my life and I want it to be for my dad.'

I was desperate to snatch some lunch, but as I left the press call I got a message that Clive wanted to speak to me privately. This was odd. He pulled me aside and asked me to follow him. He led me out of the creeper-clad hotel building, well away from anyone, and we headed through the manicured hotel grounds and down a beautiful woodland path. I was thinking, this must be bad. *Shit*, he's going to drop me. He's only just picked me and now he's changed his mind. I could see that he could detect that I was wondering what the hell was going on, but still we walked on further away.

Clive led me to a quiet spot and we stopped at a bench. I remember the shadows of the leaves under the sunlight playing on the earth around us. He quickly sat me down.

'There's no easy way for me to tell you this,' he said quietly. 'Your mum has just called and asked me to break the news that your dad passed away this morning.'

I stared at him. Sometimes, because of my poor hearing, spoken words take time for me to absorb. Clive knew nothing about my hearing problems so he couldn't possibly have understood why I was instinctively looking at his lips shaping the words that morning. Unreal words. Feeling as if I were deep under water, I did register his next comment:

'Your mum is fine and she wants you to go home and say goodbye to your dad.'

He gave me a big hug and said everyone in the England camp was there to support me, and then he looked over his shoulder. I followed his glance and saw Matt Dawson standing a discreet 40 yards behind us. It was typical Clive to think I might immediately need to be with someone I knew well, a Northampton team-mate who knew my dad and was fond of him too. Daws was six years older than me, someone I looked up to and could trust. He'd been with me a few weeks back to visit Dad when he was in the Intensive Care Unit at Queen's Medical Centre in Nottingham, so he knew what had been going on. It must have been a shock for him too, and he'd trailed at a distance to lend his support. Clive had not known how I might react.

We stood there, a trio frozen in surreal formation. There was Clive, on the cusp of preparing the cream of the country's rugby players for a massive game, England's opener in the Autumn Internationals, breaking this completely shattering news to the 22-year-old kid in his team. There was Daws, unsure how best to support me, sacrificing his time at a buzzing England camp to drive me home. And there was me: my world at an end on such a beautiful day.

CHAPTER 1

WHO LOVES YA?

Mum had had her two children and wasn't planning on having any more. My sister Sam was born in 1973, when Mum was just 21, and Justin in 1974. Dad was keen for another child. He wanted a football team. And Mum's friends were having more, but she thought carefully before considering a third child. Could they afford it? Did she have enough love to give? The answer to both must have been yes, because she was out buying a pram before she was even pregnant with me.

Love was the most important thing to my mum in creating her family. She'd had a very unhappy childhood, being moved between care homes in Surrey, Putney and Slough, and hadn't experienced love as a child. She said homes provide you with everything you need to live, except for love. There was no way she wanted her own kids to repeat what she went through. The thing she wanted for us above all was to grow up with a lot of affection and emotional security. She sort of over-loved us. There were stages when we had money and, as kids, we had everything we wanted, but, even when my parents lost everything, our family life was still based on warmth and fun. My dad never left the house without shouting 'Love ya, love ya' to my mum. 'Who loves ya?' was his regular greeting to us kids.

Mum knew instinctively I was a boy. She carried me to the front, and apparently I played football in her tummy, though the doctor said the kicking was actually hiccups. We were living in the Northampton suburb of Kingsthorpe when she went into Barratt Maternity Home and was induced to go into labour. I was born on 14 September 1978. The midwife didn't even have time to get her apron on. Within 55 minutes, labour was over and I'd arrived – bang on midday, which was funny because they'd been wondering how they should style the time on the official birth record if I was born at exactly noon (the answer is '12 o'clock midday', as it happens). I weighed in at nine pounds, twelve and three-quarter ounces, and measured 57cm in length, with a head circumference of 36cm. The doctor asked what my parents were going to call me. 'Ben,' Mum said. 'Ooh, Big Ben,' he replied.

The day I was born was the first time Mum had ever left Jay. Concerned about his feelings, she suggested Dad take him to the shops to buy him a present, and pick up one for him to give to his new brother. Dad also bought a card. Inside he wrote, 'Thank you Mum. Hello Ben, from Sam and Justin.' Like most older siblings put out by the arrival of a new baby in the household, Jay resented the time Mum spent breast-feeding me. He thought she was favouring her new child. Then she got mastitis because I had a hell of a suck. She developed a raging fever and the doctor gave her a week to dry up. After that I was on formula milk, gallons of it. There are pictures of Mum sitting up in bed holding me, with my sister holding a bottle in reserve, keen to help. I was such a hungry baby she was feeding me tiny bits of boiled egg from the age of three weeks.

My father was the youngest of three brothers. We didn't see much of Uncle Len, the eldest, who with his thick-rimmed square glasses looked a bit like Michael Caine, but Dad and his older brother George were very close.

Andrew and Anthony, Uncle George's sons, were fascinated by the feeding process and asked if they could watch Mum breastfeed me. Before my mouth got on it, milk spurted across the room and hit them. The boys still laugh about that to this day.

We never knew Dad's parents, who died before he even met Mum, so we had no grandparents on either side. In fact Mum later advertised for some in the local paper – literally paid for a small notice seeking people who might want to be honorary grandparents – but she swiftly parted ways with the couple who replied for the job. They had been attracted by our surname and thought their role was to steep us in strict Jewish ways whereas

Mum just wanted a nice old couple to indulge us with little gifts and affection! Besides, we aren't even Jewish.

Mum kept a book called *Baby Days and Ways,* which she inscribed to 'Our Dearest Son, You are forever in our Hearts'. There is no danger of any of my infant milestones being forgotten. My first word was 'Baabaa' – arguably an early indication that rugby would be 'my thing' as it matches the nickname given to the Barbarians (not that my parents would have known that). I first smiled at four weeks, sat up and crawled at seven months, stood up at ten months, and ten days later started walking. Clearly I was keen to get active, and my favourite bedtime story was *The Gingerbread Man*: 'Run, run, as fast as you can. You can't catch me I'm the gingerbread man.' Mum and Dad recorded every little target reached, writing remarks in the baby book and sticking in family photos. Mum wrote down my weight every month until I was two years old (when I hit the scales at two stone, eight pounds), the date every one of my milk teeth broke through the gum, and my melodramatic health record.

I was a very poorly baby. Ten weeks after I was born – and, with classic timing, three days before Christmas – I was taken, screaming in great pain, to Northampton General, where I was diagnosed with a hernia. The doctor taught mum how to relieve the pain and sent us all home. Basically, she had to hold me upside down and the little sac of fluid that had dropped from my abdomen would go back through the muscle gap and the pain would cease. If it didn't fall back into place by that method,

Mum had to push it up manually. She did this, but a few days later, I was writhing in agony and she rushed me to the GP, who referred her straight back to the hospital. I would need an operation to fix the muscle gap, but it was Christmas and they were short of staff so they asked us come back a few days later to have it fixed on 29 December.

A year later, I spent Christmas and New Year with chicken pox, and a few months after that I tripped on a hot water bottle, hit the dressing table in my parents' bedroom and broke a small bone in my nose. There were several incidents resulting in not-quite-broken legs and eventually a bona fide fracture. On one occasion, I saw Jay and Sam across the road coming home from school. Sam called me over. My sister was one to be obeyed. (Once, ignoring her bid to stop me jumping on the leather chesterfield, she threatened me with her horse whip – and followed through.) Rushing impetuously across the road to meet them, I was hit by a car but luckily didn't hit my head on the kerb when I landed. An ambulance took me to hospital. No bones were broken. I was just badly bruised all over and gave everyone a shock by falling into a deep sleep or mini-coma for an hour. I stayed the night for observation as all the readings on the monitors went right down. Briefly there was a panic on, but I survived!

On another occasion, aged about four or five, I was playing in the car park that Dad was running. I was at a stage when I loved wearing my wellies, whatever the weather – and thank God for those wellies. It was the end of the day and the car park was emptying out. I slipped in front of an exiting car and its wheel went right over my leg. Another ambulance. The paramedic couldn't believe my leg wasn't broken and said two things had saved me. For one thing, the car was only doing about two miles per hour, and secondly, the rubber of my beloved baggy wellies had folded around and cushioned my leg. I was a pain in the hospital, constantly jumping around. Mum was saying, 'Lie down, you're meant to be injured,' and the staff were saying, 'I think you can take the little tike home.' I was well known as a character as a small child.

Throughout these years, I also suffered from recurrent tonsillitis, adenoid problems and heavy nosebleeds. Aged just three years and ten months, I was back into hospital to have my tonsils and adenoids removed, and my nose cauterised to prevent further bleeds. I was one of the youngest children the doctors could ever remember needing to have all that done. I also had dozens of ear infections which blew up out of nowhere. Each time I became ill, I'd get a sudden high temperature, and the pressure from the infection perforated my ear drums. Over the years they became very scarred, and that's probably why I have hearing problems – though no one realised it at the time.

Despite my medical dramas, I was a happy, active child with a mop of very straight, white blond hair. As Dad was very dark, with brown eyes, I was teased and called 'the milkman's'. My favourite toys were things that moved – roller balls, cars, tractors and a push-along Panda bear.

My first summer was spent on the beach in Javea, in Spain. We travelled by caravanette, and there are photographs of me climbing over my dad, who is face down on the sand, and preparing to whack him with an inflatable hammer. In another, Dad is hovering protectively over me as I sit on a step looking like a bandit in a multi-coloured sombrero.

Shortly before my second Christmas, we moved around the corner from Birch Barn Way to Greenhills Road. That's the first house I can properly remember. There was a playroom in the garage; in fact, every house we moved to – and we moved a lot – my parents would create a den for us in the garage. Mum always knew how to turn a new house into a home, and part of that was providing space for us kids. We were a loud, loving family, always having fun. Mum loved making a big fuss of birthdays and Christmas. That was a big thing for her. Dad used to dress up as Father Christmas – I always remember that, and him carrying me up the stairs to bed every night.

This is my baby book entry at age two (so I think I may have had help from Mum): 'I'm getting quite big. I weigh about three stone. I still have blond hair. I get my clothes dirty very quickly with sweets and drink. I go to bed at 7pm. I still like my bottle. I love to play with my cars, watch cartoons and Morph. I love the Monster Munch advert.'

Aged three, Mum writes: 'Ben goes to nursery all day Tuesday to Friday. He's a very active child, but sleeps well at night. He's in the bottom bunk now. He's quite slow in talking ...'

And there, I believe, is the first indication of my deafness… Before long, quite regularly, I'd be waking up in the middle of the night in agony. I'd recognise the scenario. I'd be in great pain. I'd see the hall light on. I'd cry, and Mum and Dad would know I had another earache. It was so routine they'd almost wait to see pus on the pillow to know whatever it was had burst; then there was huge relief for everyone in knowing the pain would go.

My parents had moved from London to Northampton before I was born because Dad had been offered a job running the Grand Hotel car park in the town centre. My birth certificate boldly states that the occupation of Peter John Cohen is 'Car Park Proprietor'. He grew up in the Fulham area, living first in Walham Green and then at the top of the North End Road in West Kensington. He'd had a few jobs in London, lorry driving and working at Harrods, where he met my mum Lana Harrison, who worked as a veterinary assistant in the pet department. Harrods' pet department was more like a zoo in the late 1960s/ early 1970s; full of exotic animals, not just domestic pets. Dad was manager of the deliveries area and he first glimpsed Mum when she was pushing a wheelbarrow of animal poo. At least, that what she likes to say. She was well known among other staff on account of getting locked in one night and having to be rescued by the police. The pet department was up on the roof and she'd got trapped after closing time. The internal security doors came down and locked into position, so she had to get the staff lift down to the basement to find a phone and call the police. People talked to her a lot after that drama, and she kept hearing word that Peter Cohen in deliveries fancied her, so one day she went down to have a look. 'Where's Pete?' she asked Bob Jones, the manager, and he said, 'He's gone. His mum has died.'

It was a horrible accidental death. My grandmother was crushed by the rear wheels of an articulated lorry as she waited on the pavement at the traffic lights where Lillie Road crosses the North End Road in west London. She was on her way to work at Marley Tiles store where she was manager. One minute she was bristling with life, waving up at a window cleaner she knew as a friend of her son George; the next minute she'd been run over, her body left with indentations from the impact. The lorry was huge, and she must have thought it had gone past but it had three sets of wheels and the rear axle was still turning the tight corner. Dad was inconsolable and had to be sedated for a week. He was close to her, a true Mummy's boy. She had lost her husband, my grandfather, eight years earlier to cancer and she relied on her youngest son. It was just the two of them in the flat, and their dog. Her other sons, Len and George, had left home. Mum says it was ironic because she'd never have married Dad if his mum hadn't died. No one would have been good enough for him. His brothers fondly accepted he was the apple of their mother's eye. She'd already made a close friend of hers promise to look after him in the event of anything happening to her. As Mum tells it, when Dad came back to Harrods after the tragedy she no longer thought of him as a romantic prospect. She just felt terribly sorry for him and she ended up agreeing to go on a date. He used to go home from Harrods to walk his dog, a big yellow Labrador which he thought was a Rhodesian Ridgeback – but she, with her animal expertise, put him right!

Dad was ten years older than Mum, and quickly became her rock: a husband, lover and father figure in one. She'd had a very unhappy childhood in care, and had run away a couple of times. Mum had experienced violence, and awful things happened to her that she doesn't ever want to talk about. She had no relationship with her parents. It was my father who rescued her and gave her happiness. He adored her. And she loved his sense of humour and his kindness. He was a rough, tough guy who had been taught good manners and had the proverbial heart of gold. His sole aim was to look after her and the big happy family they planned to have together. They both needed each other. First they settled in the North End Road in Fulham, where Sam and Justin were born, and then they moved to Northampton to start afresh.

Just a few months before he died, Dad and I were in a restaurant called Sophia's in Bridge Street, Northampton, and out of the blue he started to tell me about his past and about his family. I didn't know about my parents' journey until then. I was 21 and

I'd never been curious. I find that very strange now, because there was a lot about my mum and dad I didn't know. What prompted him to tell me, I don't know.

I knew Dad was one of three boys – Len, George and Peter – and that they were brought up in Fulham. Dad told me their father Harry was a foreman gas fitter who was very popular in the community and channelled all his energy into providing for his family. Their mother Catherine, known as Kate, worked as a store manager. She was dark-haired, stout and tigerishly protective of her sons. They lived initially in Cassidy Road, Walham Green, and then in a two-bedroom flat in Burne Jones House, a new block of council flats which had gardens and a janitor, at the top of the North End Road in West Kensington – the posh bit of the borough, they joked, where people wore shoes. The boys went to Henry Compton School and post-war family life was full of love and warmth, but extremely tough as everyone struggled to pay their bills. The boys counted bread and dripping as a treat; they ate jellied eels and drank boiled cabbage water – Uncle George says he didn't taste chicken until he was 11 years old. In the collective effort to make life better, Dad would 'lift' bits of coal, just to help towards keeping the family warm. When the market closed each day, they'd see people collecting rank leaves left behind on the street – in order to feed the rabbits bred for food in tiny yards behind each block of flats.

The Cohens were a football family. Football was at the heart of the working-class community and support for the local club,

Fulham FC, a proud expression of local identity. My grandfather played football for the London Business Houses; Len, a tremendous sprinter, played for the gas board. George, of course, was the star who went on to play for Fulham and England. Dad, too, was very good at football – some say better than George. At five foot eight, he was the shortest of the brothers, powerfully built and extremely nippy. He was strong and determined; nobody who played against him liked the experience. He was on the books at Southend United for a while until a knee injury forced him to give up. Speed must run in the family, because George and Dad were no slouches. They used to train together, and George was once timed at 10.3 seconds over 100 yards.

I never met my grandparents but I can see they had a huge influence on Dad. His mother's attitude towards George's desire to go into professional football – waiving concerns about the need for him to have a back-up qualification in a trade – was exactly how Dad mentored my approach into professional rugby. 'If you do anything, you should throw yourself into it, give it 100 per cent because that's the only way you have a chance of being a real success,' she said, according to family legend. 'George has a talent for football. He should see where it takes him. Until he has done that, he shouldn't mess about with anything else.' Dad's father exemplified an attitude of doing the very best you can with what you have – an admirable set of values. My grandparents were modest and hard-working, good friends and neighbours, and never thought of themselves before their children. Staying grounded and never forgetting your roots was the unofficial family motto.

Cohen, of course, is a very common Jewish name, but our Cohens have long been Church of England, and Mum was brought up a Roman Catholic. Traditionally Jewish status passes down through the mother. According to Uncle George, the Jewish bloodline ceased to be pure when my grandfather Harry was born in 1903, because his father – my great-grandfather Jacob Solomon Cohen – had married a Gentile woman from Chelsea called Sarah Mann. My grandfather then married Catherine Gibbs, also a Christian, and so on down the generations. In less politically correct times when intolerance was rife, my grandmother sometimes styled herself 'Mrs Cowan' to avoid any potential abuse. Uncle George tells how he was referred to as 'the Rabbi' by his own fans at Fulham. Sport is a world heavy on banter, and I'd be lying if I said I wasn't called 'Jew boy' at times, but it has always – quite literally – fallen on deaf ears.

What is interesting about the Cohen line is that it has produced a champion in different sports in three successive generations. At the turn of the 20th century, a great-great-uncle called Abraham Benjamin Cohen, aka Jewey Cooke, made a name for himself as a talented bareknuckle fighter and champion of the boxing booths. Fighting in the halls of east London and in rings all around England, he was the 1903 lightweight champion of Great Britain and won the original ruby-studded Lonsdale belt at that weight (bequeathed via Jewey's wife to Uncle George minus the rubies). During a spell in South Africa, he won the country's middleweight title, but, following a trial of which the details were said at the time to be 'too revolting to publish', Jewey Cooke was also found guilty of rape and sentenced to eight years' hard labour and ten lashes. Uncle George did a lot of research in South Africa to get to the bottom of the story and discovered that, although it seems that Cooke was eventually cleared and freed, none of the circumstances of the case were particularly nice.

George himself, however, was a bona fide hero. In my baby book, Mum and Dad stuck in a photograph of me as a boy of five, sitting in a leather armchair wearing my uncle's 1966 Jules Rimet silver-trimmed felt cap and holding up his solid gold World Cup winner's medal in its velvet-lined presentation box. I have a big confident grin on my face, as if the victor's pose was natural to me. To be honest, it wasn't until Euro '96, when I heard that song, 'Three lions on a shirt … thirty years of hurt', that the significance of the 1966 victory hit home. By then I was nearly 18, about to start out as a professional sportsman, and the full impact of what my uncle had achieved made that level of achievement a potential reality rather than a remote dream. My own father's brother had played for his country and become a world champion, a national hero. And my own father had seen how he'd gone about it every step of the way.

CHAPTER 2

A BRAT AND A HERO

By the time I'd come along Dad and Mum had settled in Northampton. My first memories of family life stem from when we moved from Greenhill Road to nearby Acre Lane, still in Kingsthorpe. Dad converted the garage into a kids' playroom. I shared a bedroom with my brother and loved hanging around with him and his older friends, more than with kids my own age. I was quite a handful, mischievous, into everything. Wherever Jay went, I followed. I was the annoying little brat of a brother. I used to steal his Matchbox cars, so he'd hide them under a loose floorboard at the top of the stairs. What he doesn't know is that I knew that. I imagine there are still little cars in there now. According to Mum, I showed all the signs of a typical Virgo: strong-headed, perfectionist and determined to live life on my own terms. I was also quite a tough, physical boy. A little girl once came running round to tell Mum I was in a fight. She ran to the park to find me, aged six, pinning down a chunky 11-year-old – the reverse of the scenario she'd imagined.

Mum always loved animals. We had so many pets: a dog, cats, mice and my brother had ferrets. Sometime foxes or birds of prey would get the ferrets. We used to find them half eaten in the park behind the house where we'd kick a football around. My sister Sam killed one accidentally by shutting it in a door.

I had a grey cockatiel called Spike. He was kept up in my bedroom but he'd chirp as soon as I came in the door; he always knew when I was in the house. I learnt to ride a bike on the concrete patch in front of the garages with a boy called Richard Chattaway; then Dad bought me a big red Honda all-terrain trike – like a mini quad bike. Jay was into motocross, so it was an early introduction into the world of speed. My sister Sam was a demon on my trike, haring around the recreation ground behind our house. The park was quite an expanse of green, with an impressively steep dip in it. When it snowed we used to drag everyone around on big plastic sheets attached to the back of it. I exasperated everyone, always trying to keep up. Dad took Jay and me to Pittsford Quarry for one outing; they had motorbikes and I was on the three-wheeler. I was good in a straight line but not great around a corner. I came off trying to prove myself. My leg was cut and bleeding profusely. Jay grabbed it, and tried to stem the bleeding by holding it together, while I screamed my head off. This time the leg was properly broken – and then I became the little pest on crutches.

The house was perfectly situated with the park behind, woods at the back and the river down on the other side of the main road which Mum hated us crossing. When it rained, we'd watch videos. I remember Justin and his mates watching *An American Werewolf* and *Police Academy*. It was the time when every neighbourhood had a video rental shop, and we used to ride or walk to the little parade of shops to buy bags of Monster Munch, racing through a little cut-through. More often we'd play outside and venture off into the wild woods called the Little Spinney to build dens. Further afield, we'd cross the dreaded main road and head towards one of Kingsthorpe's three original water mills and mess around by the river where there was still a bit of a weir. On one occasion, Justin fell in and I saved him by grabbing hold of his arm to prevent him being pulled under the flood-swollen waters of the River Nene. This prompted a big article in the *Northampton Chronicle and Echo*, which my parents framed and hung in the hall as a constant reminder of my heroic exploits. In purple prose, I am given the full superhero treatment under the headline: RAGING RIVER RESCUER 'RAMBO' (AGED 7) IS HAILED: BRAVE BEN SAVES HIS BROTHER FROM DROWNING – AND THEIR PALS HELP.

The exact circumstances are still the subject of sibling debate today. Jay would say it wasn't quite like that: the water was shallow and he was simply scrambling to get back up the slope and asked for my hand. But I can remember him struggling, his feet stirring up lots of mud and muck in the swirling, icy water. He could have got his legs caught and been pulled under. When I ran back and told Mum, she thought I was amazing and called the local paper, who sent a reporter around. I loved the attention: I was written up as 'have-a-go Ben, the pint-sized Superman'. The whole episode made a huge impression. I remember running to the shop barefoot in the snow to buy that newspaper and having to thaw out in a bath afterwards. Whenever I get into a really hot bath now, I think of that house, my frozen feet and that newspaper cutting.

That may have been the first time I was described with adjectives such as plucky, brave and fearless, but what I remember of that time as a very young lad is snuggling up to my mum in bed. Dad used to get turfed out to the bunk bed I'd left. I was on the top bunk by then, so he had to get my brother to swap bunks in case they collapsed under his weight on the top! That happened once – nailing my brother's arm. No major damage, however, and it went into family folklore, filed under comedy.

It was a laugh too whenever we used to go to visit Uncle George, Aunt Daphne and my cousins, Anthony and Andrew. They lived in a beautiful village called Bidborough, overlooking the Weald in Kent. It was a long, long drive from Northampton and Dad never liked to stop. On one trip, I was absolutely bursting by the time we arrived. I ran down all the steps to rush inside, but I didn't know where to find the toilet. There, on a low-lying table in front of me, I saw the perfect receptacle: a large, cut-glass bowl. I weed into it, a very long wee, with everyone watching me aghast. Mum and Dad were horrified, but Aunt Daphne was amused. 'Don't stop him,' she cried, in case I redirected my aim and continued over the Persian carpet. I finished and looked up sheepishly. Daphne gently carried the bowl away to empty. I've never been allowed to forget the incident – the bowl was a special memento presented to George by the great Dutch football club, Feyenoord.

My status as a nightmare brat continued for several years as Andrew and I only had to look at each other and *whack!* We exulted in our rough and tumbles. Once we almost wrecked an entire cabinet of Meissen porcelain. 'Get them out in the garden' was the inevitable cry. A few years on, I'd head straight for the kitchen and ask what there was to eat. George would compare me to a small rhino. Or joke that I'd half-volleyed the cat. As I got taller, he'd say, 'Is it cold up there, Ben?' You had to take it on the chin.

By then my Dad was working as a bouncer on the doors of a nightclub at night and managing the car park in the city centre during the day. I don't think any of the family liked the idea of the nightclub business, but it suited Dad. He loved people; he loved a chat and a chuckle. Northampton then was a bustling, thriving town, with life and soul. The car park was on a site which is now a block of flats. I loved going to see my dad in that car park, in his little hut, because it was always full of people who'd dropped by.

Dad knew everyone; it was a sociable job. People would go and do deals with him. His hut was always full of chocolate Advent calendars or Matchbox cars or things acquired cheaply in bulk, and he would be selling them on. Sometimes space was tight and people would get him to park their car. I was always hearing them marvel, 'That guy could park a car anywhere.' Inspired by his manoeuvring skills, I once climbed up onto a steam roller that was parked outside the car park and somehow got it to move … and steered it straight into the back of a trailer carrying new cars. Not so impressive.

Dad's companion was an Alsatian called Seb, a former police dog, a beautiful, friendly animal which on command could switch into serious guard dog mode, ready to go. On one occasion a thief had targeted Michael Jones jewellers at the top of the road. My dad, standing outside the hut in the car park, saw these guys chasing the thief down the road and set the dog after them. Seb pounced, got the thief and rescued all the stolen valuables. He got a gigantic bone as reward. People still come up to me in Northampton to reminisce about Dad from those days.

At Whitehills Lower School. I got on well with the teachers, but I didn't do well at lessons. No one picked up on my hearing issues, though they were clearly a serious hindrance to a classroom education. I learnt subconsciously from a very young age to adapt, to lip read and position myself at the front of a large group, close to a speaker.

In 1986, when I was eight, we moved out of Northampton to Whilton, a lovely village about ten miles west of Northampton and four miles from Daventry. My parents had started small, but kept moving to bigger houses in better locations. This house was called Rustlings, in Brington Lane, and it was their country idyll. The house had a few acres of land and a stable for my sister's horse. We used to play on the village green and mess around by the church which was mentioned in the Domesday Book, or burn around the roads on a bike. It was a lovely little community.

My friend Barry Crane lived nearby and we used to stay over at each other's houses. We shared a birthday but he was one year older. His father was called Trevor and he took us once to a sports ground, leaving us to mess around on the grass while he went into the gym which was housed beneath an old wooden grandstand. Years later I realised it was Franklin's Gardens and that Trevor was a Saints player, a flanker – and those were my first steps on the pitch of Northampton Saints Rugby Union Football Club. I hadn't a clue. Rugby would not be on my radar for another six years.

Whilton and the surrounding area was a great place for us to play outside. We used to run or bike down the path to Brington and have adventures in the woods at the back of the house. Very handily, there was a gate leading out of the back of the property. When it snowed, we could feel quite isolated. The lanes would get drifts four or five feet deep. One night, or very early morning, Dad got stuck while coming back from Top of the Town nightclub where he worked and dropped a bag of 50p pieces – about £10 worth – in deep snow. The next morning, he marshalled us all to walk down and try and find it. I spotted it, and the others tried to mug me all the way home. That was typical Dad, creating fun out of a chore.

When we lived here, I went to Little Brington Village School. The school is a classic Victorian village building with just two classrooms and a beautiful hall. The teachers used to pull out apparatus from wall brackets for indoor games. I remember quite often being sent out of the classroom and told to stand outside the Gothic arched door of the classroom, staring at the wall. It was a nice little school. I sang in the choir. With my blond hair cut in a long page-boy style – thanks, Mum – I looked deceptively angelic. It's funny how we all hark back to school dinners. I loved lunchtime at Little Brington – until the day we were given a trifle with fruit and jelly. I hated it. They made you eat everything on your plate in those days, and I remember heaving. I can't eat trifle to this day. I was there for three years, until I was eight or nine. I remember the Portakabin classroom out the back, the hopscotch that was painted on the tarmac at the front of the school and the huge holly bushes that bordered the playground. It was painful retrieving the ball from those bushes.

I liked football, but I was awful at it. I wasn't skilful and I didn't understand the offside rule. I had a go playing for the Little Brington village team on the field there, but it was obvious I was no good. I just had no finesse. There was no point anyone saying that even Uncle George was not a great crosser of the ball; football was never going to be my thing. I had no natural attributes to work on. Interestingly, the Cohens who have achieved success are known not to be as innately skilful as other sportsmen, but we all worked hard at our respective sports. I never pretended I was something I wasn't. When I was a young lad, Dad helped me to see that we all had individual strengths and weaknesses, and we started to work out where I could excel. We used to take part in a race between Great and Little Brington – known as the Great Brington Run. When I was nine, running in plimsolls, I came second out of 25 adults and 25 children and took great pride in my medal and certificate. Speed and fitness were my thing; I was always very fast in a straight line, very athletic.

For a period Dad earned a good salary and every summer we'd travel to Alicante in Spain and stay in a villa in Javea for three weeks or so. We'd drive there in a caravanette, which was an adventure in itself. Dad loved Spain and decided to move there and set up a bar with a guy called Terry. He wanted a good life in the sun for his family. That was the plan, so we said goodbye to Northamptonshire and moved to the Costa Blanca, where I attended the Laude Lady Elizabeth School in Javea, which taught the English national curriculum. We bought a beautiful house, and to me our Spanish interlude was a blur of lovely long sunny days on the beach. I discovered I excelled at trampolining. We'd have breakfast on the beach and I'd go to the big beach trampoline and stay there all day with my friends. It was very safe. The man who ran it encouraged me to come every day, and he let me on the trampoline free because I drew an audience. He had 12 trampolines, linked in two rows of six. I loved it, bouncing high, doing backflips, tucks and acrobatic twists. My party piece was to backflip all the way down the line and back. I never worried that I'd hurt myself. I've never been risk averse. Meanwhile, Dad was still musing on setting up his bar. When it came down to it, however, the deal they'd been offered didn't look good enough for him to sign. He tried to persuade Terry not to sign either, but Terry went ahead by himself and I think ended up losing a lot of money.

What next for Dad? Our life moved where his work ambitions took him, and so it was back to Northampton. He had been offered an opportunity to buy the Top of the Town nightclub in Great Russell Street, where he'd previously been the manager. It had been built as a working men's club in 1978, but by the late 1980s it was the leading nightclub in the town. To someone with his sociable nature and so many friends in the town community, it was an exciting prospect, so we abandoned beach life for the English countryside again, surfing back on a huge wave of optimism. So much so, I started at a private school called Quinton House. My education was not going well and Mum and Dad thought I'd catch up more thoroughly at a private school. I'd never have been accepted by the school if I'd had to pass an entrance exam, but luckily they were short of numbers. I didn't do well at my new school, and I was rarely there because we were still travelling to and from Spain. I didn't enjoy the formality and hated being told what to do; I preferred to learn things for myself. I started getting into scuffles, so my parents decided to take me out of the private system. Before I left, though, I went on a school trip to Germany and, because I knew I was leaving, I was a bit disruptive and carefree. On a tour around a vineyard, I nicked a couple of bottles of wine and gave them to the older boys. I was still only 11 and not interested in drinking it myself, but someone grassed on me and I was officially asked to leave.

Life felt quite unsettled at that stage, but it steadied after I started at Kingsthorpe Middle School. We moved to Upper Stowe to live in Leys House, a gorgeous old barn conversion-cum-farmhouse built from Northampton sandstone and with a thatched roof. The property was a visible sign that Dad's business at Tops, as we called the nightclub, was going well. We were able to have horses, which were still Sam's passion, as the house had stables, a field and a manege or indoor riding school. When we owned it, the house and stables were joined by a courtyard. It was a large house with a massive extension and a snooker room. It's since been made into two separate properties.

My brother Jay had started working as a DJ, putting on mobile discos. He was good at it; he entered competitions and came second in a national contest. He had the top bedroom in the loft, where he installed turbo-charged loudspeakers, four or five foot high, and turned up the bass so high that the roof vibrated and bits of thatch fell off. He'd placed his decks so that they faced down to the field, and for amusement I used to take pot shots at him with my pellet gun from below – until he went down one day with a hole in his shoulder.

My ambition was to become a fireman, but my understanding of the role must have been a bit hazy. One day, when Dad and Mum were out, I was helping my sister Sam eradicate stinging nettles in the manege with a weed sprayer. I filled it with petrol, lit it and tried to burn the nettles. When I struck the match, everything seemed to burst into flames and I panicked. The weed-sprayer nozzle spun round my legs, spraying more petrol, and the flames whirled right up to the top of my leg. The pain was horrific. I ran to my sister, who sensibly shoved me in a cold bath with salt, and she rushed to find Dad to whisk me into hospital. I remember our white Vauxhall Nova practically taking off over the hump of Heyford Wharf Bridge as we raced over the canal towards Northampton General A & E department. I was treated for second-degree burns and had to have a skin graft. I'll never forget the look on my dad's face – not angry, just resigned to helping me recover from the aftermath of yet another scrape. It was bloody painful, changing the dressing every day for weeks, and I still bear the scars.

Dad had a tremendous sense of humour and loved a good story. He used to teach me how to count money in his office at the back of the nightclub, and he spoke a lot about the nature of earning, deal making and enjoying the rewards of your efforts.

When I was 11, I won £100 on the fruit machine in his club. Typically, he wanted to strike a deal. He suggested we go 50-50, but Mum intervened and said, 'It's yours, Ben. You won it fair and square.'

That summer of 1990, I went off the rails a bit. I liked hanging out with kids older than me and I loitered around a youth club nearby in Nether Heyford, a single-storey red-brick clubhouse tucked away off Furnace Lane. I used to walk it or bike it and I was a bit of a brat, doing a bit of drinking and smoking and 'going out' with a girl from the nearby village of Nether Stowe. She was 16! My bad phase culminated in me stealing money off Mum and Dad. I got caught taking cash from Dad's drawer and in my shame I ran away from home for a few hours. It was the classic kid's escapade. I hid in the woods, made a campfire and thought I was ever so independent. I'll never forget seeing the silhouette of Dad stomping through the trees coming to get me. He gave me a right ear bashing.

My parents wanted me to know right from wrong, but they were big softies. By example, they showed me the importance of having a kind heart. Dad was everyone's mate and supported any good cause. He used to put on fund-raising events for St Crispin's – a large psychiatric hospital for severely handicapped people on the outskirts of Duston. Mum took me there with her once. I remember being mesmerised by a big, tall lad whose tic was to twiddle his pencil incessantly. I could see the pencil was important to him, his security prop. When he dropped it, I was so scared of how his mood might turn that I rushed to pick it up and handed it back to him, and Mum was proud of me. On another occasion, she was late driving to the nightclub and out of the car window I saw someone had fallen over on the pavement. I screamed at her to stop to go and help, and was really angry when she wouldn't because we were running so late.

My parents had lots of good friends, and they'd help out anyone who needed a bed for the night or longer. Our door was always open. We used to have exchange people over, people who'd been in a home, women who wanted to escape their partner, all sorts. Some of my dad's friends sailed close to the wind, but my parents were very accepting and unquestioning of everyone. One night there was a knock on the door and some guy asked if he could leave some stuff in our house for a bit. Of course he could. Leys House was big. We had no idea he'd just burgled a property. After several days the police came around with a warrant, and there I was quite innocently watching a pirate video on the stolen television with the stolen VHS player. Another time Sam's ex-boyfriend was driving back from Spain and died in a car accident. This was a great shock to all of us anyway, but in the back of his car he had all these imitation firearms and, because he'd been staying with my sister, carloads of armed police turned up at our home. It was crazy. There were always a lot of characters about. We were a loud, happy, loving family and that drew people in.

Leys House was perfect for my parents in that way, for having lots of people around and looking after them with a cup of tea.

Dad always had a cuppa in his hand. He was teetotal to the point of drinking totally tea. But that house skinted them. The property was a work in progress; Dad was always labouring on it, but his DIY skills weren't great and the recession of the early 1990s hit the nightclub business hard. Slowly but surely, no one seemed to have spare cash to burn on drinks and a night out any longer. In 1991 Top of the Town went bankrupt. The receivers came in; Dad was stabbed in the back by the manager and pushed out. He went from wanting for nothing – and providing for his family in the way he wanted – to leaving that day with 16p in his pocket. That house broke my dad financially, but handing back the keys broke him in another way. It was a massive turning point.

Reluctantly, we packed up our belongings and swapped our big house in the countryside for a basic rented house in Saffron Close, West Hunsbury, a large housing estate to the south of Northampton. Every time we packed up a house, we did the removal ourselves. On this move Dad got the lorry stuck under the low railway bridge in Furnace Lane, near Nether Heyford. That lightened everyone's mood – once we'd let the air out of the tyres and reversed it out to try another route. For a long time, you could still see the scrape lines along the brickwork.

The 'change in circumstances' was dramatic and difficult for us all to adjust to. Sam and Jay had pretty much left home, and I was a spoilt brat, just no longer in the materialistic sense. Things were tough. Dad was out of work and out of pocket. Mum struggled to put food on the table. Every day there was tense talk about where the next pennies were coming from. There were fiery arguments. It was horrible. I remember Dad losing it a few times – not with us, just because of what had happened. We were absolutely skint. It seemed like I was being farmed out to friends for tea after school, mainly so I would be fed a decent meal. There were some weeks when I remember eating nothing but cereal. I often used to stay with Richard and Rob Bavey. Their mum was a teacher and they lived in a house which looked like a small castle, surrounded by lots of modern houses built on its former grounds. We had to use the excuse that the car had broken down. Again.

With the atmosphere tense at home, it was even more important for me to find an outside interest to occupy me. I still hadn't found anything that consumed me, unlike Sam, with her love of horses, or Justin with his music and motocross. Mum was very keen for me to find a pastime to pursue too. Initially she thought I could get something out of my beach trampolining prowess. The man on the beach in Javea had told her I was 'absolutely outstanding', but when we tried to continue trampolining as a sport in England, I was told to stop immediately. Apparently my technique was dangerous – and I couldn't un-learn it. One awkward fall, I was told, and I'd break my neck. Next, we tried swimming, as I'd started early in our pool in Spain. And I did swim like a fish, but underwater. I didn't like swimming on the surface. No good.

Our house move coincided with me starting at Kingsthorpe Upper School, but for some reason my year of birth was registered as 1977, not 1978, and they put me in the wrong year – the year above. I had been struggling with academic work in my own year group; in the year above, I was completely floundering. Physically I still looked like a choirboy while others had reached puberty and had started to shave. It was a whole new learning curve in social terms as well as educationally. My schooling had not been very consistent. We'd lived in Spain, then I'd had a spell at the private school – where I'd been a tearaway, not academically strong. When I turned up at the state school I found it hard to make friends. In fact for a while I wasn't even there very much. Mum and Dad practised reverse psychology; if I said I didn't want to go, they didn't force me. I felt a bit of an outsider, and I became alert to others who also hadn't found a way to feel involved in school life. I particularly recall seeing one young lad being bullied. The bullies had thrown his shoe in the toilet. I was running late for whatever classroom I was supposed to be in next, but I remember going into the toilets and retrieving the shoe for the boy. The world seemed a hard place for some of us.

Sport was the only area in which I could excel. I was a good all-round athlete. I ran sprint relays and solo sprints, and I think I still hold the school shot put record. The school offered nearly every sport you could think of, except rugby.

Christmas that year was particularly tense because my parents loved to spoil their kids; that year they didn't have the financial means to make it as special a time as usual. We were always spoilt with love, but we'd lost a familiar ease with life. We were unsettled and we battled to adjust. I could hear Mum and Dad arguing. Where's the next money coming from? How can we survive like this? They both tried to find work, any work. Mum worked in a kennels, in a shoe company and as a fruit picker. I had a Saturday job at John Sargeant butchers in Alexandra Terrace, washing up disgusting trays and implements after the butchers had cooked the hams and prepared the day's display. It was a terrible time. I was only 13. I didn't understand what had happened. The house, the cars, the disposable income had gone and, with them, the carefree atmosphere. I look back and wonder if it affected our family bond, and it didn't. We were all in it together and Mum and Dad kept us away from the nitty gritty of their financial problems. We still had a wealth of love, and my dad could conjure fun from nothing. He didn't like sitting around. There'd be a blow-up about money and he'd say, 'Come on, let's go play in the garden.'

As the saying goes, above the clouds the sky is always blue. Gradually I started to appreciate school. It became a good place to go. I liked the routine and structure and I'd become friends with a sporty boy called Trevor Evans after an initial bit of tension between us. We'd had a couple of schoolboy scuffles and set-tos, and ended up with a lot of mutual respect. One Friday night in late spring 1992, I'd stayed over at his house and the next morning got dragged along to watch him do his Saturday sport – rugby. Because we were at a state school, it wasn't on the curriculum. This was a drop-in Saturday activity which volunteers would organise on the school fields. It was a damp, overcast day, a realistic introduction to the game. They were short of people so I was roped in to play. I didn't have kit, but I had no choice. They needed more legs on the pitch. The position that needed filling was prop. I hadn't heard of any of the positions. Prop was not where I stayed long, that was for sure. It was full contact. We were all shitting ourselves. I went pretty much from one to 15 in that session, running around, now knowing what to do. That was pretty much the last rugby of the season. I joined in that one game and enjoyed it. What I loved was the physicality and the freedom to run as part of a team. I had a lot of energy to expend.

Back at school after the summer, a notice on the board advertising the 'Northampton Old Scouts RFC Open Day' caught my eye and I took down the details. I thought I might go; I was curious to find out more about rugby. It was billed as an introductory session, so everyone else would be starting from scratch. When I mentioned it at home, I was well teased for wanting to play a game with the wrong-shaped ball, but Mum told Dad he should let me try. She wanted me to do something to get me out of the house, and Dad drove me down there. The pitches were already teeming when we arrived. When I had played with Trevor I didn't have any kit, but this time I came prepared. I had no sports kit or boots of my own, and I didn't want to ask my parents as money was still tight, but I had raided the Lost Property box at school and equipped myself with odd boots and odd socks. I think I must have looked quite odd in my unclaimed, mismatched kit. I spent the day there and loved it. We did lots of drills – hitting tackle shields, running with the ball, passing and catching, basic stuff. It was dark when I left, and as I was leaving the Portakabin changing-room, walking behind the brick clubhouse towards the car park, I wondered what happened next. I heard a call, and saw a man I later knew to be a parent-coach called Keith Bramhall looking out after me.

'Are you going to come back then?'

'Yeah,' I said. 'Yeah, I'd love to.'

From then on, every Tuesday and Thursday night, I'd go down to Rushmere Road and train under the lights. On Saturday and Sunday we'd play league matches against clubs like Kettering, Olney, Long Buckby, Bugbrooke, the Towcestrians and Old Northamptonians. Dad came down to keep an eye on me, and he soon joined the Scouts, too, to help out with fitness training. It turned out he knew one of the coaches, Bill Conisbee, from way back. We set out together, father and son. It was our little hobby. It gave our week a rhythm and a purpose, and it got us both out of the house. I was not a natural rugby talent and Dad was resolutely a football man, but we started out, this unlikely duo, on a rugby journey together.

CHAPTER 3

A POINT TO PROVE

'Ben, is it? Where do you play then?'

When I first arrived at the Scouts for a proper training session, I was again asked my position and I still didn't have an answer. This time I went from one to ten, but I was useless so they stuck me out on the wing. At that stage, I didn't know the point of the game I was trying to play so I didn't understand what it meant when I was told to straighten up my run. As time went on I realised it was about gaining metre-age on the field and I had to see imaginary channels on the pitch – inside, outside, the wings. I found tactical things hard to grasp; I was putting everybody offside. I had never followed the Five Nations on television or seen a match in the flesh, but it was obvious I loved the athletic side of sport and that I was a fit kid. The physicality of the game appealed to me, but I was very conscious I didn't have specific skills. Whatever the coaches suggested I work on, I'd practise over and over again to try to master that skill; they had to tell me it was okay to stop because I'd never give up.

At the age of 13, I was slow at learning but I tried hard. Because of my hearing issues, I was a visual learner but no one picked up on that for a while. I could only learn a skill or a move if I was shown it physically on the field, and then I'd try it myself, and keep trying until it became instinctive. Once I'd learnt something, I never lost it. I liked to please the coaches and, in seeking their approval, I was discovering something else about myself: I *really* liked to be the best. Rugby unleashed a competitive instinct I didn't know I had. If I was good at a particular skill or move, I became determined to work on it until I was the best. Fully accepting my bottom-of-the-class status at school, I knew I had to concentrate, focus and practise if I was going to learn anything well. I never thought for one minute that I would have a future in the game; I simply wanted to stand out among my peers as good at something. Rugby, at junior club level, had a great ability to be inclusive. What I loved was the sense of belonging that Dad and I found at the Old Scouts: the camaraderie, the banter, the opportunity to contribute and be noticed. People's wealth, their social background, school, ego – all that was left at the gate; there was a warm welcome for a broad spectrum of abilities and types. The family environment of rugby was my saviour.

The coaches, Keith Bramhall and Bill Conisbee, created a terrific environment that embraced everyone. Bill, a lovely man, recognised Dad from in and around Northampton the minute he turned up with me. To be honest Dad was hard to forget even if you'd only met him briefly. His heart was hidden under a pretty formidable exterior. He looked like your archetypal bruiser: short, rugged, fearsome-looking when he wasn't smiling, and built like the proverbial outhouse. But his demeanour was the opposite of the man inside; he was universally received as a lovable chap who was always up for a chat and a laugh. He would do anything for anyone. Very quickly Bill had invited Dad down to help out with the fitness side of training and, later, to be the first aider. He became part of the set-up.

On weekday evenings, Dad would take us all for the first 15 minutes to warm up. He'd wear a long black coat and baggy tracksuit bottoms tucked into wellies, an unlikely figure of authority to command our attention, but he did that all right.

'Right, stand along here,' he'd say, indicating one end of the pitch.

'Now look at my fist. I've got something in here from the long grass down the other end of the field. I want you to run there, get some too, and run back. If it matches what's in my fist, you can stop running.'

We'd run there and back, and arrive clutching handfuls of green stalks to show him.

'No! It's not that type of grass!'

And he'd send us back again, chuckling to himself. The joke was always on us. We could never come back with the right kind of grass. He was full of schemes like that. After our warm-up, the coaches took the forwards off to do scrummaging while we backs would do exercises and drills. We'd practise moves over and over again. We might be made to stand in a line across the pitch, passing to the man on the left. I'd be the last man, five or six passes down the line on the wing; I'd catch it and sprint to the line. We learnt how to tackle on crash mats and tackle bags, where to put our head, how to fall, how to maul. To teach us to keep our heads down, Dad and Bill took a length of thick plastic piping or a corner flag and made us run under it virtually bent over double. If we weren't low enough, they'd give us a flick on the ear which made us scream in the cold. It was good fun. A lot of the boys wanted to mess around, but we learnt a lot.

Bill was an extraordinary example of commitment. At one stage he was working in Glasgow but he'd drive down each weekend to take the training sessions. His dedication paid off because it inspired lads like me to share that passion for the Scouts' success. I started to live rugby. I loved it and I wanted to work hard to acquire the skills. I had to. I was a late starter in the game and it pissed me off to hear that Keith Bramhall, an excellent coach, had said: 'Ben Cohen will never be a rugby player as long as he has a hole in his arse.' He may have said it in jest, but the way it was relayed to me just made me want to prove him wrong. I was fast and able to score tries with ease thanks to my speed, whereas his son, James, who was my contemporary, was much more skilled but getting less glory. Bill told Dad that while it was true I had more holes in my game than a string bag, he was sure I had 'something'.

Bill used to get exasperated by the way I couldn't present the ball after I'd been tackled. It was always being knocked on. He spent hours with me – hit, present the ball, hit, present the ball, hundreds of times – teaching me to keep my hands and elbow close to the body as I hit the pitch, showing me different methods to make the ball available after the tackle and keep the attack going. Five years later, in my first match for the Saints as a professional, that was all I heard from him and Dad – how thrilled they'd been to see my first bit of pro action was to present the ball on the floor for my team-mates with textbook aplomb.

Games on Saturday and Sunday were not fun – they were seriously competitive. The coaches drilled us in fitness and tactics in preparation for each match, and applied their own psychology to get the results they wanted. They knew us all well as individual lads and took pride in working out how best to motivate us. At the end of that first year, for example, we were through to the final of the Milton Keynes Sevens. I asked if could play in the final. They flatly refused, saying I wasn't good enough. Andy Herlock started instead of me and I was named as a sub. After a few minutes he fell down injured and I was brought on. Furious at not being 'good enough' to start, I stormed around that pitch with something to prove and scored four tries. The coaches thought it was hysterical. They later told me they'd decided I would be their match-winner days beforehand, but knew that to get the best from me they'd have to put some reverse psychology into play. Unbeknownst to me, Andy Herlock went on to the field with the order to go down and pretend he was injured – and then they'd bring me on. They knew I'd be steamed up. Their ploy worked perfectly.

Dad and I both grew close to Bill, who was so passionate about rugby. He'd rope everyone in who wanted to help, whether it was volunteering for car shares or organising summer tours. People gave up their time to make it happen; somehow it was made affordable for everyone. In between Thursday evening training and Saturday morning games, especially before away matches, there was a lot of horse trading going on over the phone to make sure all the boys somehow got transport. 'We need ten cars … how many have we got?' It was a big sacrifice in time and money for parents to volunteer to drive – some matches were as far afield as Birmingham or Luton. At first Dad and I got lifts everywhere. We were always in a car share because we couldn't afford the fuel. There were never quite enough parents with cars to take all of us. It was touch and go whether we'd get a lift or not – and whether we'd have a full team. The coaches were very aware of everyone's circumstances and sympathetic. A huge effort went into making sure kids didn't miss out. I was unaware of the anxiety about getting to games, but it would have worried Dad. He wouldn't want to let me down. Sometimes Bill would give Dad money to take a group of lads. When we did use our car, or later on Dad's white transit van, I swear it ran on vapours. Dad never filled it up with fuel. We were always running out of petrol and pushing the car over a roundabout towards the nearest garage. But somehow it felt part of the fun.

The team that formed around my age group grew up together – as Under 13s, Under 14s and Under 15s. Many of us had started rugby the autumn of the 1991 World Cup, and when people saw the final on TV it gave my newfound sport extra validation. Justin looked on with rare elder brother approval: 'Rugby? Well, that's cool.' I can't recall a thing about that final beyond the result. I didn't have enough finesse to relate the game I was watching on TV to the one I was playing, but the crazy thing that strikes me now is that Jason Leonard was in that team, and he would still be in the team 12 years later, offering welcoming banter and a cup of coffee to the new boys. He always had time for people.

Our Scouts outfit bonded astonishingly well. We were un-beaten for two seasons. Sometimes we'd only have 12 players – people were sick or had family commitments or couldn't get lifts – and we'd still win. It was insane, just crazy. Bill and Keith, my dad and the other parents sacrificed a lot of time and spare cash, and went over and beyond to support us and set our ambitions high. That paved a way for those of us good enough that might otherwise have not been there – though we never realised it at the time. We developed together and many of us went on to be invited to join Northampton Saints Academy. Six of us eventually made it into the Northampton Saints first team, and two progressed from club rugby to play for England, the British Lions and to win the World Cup in 2003, which is incredible from one small local club. The Old Scouts club now bills itself as 'The only junior club in England with two World Cup winners!'

My great pal by this time was Steve Thompson, who was then known as Steve Walter. He was adopted as a child and only later reverted to his natural father's name. A former British roller-skating champion, he arrived at the Scouts a year after me and for a long time played in the back row. He was always known as Wally – half-witted and the spitting image of Shrek. Anyone who has known us both a long time will confirm our conversation has always been based on exchanges of insults. If you overheard us, you'd think we were each other's worst enemies, sniping and bickering away, but it's rooted in affection. Wally is black and white. He has a heart of gold. He'd do anything for you, give you everything he had. Off the pitch, our coaches had us down as reprobates, but on the field we were both enthusiastic boys. And there was a bond, too, in that neither of us was from a typical rugby background.

Our summer tours replaced the family holidays in Spain that we could no longer afford. The first rugby tour took us to Devon. I absolutely loved it. It was boys being boys, messing around in the hostel on the bunk beds, great times. We found a way of introducing ourselves to a little bit of alcohol – or what the Americans call 'the third half' of the game. We stayed in a castle of sorts. In one of the ground-floor rooms there was a beautiful grand piano, with a sign that clearly said, 'Do not play the piano.' One of the lads could play a bit, and couldn't resist. The lady came out to have a go at us and everyone ran upstairs, de-activated the smoke alarm and lit up fags. Meanwhile out in public our coaches would be congratulated on the good behaviour of their lovely lads! As a group we were a handful, and I was certainly no angel. That's what rugby was all about.

Our second tour was to Bristol. Dad came on that one, a useful reinforcement for the coaches charged with managing a gang of pumped-up 14-year-olds. We stayed in a youth hostel, four or five storeys above pavement level, next to a convenience shop which sold sweets, milk and random toiletries – ammunition for fun, as we saw it. All the lads popped in and bought plastic bottles of milk and then bolted upstairs to drop them from our dormitory windows so they exploded on the pavement. This behaviour prompted a knock on the door from the hostel manager with a warning: any more trouble and we'd be kicked out. To the horror of the adults, we'd also stocked up on shaving foam – the plan was to shave each other's eyebrows and hair at night – and we were running down the corridors throwing foam at each other, oblivious to the manager's ultimatum. The only way to stop us, our coaches decided, was to ambush the main culprits. They went to the trouble-makers' room and hid, ready to snare the boys and give them a good hiding. When the door opened, they leapt on the first boy in – but it was the hostel manager. He was glad to see the back of us.

The team grew strong as Under 14s, and I began to realise rugby was something I could be truly good at. I went to bed every night watching a video featuring back-to-back England tries, not taking much notice of the players in the England jersey, just revelling in the art of scoring. The Scouts' coaches suggested I ask my headmaster, David Moore, if he could put me forward for a county trial. He did, and I was picked for the Northamptonshire U14s where I came to the notice of David Palethorpe, the regional director who coached the East Midlands U14 schoolboys. An English teacher at my school was chairman of East Midlands Rugby and he called David:

'I have a fine specimen of a boy for you.'

'A big lad, then?'

'Oh no, I said he's a *fine* specimen.'

The teacher was called Bob Bunting and it was typical of him to be specific about the precise meaning of a word. He took the advanced English classes; I was in the remedial group. He'd once brought me up short for saying I had 'slipped discs' in my back. I was just using a phrase I'd heard associated with back pain, and I received the full lecture on incorrect use of language and how this could not be the case because I would be in agony, et cetera. It was an extraordinary moment to realise now that this teacher – who was a known disciplinarian at school and an absolute prat as far as the non-academic 14-year-olds were concerned – had made the effort to promote me beyond school. As a nurturer of young talent he was fantastic. He had noticed something commendable in my attitude and approach on the rugby field, and he was keen to direct me towards something I was good at. I got into the East Midlands team and came to know Bob well. It turned out he was a great guy, quite unlike the pedantic figure he presented at school. He smoked!

I went on to win selection for the Under 15s and Under 16s. When David Palethorpe told me that it was very unusual to make my mark so early, coming from a non-rugby playing school, I didn't understand what he meant by that; I was unaware of the bigger picture. I didn't know there were two routes to the top of the game. The main route was the England Schools path, where boys were selected from traditional rugby-playing grammar schools and public schools at each age level until Under 18s; and there was a wider path to England Colts (Under 19 in my day) where lads were selected via county, region and division (i.e. Northampton, East Midlands, Midlands). At the age of 15, I was selected for the Midland Schools team – on the England Schools path – but then I seemed to disappear from the radar. I was playing better rugby than ever, but I had mysteriously become invisible to the selecting coaches. What really pissed me off was the emphasis on what school we went to. It drove me nuts. And that frustration boiled over in 1993 when I didn't get selected for the England Schools Under 16 trials at Castlecroft,

Wolverhampton. Why not? I sat in the car on the way home, fuming with anger and disillusionment.

Maybe, given a taste of the ladder I could go up, my expectations were too high? I look back now and I get it. I didn't go to the right school. Traditional rugby-playing schools had a long, reliable history of churning out well-coached boys who played regularly against schools of a similar standard, in contrast to boys like me whose state schools didn't offer rugby for health and safety reasons. Boys like me were at best unknown entities and at worst oiks. David Palethorpe had told Dad beforehand not to get his hopes up high. 'They will look at Ben and they will look at his socks,' he said. It's different now, when the selection process is broader, but in those days the boys on the radar came from Rugby, Stowe, Oakham, Wellington and some of the Somerset schools. It was always going to be near impossible for a lad from Kingsthorpe Upper School. David felt so strongly about my not getting picked that he talked to the selectors.

'Why not Ben Cohen?'

He was told I lacked pace. David pointed out I was a 100-metre sprinter.

'Ah,' they said. 'But he lacks *acceleration*.'

He shook his head and said that if he'd put me in Wellington College socks, I'd have got it.

I raged at Dad about it. I was very disappointed, and Dad was disappointed for me. 'We'll show them, son,' he said. 'You have to be positive, get out there and work harder.' Privately

David reassured Dad. He said I'd have the last laugh because a lot of the others would just drift on. 'He'll wear an England shirt one day,' he declared. 'I don't know about a full senior one, but I'm certain from the way he is progressing that he'll play for England Under 19s.'

That was good enough for Dad, but it marked a turning point. I got the bit between my teeth. Talent should be encouraged and nurtured wherever it comes from. But there was a strong, suffocating sense that I would never get there by rights. It resonated with Keith Bramhall's opinion, and added to the list of people I wanted to prove wrong. I found it incredibly frustrating, but it was part of my learning curve. I became more determined than ever to succeed, and more aware of the weaknesses I needed to work on and skills I needed to acquire. I think everyone is born with an X factor. Mine was definitely a motivation that goes 'Fuck you, I'm going to prove you wrong.' In any given field, millions of people may share a similar amount of talent but, mentally, they'll all be in different places along the spectrum of self-motivation. Whenever I am deemed to be not good enough or to have failed, I've always been determined to prove people wrong. My mindset won't stand for failure. I have to keep striving for success and not let failure define me. You can't dwell on disappointments too long. You have to go out and improve. The only person who can do that is you. I'm always dreaming about how I'm going to be better at something.

I wanted to get noticed, but at the same time the early fun had gone out of it. I could see it was going to be an uphill battle, hard work, and I went through a brief phase of wondering whether to give up rugby. It required so much commitment, but for what? To be ignored by the higher level because of your school background? That was something I could never change. Then I thought I'd like to change position to be a back row, but I got told no, I was best on the wing.

Dad and I talked a lot about my situation. He always said that he couldn't advise me about rugby because he didn't understand the intricacies of the game, but he was good at drawing parallels between his business setbacks and my thwarted rugby goals. Life lessons, I suppose. We talked about everything. He had to work hard for every penny, but that didn't stop him being a dreamer. There was always some big plan in the pipeline. I remember one of his friends bought the old Mersey ferry in Liverpool, which he turned into the largest floating disco in Europe. Dad was helping out, and once, while it was moored on the Mersey docks, Jay and I went along with him to look around. It was the time of the James Bulger murder, and bizarrely Jay and I were nearly arrested because we looked like boys up to no good.

Dad taught us the importance of keeping your eyes open for opportunities, having a vision and a strategy. He said it was important to harbour an ambition and that part of the process was to stop occasionally and re-evaluate. We'd often fantasise about Dad getting back the nightclub that he'd lost, or me playing for the Saints, or for England. We dared to dream that he would have Top of the Town up and running as a big success again, and that one day I might be selected to go on a Lions tour.

My dad was very naïve about rugby, and so was I. In his regular telephone calls to Uncle George, talking about life in general, he'd let him know how I was getting on. George always emphasised the value of doing a little bit of extra fitness training to make me a different class of player. We didn't know what could happen, how far it could go, but I had the family work ethic. My dad was a grafter and I inherited that from him. For us there was no resigning yourself to coming second for want of trying.

Dad's enthusiasm fuelled me. He never got the rules of rugby, but he absolutely fell in love with the game, and the boys at the Old Scouts and East Midlands loved him. There was no pressure on me – as I could see there was from some fathers on their sons. For Dad, going to rugby was about the camaraderie and 'the boys'. At the end of the season, he would set up paintball equipment and we'd have great fun. He loved being involved, being with the young lads and getting them off the streets. He'd protect all the kids like his own. All the coaches did. We must have looked a funny pair. Dad was short, dark, stocky and bald and I had overtaken him in height by the time I was 14 or 15. Quick-witted and charismatic, he was instantly likeable, whereas I probably take longer to get to know. Dad was extremely proud of me, but rugby was his release too as he tried to reinvent himself after going bankrupt. He always had a new wheeze, a new prospect. Some worked, some didn't. Rugby provided continuity for him, while he provided continuity for me.

He never did know what offside was. In one end-of-season game, coaches versus parents, Dad was playing at full-back. In theory, he could catch a ball, but he was never in the right position. He'd call 'Here, me!' when he was ten metres in front of the player with the ball. He was the first aid man, but it was questionable what he considered his most vital piece of kit: his flask of tea or his collection of bucket, sponge and spray. He always had his back to the pitch, chatting to the other parents. In one game, a Scouts player went down at the same time as one of the opposition's. Dad ran on towards the opposition's injured lad. You could hear Bill shouting, 'No, Peter, *our* player!' The referee hadn't whistled, and there was Dad running through the opposition's backs, with all our lads screaming, 'Give Pete the ball – he'll score!'

Home life remained tough financially. Eking out a day-to-day existence was challenging for my parents, but we'd become accustomed to our situation. For Dad and me at least, rugby tours were making up for the lack of holidays. As for clothes, I was still raiding the lost property box at school. And I had a pair of huge trainers that could double up as school shoes and sports shoes.

Things perked up when Dad secured a job on the council helping to run a community sport programme called Comm Sport. In this role he was responsible for promoting recreational sport in villages all around Northampton, and it was fantastic for us. He'd travel to local sports grounds and village greens with the van filled with gear and equipment, introducing kids to different sports. By the time we moved to Underbank Lane, Woodrush Way, in Moulton – a large village four miles north of Northampton centre – things were getting easier. Mum had started working at a dog kennels. Every night we'd go out in the Comm Sport van and do something. Dad wasn't one for sitting around. We'd go to a different village and play indoor bowls. That van was brilliant. We had a motor with fuel in it! Climbing into it always meant an adventure. I absolutely loved it.

A lot of teenage boys get self-conscious with their parents hanging around their mates, but I was never like that about Dad coming to rugby. I don't recall any boys feeling embarrassed by their dads at the Scouts either. He enjoyed seeing what I got from rugby and everyone felt secure with him around; he was also the overseer of all the japes. The boys loved him because he was a big kid himself. With the arrival of the Comm Sport van, he'd do his share of taking boys to away games. He allowed himself to be a figure of fun. The boys would tap him on his head as he drove along, because he was bald, and they knew it would wind him up. They'd even put jam sandwiches on his head. One time we were in Leicester and he'd parked in the Nelson Mandela Park in the city centre. On our way back to it after the game, one of the boys said, 'Pete, look, someone's breaking into your van.' Dad bolted ahead, grabbed the bloke, hauled him out of the van … another white van, as it turned out, parked close to his.

He also used to love winding up Bill by asking stupid quest-ions. Bill had always made it clear that the changing-room was a sacred place before a match, a private zone for players to focus and concentrate on the game plan, but Dad would run in and out asking daft questions. 'Have you got oranges?' … 'How many corner flags shall I put out, four or five?' He would do it with a big stupid grin on his face and would chuckle away as Bill exploded.

Bill was instrumental to my rugby development, and he was a key figure for Dad too at that stage in his life. When I graduated to the Saints academy, Dad stayed in his role at the Scouts.

At the age of 16, a lot of the lads wanted to go down to Franklin's Gardens for a trial at the Academy. This was after my England Schools disappointment and I begged Bill to let me go along. I looked a good few years older than my age, but the Scouts coaches thought I wasn't mature enough. Physically, I was what the coaches called 'well put together'. I had the framework on which to develop a strong physique as I matured. At this point Dad got strict with me. He was the fitness man, after all. Privately he set a training regime to give me that extra edge Uncle George talked about. He'd tie a rope around my waist and send me around the park dragging a tyre to build up my legs.

Meanwhile Bill wanted to keep me at the Scouts; he didn't think I would be able to cope. He thought I was still too much of a boy to go into a man's environment. He'd warn me and Wally, 'When you make the transition from Colts to seniors, it's not a game any more, it's a war. It's not your Saturday afternoon recreation, it's a job.'

Dad asked what would happen if I didn't make it. Bill said I'd come back to the Scouts and try again a year later. But Dad was a man's man and he took it for granted that I would cope. So when David Palethorpe told Keith Shurville, President of the Old Scouts, that they'd like to take me to the Saints, Keith agreed, but said, 'If he doesn't make it, will you make sure he comes back to us?'

'Yes, but you won't get him back,' David replied. 'He'll be in the first team before you know it.'

CHAPTER 4

ACADEMY

When I was 16, I was invited to join the new Saints youth academy. That summons was a big deal, not natural progress you take for granted: those at the Scouts who didn't get an official request to come down to the home of Northampton Saints at Franklin's Gardens were left disappointed. I'd left school with few opportunities beyond going into a trade; success at rugby was my dream. I'd found something I was good at, and I wanted to see how far I could go. On an early tour of Franklin's Gardens, I eyed up three framed display cases of ties on the clubhouse wall, close to the trophy cabinet. They must have contained a hundred ties, and my aim was to get all the ones that could be awarded from youth to senior levels by the Northampton and District Rugby Alliance, the East Midlands Rugby Union and the Midlands Rugby Union.

I took great pride in wearing my Saints youth blazer and tie in that 1994/95 season. They were symbols that I had reached a certain level. And I loved being in and around the seniors at the club. I was so ignorant about rugby, though, that I wouldn't have recognised the world-class figures that were part of the first team then. I never got caught up in the 'That's X' or 'That's Y' kind of star-spotting. A few years earlier I'd got a poster of the Saints captain Tim Rodber in a goodie bag at a local RFU Open Day, but I didn't know his player record or even how to pronounce his name. I think that innocence helped me no end. Basically I didn't give a shit about reputations. I just tried hard, and I knew the person at the ultimate head of the Academy set-up I was joining was a quiet, tracksuited figure called Ian McGeechan who always looked so happy to be at work. I hadn't a clue about his great reputation with the Lions. I just heard that Geech's knowledge of the game was phenomenal – and he had a charming way about him. To join the Saints when I did was definitely a 'right time, right place' opportunity.

I'd found work in the Burton's warehouse, packing up huge orders to be delivered to stores around the country. It was here among the fork-lift trucks and pallets that I met Abby. She was tall, slim, with long brown curly hair. I fancied her but she didn't really fancy me. I was shy, and dressed badly. We were both 16 and got chatting in an awkward teenage way one day as we sat on the same table with the other new young workers in the factory. We went on a first date to see *Forrest Gump*, and both got collected from the cinema by our parents. She soon got sacked from Burton's for talking too much, but we carried on seeing each other. I worshipped the ground she walked on and started to spend most of my spare time with her. My days were long – I'd leave at 5.30am to get to work for the 6am to 2.30pm shift in the factory, then go home to eat, rest for a few hours, then get down to the Saints to go to the gym. Training was on Tuesday and Thursday evenings, games on Saturday – the same structure as the Scouts. It was a tiring schedule. I might stay at Abby's mum's house with her. As a result I saw less of Dad, and that started to cause a bit of upset.

'Your dad misses you,' Mum would say. 'Make sure you ring him.'

Rugby, even more than before, became valued time we shared.

I took on an assortment of odd jobs – assisting a plasterer, driving a white van, guillotining and folding paper for a print finishing company. Not for long, however, would I have to cope with the unsatisfactory amateur player routine of trying to combine wage-earning work with training, and not doing quite enough of either. On 26 August 1995, the International Rugby Board declared rugby union an 'open' game and thus removed all restrictions on payments and benefits. That same summer, the Heineken Cup was formed as an elite competition for 12 European clubs to provide a new level of cross-border competition. The professional era had dawned, and Northampton Saints was a great place to be if you were looking to convert 'youthful promise' to success at the highest level.

Northampton is a passionate rugby town. The Saints, one of the oldest rugby clubs in the country, has always been well supported. Even for training sessions there was a responsive crowd on the touchline, including my dad, an ever-present, and often Ian McGeechan's wife. As a player at any level, you knew you were representing the town. The club had been established in 1880 under the original title of Northampton St James (hence its name – the Northampton Saints). The curate of St James Church, the Rev Samuel Wathen Wigg, wanted to encourage orderliness in his younger parish members by creating a youth rugby club. It started as an improvement class to let high-spirited boys let off steam in a constructive way, promoting rugby as a 'hooligan sport designed to turn them into gentlemen'.

Franklin's Gardens was originally a popular pleasure park known as Melbourne Gardens, which included a zoo, and its name was taken from John Franklin, a hotelier who bought the site in 1886. Local farmer Harry Weston became the first to be capped as an England player; the Saints soon produced a national captain too in Edgar Mobbs, whose wartime bravery is commemorated with an annual game against the Barbarians. Denied a commission to fight in the First World War because he was too old, Mobbs formed his own corps that became known as the Sportsman's Battalion. Within 18 months he was battalion commander, but sadly died in combat. Legend has it that on 29 July 1917, in the Third Battle of Ypres, otherwise known as the Battle of Passchendaele, he led his men 'over the top' to charge a German machine-gun nest by kicking a rugby ball into no man's land; his body was never found. The inscription on the war memorial at Franklin's Gardens for players lost in the two world wars reads, 'They Played the Game'.

The club motto, 'Nothing without labour', reflects the town's ethos of hard work, and its modest anticipation of reward for that hard work. Following the club was like an adventure. Fathers like my dad, and Matt Dawson's, found satisfaction in watching their young sons develop before their eyes and achieve a standing that was appreciated by a lot of other locals, and seeing us mature in the way you'd want a son to grow up. Geech emphasised to us as players the strong relationship the club had with the town, the supporters, our parents and schools. He took the entire senior squad on a factory tour of nearby Church's Shoes, who sponsored the rugby club. We met the workforce and saw how the high-quality shoes are made. On our tour we were introduced to one of the top craftsmen, who long ago had served a seven-year apprenticeship and had spent 30 years earning the right to do the finishing stitching on the highest quality shoes. He'd started at one end of the bench, 12 feet away from his current top perch, and gradually moved up to become top craftsman. As a season ticket holder, a precious percentage of his wages was spent coming to watch the Saints on a Saturday. That was his pleasure, his outlet, and it was drummed into us that he had a right to expect something back in terms of our commitment and performance. 'Remember the man from Church's Shoes' became one of the coaches' mantras. Geech made me see that my dad's pride in me was part of a wider dynamic. I was growing up as a representative, not just of my own family, but of these people who don't have a lot of money and are dedicated craftsmen in their own right, and choose to spend their spare cash and leisure watching what we could do as players to boost the town.

Our captain Tim Rodber would admit that in the 1990s the club had been a bit of a pretender, boasting loads of potential with England players like himself, Ian Hunter, Paul Grayson, Nick Beal and Matt Dawson, but failing to achieve success. Once the game had gone professional in 1995, the approach changed. The club was taken over by local businessman Keith Barwell. He had a passion for success, an ambitious vision for how to achieve it, and he put his money where his mouth was. Ian McGeechan had arrived as Director of Rugby the previous season, and although the club was relegated in his first season of re-structuring, they returned in style the next season, winning every single game of their campaign and averaging 50 points a game as they demolished their opponents.

Everyone around the club was energised by the return to the Premiership and the momentum behind it. The atmosphere at Franklin's Gardens on match days was buzzing. I remember sitting outside the clubhouse when the first team played Wasps – Harvey Thorneycroft's name had just been announced – and thinking how could anyone ever tire of hearing that passionate roar from the home crowd: 'Har-vee, Har-vee.' I loved the fans' chants – 'Gloucester, you're like a tea bag – never in a cup for long!' The competitive atmosphere was intoxicating.

To get into the senior squad there was a clear ladder to climb – from the youth squad to the development squad to the Wanderers, as the second XV were known. For me, in parallel to the big question of how the club was going to shape up in rugby union's new professional era, was the question of how quickly I could establish myself as an up-and-coming talent. Geech and the board had set up the Academy and Player Development Programme to try and recognise local talent to bring into the club, developing us through the Under 18 and Under 21 teams. My peer group was to be literally the first onto that conveyor belt and not all of us would be getting off it into the first team.

The approach was: here's a talent, what's the best way of bringing him on? Geech and the coaching staff were trying to shift the game along and do things a little differently. The coaching system was excellent, and integrated from the youth squad (manager Keith Picton, coaches Allan Baxter and Matt Bridge) and the development squad (coach Doug Ferguson) to the second XV (coach Alan Hughes) and the first team under Geech and Paul Larkin, with Phil Pask doubling up as both strength and conditioning coach and physiotherapist. There was a uniformity to the coaching methods to bring through players suited for the expansive, high-tempo style of play they advocated. We set out to play a game different to other teams. It would take two or three years to get to where Geech wanted to be – to shape a team capable of pretty rugby that was also ruthlessly effective – but we were all on the journey together.

There was a wonderful inclusivity from the most junior level up to the first team. The coaches shared information, and on a Saturday evening after all the teams had played they would go out with their wives and discuss the players coming through. The game was evolving fast and it was players like me who had the opportunity to change what it looked like. There was an open-minded view of what your role could be, and because we had a group of world-class coaches professionally appraising what we were doing, the perception of what was possible changed too.

I went down to the Saints as a centre, because I'd been playing in that position for East Midlands, but the coaches saw I had the potential to be a new breed of winger. Geech believed in directing players according to their strengths, and mine were my pace, power and enthusiasm to be involved. The advent of professionalism encouraged me to think ahead and strategise: just how far could I go if I set my mind to it? I could see that wingers before me had achieved their success by training two nights a week. If I signed as a professional at 19 or 20, I could work full-time at developing into something special.

Dad and I discussed it and agreed that fitness was the key. Like my grandmother with Uncle George, he backed me to throw myself into the game and give it 100 per cent effort. It pisses me off when people say I was lucky. I agree up to a point, but I also believe you make your luck. Everyone gets opportunities in life, big or small, but it's every individual's choice to take them or not. I got the opportunity to learn about rugby at the Scouts and I grasped it. I then got the opportunity to go down to the Saints, and I didn't stop there. I was in the right place at the right time, and I took advantage of that. There were plenty of others who had the same openings but didn't channel their energy and commitment. I wanted to develop, improve and work harder and harder at my game. For me, it was definitely 'nothing without labour'.

At club level, I benefited hugely from the coaching, from watching the senior teams train – I was always running around the edge of the field asking Alan Hughes, the backs coach and second XV coach, if I could join in – and from the drive forward Northampton Saints was embarking on collectively. I was also selected for East Midlands for a further two years, as we made the Under 19s County Championship final at Twickenham in two successive years, and those games proved to be my shop window for the England selectors.

Dad was now the established first aid man for the East Midlands team. It was pretty agricultural. Dad had big, shovel-like hands, chapped from working outdoors, and he'd readily admit himself he didn't know what he was doing. They had a physio's table, purloined from somewhere, and he'd have this lad on it for treatment. Alan Hughes, who coached East Midlands as well as the Saints, would catch Dad's eye and he'd shrug his shoulders as if to say, 'I've seen this done but I don't know what

I'm doing ...' These were fledgling, future World Cup winners and there was Dad putting a cold sponge over the top of their heads, saying, 'You're fine now, son.' When you think of the concussion protocols now ... But this was 20 years ago. Alan remembers us playing in Plymouth, in the quarter-final of a competition, and one of the boys seemed a bit out of it. 'Are you sure he's all right?' he'd ask Dad. 'He's fine!' he replied, even though the boy in question was running in the wrong direction.

Quite a number of the dads helped out, but Dad actually came on board as part of the support team. Everyone shared lifts, stood on the touchline, offered support and lapped up the atmosphere. I think Dad knew, deep down, that I could go the distance in the sport. He was as close as he could get to participating as a non-rugby man. Alan viewed him as his 'guardian angel' because they were often up to a little bit of mischief in the course of travelling to and from games, and Dad's formidable bearing silenced any challenges. There was a lot of banter.

It was a long time before the coaches realised that 'George', as in Peter's brother and Ben's uncle, was George Cohen from 1966 and all that. George is extremely modest, and for my father he was just family. Until the discovery was made, I didn't fully realise the status George had, but the Saints coaches found it a source of fascination. Alan Hughes had often told me how, as a nine-year-old boy, he had watched England's World Cup victory, and George's performance was etched on his memory. Geech's, too. I have no doubt the Cohen connection made them more curious about how I might develop. There was always that reference, that I had a World Cup winning relation, so I thought it would be nice, as a surprise, to ask George if he would bring his World Cup winner's cap to the dressing-room at Twickenham before we played in the 1995 County Championship Cup final – East Midlands v Hertfordshire. It was a huge, huge day for us – a cup final – and George duly arrived to wish us luck, modest as ever, with his Jules Rimet cap carried discreetly in a Tesco plastic bag. He came into the dressing-room and was bowled over by the sight of 'kids like trees'. He's five foot nine or ten, and there were all of us lads of 17 or 18, well over six foot and a stone or two heavier. Afterwards he told me he was amused to hear from one 'man mountain' – a boy of 16 – that he wasn't playing. 'I'm too young, Mr Cohen,' he said, gazing down from his great height.

I think of that 1994/95 season as the 'Bob Bunting year'. He got me through into selection for East Midlands Under 19s and we had the best time, winning every game. I wasn't playing on the wing, I was at centre right through to the quarter-finals of the County Championship. Every time we won we used to go into town and get pissed. I was in a pub toilet when Alan, our coach, said, 'Look, Ben, I want a word. I'm thinking of bringing in two other players ...' One was called Matt Oliver. It was when Bedford was in the Premiership (East Midlands comprises Northamptonshire, Bedfordshire and part of Cambridgeshire), and these two lads had already played in the Premiership. So I was shifted out to the wing and Matt Oliver went to centre. That team was amazing. It was a game we won against the odds.

The 1995/96 season culminated with East Midlands again reaching the Under 19s County Championship cup final. In the semi-finals we played at Castlecroft, Wolverhampton, and we ended up winning in the last minute of the game by scoring a try underneath the sticks. Simon Hepher scored the try that sent us to Twickenham. The final was my chance to show the England Colts selectors what I could do, and I was determined to do that emphatically. I scored two tries, including a spectacular solo effort, picking up the ball and running at speed. I scored an interception try from about 30 metres out from our line, displaying quick reactions. I didn't half take off. David Palethorpe, sitting with the England selectors, turned to them and said, 'I told you Ben Cohen was impressive. You need to watch him.'

From that moment on, I was in the England frame.

By this stage Mum and Dad had moved again, to Fuller Road in Moulton, next to a dairy farm which exuded the strong stench of cowshit all year round. Jay had pretty much left home, but Sam had moved back after living in Spain for a while. We were a household of four, going about our routines. We all worked hard, but it was subsistence stuff. I upped my efforts because I wanted more than that. I worked as a labourer during the holidays; I hung out with friends. I trained hard – and then my breakthrough moment arrived.

CHAPTER 5

WHEN THE SAINTS

In the summer of 1996, when I was 17, I was invited to join a practice session with the senior players in preparation for the Henley Sevens, a popular tournament that clubs would go to every year. Northampton were intending to compete with an established England 'A' or full international group of players; I'd been asked to join in the practice as cannon fodder but I decided to take the opportunity to make my mark. Harvey Thorneycroft was the long-established winger at the Saints and a local legend. The Academy lads called him Suavey Thorneycroft. We'd see his big Rover with his name emblazoned down the side and think how we'd love to have a car like that until we realised that we wouldn't – one bad game and the fans would key it! If I wanted to make an impression, Harvey was going to have to make way.

He was ten years my senior and we were polar opposites: Harvey, your archetypal public schoolboy, and me, the backstreet kid who rolled up his sleeves and got stuck in. The Sevens practice session was touch rugby, but every time Harvey got the ball, I absolutely mullahed him. I pushed him, dumped him on his arse, ran through him. Every time. He became really, really, really wound up. I was tall, skinny, quick and very aggressive. I didn't care who anyone was.

In those days Sevens was about your first-choice players, not youngsters, so it was incredible to be training alongside Tim Rodber, who I later learnt was in the England Sevens team. I had an inkling he was a great player because he featured on that poster I'd received in a goodie bag from an RFU open day at the club. And he was imposing. Off the pitch, he had an authoritative, military air – you could tell he was a graduate from the Royal Military Academy in Sandhurst. On the pitch, he was also a warrior. Every time I did something notable in that practice, he'd give me a shove, a kick or a dig, to see if I'd be fazed by that. I wasn't. Everyone could see I was raw and had an amazing desire to play, so they picked me to travel to Henley. And I shone in that tournament. I was ready to seize my moment.

Phil Pask, a former Saints player who was our strength and conditioning coach and physio – and still works as the England physio – saw a little bit of talent in me. After the Henley Sevens, he took me along with several of the Saints first-team players to the National Pub Sevens in Harpenden, a Sunday tournament that had started casually as a pre-season warm-up in the days when the RFU forbade Sunday games. This was an annual challenge for Pasky; he was fed up with always losing in the semis or final to a bunch of Welsh or the White Hart Marauders from London, full of first-class players 'in disguise'. Gambling on injecting a bit of speed into the usual mix, he invited me to join the pretence as a team from the Black Bottom Pub or something. It was a great day, though we still lost in the final – and we got back to find Pasky had nearly lost his job. He was in serious trouble for taking me without asking permission. For me, accompanying and playing against senior players in those Sevens tournaments was great experience. I had that sniff of being in and around the first team.

Driving into Franklin's Gardens soon started to feel like entering a home from home. It has changed a lot, but I remember it so clearly: the two nightclubs at the gate, the Ritzy and the Zone; the car park where I'd later do donuts in my sponsored Mercedes; the gym in the shed, and the lake, where we used to swim after training to cool down or be chucked in as a punishment. As they redeveloped the ground, we had mobile changing-rooms. Sometimes, if we'd had a night out, we'd climb the walls to get into the ground and sleep in the Portakabins.

For all my lofty ambitions to join the likes of Harvey and Tim, I was still in the development squad, still young and prone to doing stupid things. One night when Abby and I were out, we saw a guy we knew kissing a girl who wasn't his girlfriend.

He and I never got on, but his girlfriend was Abby's best friend … so, fired by alcohol, we were outraged. I went over and said, 'What are you doing? You're playing with fire.' He and I were both drunk. He pushed past me and I punched him. I can't remember it, but I simultaneously cut his lip and my hand on his teeth. Within a few days, the wound had pus oozing out of it. I was working as a white van driver for Avalon, commercial printers who were very supportive of my rugby. Print finishing was going to be my trade. (I had really wanted to be a fireman, but there was a limited intake in the year I applied.) I couldn't drive. With my hand on the steering wheel, the pain was agony. My veins had gone red and inflamed. I went to the hospital and they diagnosed septicaemia. I'd got an infection from his saliva. I had to stay in hospital so they could operate on the wound and flush out the poison. Just before a 'nil by mouth' sign went up above my bed, in walked Wally, bringing me a massive box of Maltesers and bag of McDonalds. I appreciated that, but I realised I had jeopardised by rugby career. Mum made me write an apology card to Geech, who must have thought I was an idiot. Dad told me to say sorry and make up. Which we did, later becoming good friends.

Early in the 1996/97 season I moved up to the senior squad. Paul Larkin, the first-team backs coach, had travelled specifically to watch me play in my first senior game, for the second XV against Moseley in Birmingham. That game told him two things about me: first, that I had the physical stature for a rugby player even at the age of 17, and second, that I had natural pace and power. Technical skills could be added if I listened and learnt. I didn't have great technical abilities, and Paul was tactful enough to suggest I hadn't needed them to date. I was okay at passing, but I hadn't had a lot of practice because when I got the ball, I ran over the top of players and scored. Tackling? I caught up and sat on them. I started to stay out a bit longer after training to practise kicking, catching and passing.

Geech and Paul were both schoolmasterly in their approach, and gave us thorough end-of-season reports outlining our strengths, weaknesses and proposed areas for improvement. I loved these reports. I always treated my rugby as a learning curve; I still had an insatiable desire to improve. I'd see what they picked up on in the team performance and in my own individual performance. By the end of that first year, Paul noted my 'equanimity of character'. I was calm; I concentrated (and lip-read); I took things in. In other words, I was coachable. And I was fortunate in the timing of my career: I would benefit from some of the very best coaches in the world – Geech and Wayne Smith at Northampton, and eventually Clive Woodward with England. I made sure I learnt all I could from them.

I made my first-team debut at Franklin's Gardens on 10 September 1996 in the 51–8 victory over Treorchy in the Anglo-Welsh League. I was paid £450 to play. Incredible! At 17, playing rugby was joyful. It wasn't a job. When you're named in the first-team squad, you get your tie – another tie! – and a stash of kit. Getting stashed out meant collecting a bundle of shorts, tracksuits, training tops, T-shirts, hoodies, hats, some cool Puma King boots and all the formal wear. I got it home and laid it out on my bed. For a boy who'd clothed himself for years from lost property, it felt like one hell of a milestone. I loved that side of rugby, the tradition of wearing a suit and your first-team tie after games. Every year we were given a new suit and a pair of Church's shoes.

I was tall, quite slight, but extremely quick. I really wanted to establish myself and in the last three months of the season, I made six more first-team appearances. The left wing was not a position I could walk into. As well as Harvey, there was Craig Moir, the Scotland winger. He was a fantastic player, solid, incredibly fit, very strong and powerful. He made his mistakes but when he went into a game, he'd give you a hundred per cent in honesty. He was good competition for me. And by the end of the season, in the summer of 1997, Jon Sleightholme would arrive. An England winger leaving Bath to join Northampton. I didn't believe it. But you have to do your talking on the pitch. You have to go over and beyond. You're professional and you're still learning. I had no rights to that position. There was never going to be a gap I could just slot into. I had to claim my place, but I had a good rapport with the big stars like Tim Rodber, Matt Dawson, Nick Beal and Paul Grayson. They could see my potential and liked my attitude – on the rugby pitch at least.

Off it, everyone thought I was very, very rude. First, I say it as I see it, and second, I seemed to ignore people. I never told anyone about my hearing limitations. At home, everyone knew to say things twice. It would be, 'Ben, what do you think? BEN, WHAT DO YOU THINK?'

At some stage early in my Saints career I did mention my hearing, very casually, probably making it sound temporary. I didn't want to jeopardise my chance in the team. I didn't want to present a weakness. Players thought I was loud and rude and cocky. What I didn't hear, I obviously ignored. If I wasn't in front of someone watching their lips move, I wouldn't hear them address me. The coaches, on the other hand, considered me a very conscientious student of the game as I was always in the front at team talks, and I often used to come up after a tactics discussion to clarify something. I asked lots of questions – because I didn't want to miss anything. I'd learnt instinctively to read people's mannerisms, body language, tone and posture, but I also became very vocal on the pitch. In my urgent need to know the calls, I'd confirm endlessly what was going on and became known as the clearest and loudest communicator.

It wasn't until after I finished playing rugby that I was diagnosed as being clinically deaf in both ears. Curious to get a specialist assessment back in 2004, I popped into a Specsavers Hearing Centre. At the end of a series of tests on the clarity of my hearing at various decibel levels in both ears, the audiologist sat back and said, 'Wow. How on earth have you coped?'

Four years ago, Sir Elton John – who I'd met through my Foundation – kindly referred me to the American hearing aid specialist Starkey. They tested my hearing more thoroughly and diagnosed a deteriorating condition. I now had 53 per cent hearing loss as well as bad tinnitus – a really annoying, constant ringing in my ears – and that pushed me into the 'profound hearing loss' category.

Of course I'd known all my life that there was a problem with my hearing but I'd found a way of getting by. Clive Woodward, for example, never knew I had hearing issues. In my little bubble, I missed countless crucial pre-match calls to arms, direct questions and bits of banter, but I let everyone think I was arrogant and rude. I didn't let it bother me because I'd worked out that I could get what I wanted on the rugby pitch by being the loudest; I'd shout for the ball and get it. I liked to joke that there was a reason why I was a prolific try scorer – I never heard anyone else call for the ball!

Geech used the Anglo-Welsh Cup to provide fringe players like me with competitive first-team rugby. On Tuesday, 11 March, he also picked me for a friendly at home against the RAF, playing with old hands such as Martin Bayfield and Michael Dods. The *Northampton Chronicle and Echo* previewed the game – 'The up and coming players whose careers should start taking off are jet-powered winger Ben Cohen, scrum-half James Bramhall, centre Phil Greaves and lock Matt Birke.' I scored my first try for the club, which was written up by Terry Morris, the local reporter: 'England Colts winger Ben Cohen, when given the space, produced an electrifying turn of speed for a second half try that will rank among the best at the Gardens this season.'

I was selected on the wing for another game in the Anglo-Welsh League, away to Newport on 22 March, with Richard Jackson, a Bedford School boy who made his first-team debut at full-back against the RAF. I managed another try in the tenth minute and we won 53–7.

My league debut against Orrell up in Wigan, a week later, was particularly memorable. Mum and Dad had travelled up on the supporters' coach with Sam. It was a massive occasion for me. I was sitting in the changing-room pulling on my boots when a guy called Tim, who was playing hooker, glanced at my boots and said, 'You've got to give yourself a chance, mate.' I must have looked puzzled. 'You need to put studs in your boots, son,' he continued. 'There're hardly any in there. There are studs on the table. Go and put some new ones in.' I went out and played well. We won 50–14 and I scored a crazy try. Orrell's Michael Worsley slung out a pass close to our try-line which I intercepted and ran the length of the field to score. I was playing against Nigel Heslop, the current England winger, and I gave him a right punch in the face. I don't know why.

My press image, courtesy of the latest Terry Morris report, had progressed to being 'no shrinking violet'. I wasn't going to work my way quietly into the reckoning; I wanted to make a big impact.

We celebrated winning the game with a couple of drinks. Well fuelled then, I went up to Harvey on the bus on the way home and said: 'My dad says I have to have the attitude that when Harvey Thorneycroft wakes up and looks in the mirror in the morning he will wish Ben Cohen had never been born.' It was very arrogant, and I didn't stop there. I then turned around and challenged him: 'I give you six months before I take your position.' I did as well. We had some right battles on the training ground. I liked Harvey a lot, and still do. It's something we've always laughed about. At our weddings, each of us gave the other a mirror with a note saying, 'Every time you look in the mirror you'll wish I'd never been born.' I look back and cringe. I was 18 and I didn't have a clue. Everything was so far removed from anything I'd ever experienced.

A few weeks later I was called up for the England Colts to play against Wales. We played at Iffley Road in Oxford, where Roger Bannister broke the four-minute mile in 1954. For all my personal euphoric highs, however, Saints as a club was engulfed in an injury crisis that sent us sliding towards the relegation play-offs. I was learning how to live with parallel ups and downs. Tim Rodber, Martin Bayfield, Paul Grayson, Shem Tatupu, Don Mackinnon and Craig Moir were all sidelined and I came on as a sub against Bristol, an encounter we lost 20–11, and away at The Stoop, where Harlequins won 36–16.

In spite of those results the Saints' season ended safely, but with the publicly stated aim that next season, 1997/98, Geech had to take us from being good losers to winners.

*

The Saints side I had progressed to was made up of world-class players, overseen by a world-class coach in Ian McGeechan. I was lucky that he saw something in me and gave me the opportunity. He related to me because, like him, I'd come from a state school without any family rugby background. Geech gave me good advice at key times; he wanted to give me the best information and steer me in the right direction to keep my development on track. The rugby he wanted the Saints to play suited me. We were playing better and better, partly because we had players like me who were being moulded and developed in a particular way to fit the team, and we, in turn, helped the team develop. There was a recognition that using me correctly, according to the coaches' vision, would open up opportunities for others. Traditionally, wingers were finishers; but Geech wanted me to be more than a finisher. I was a powerful runner who others could latch on to. His guidance gave me confidence.

The Saints changing-room was intimidating, full of seasoned tough guys. Tim Rodber, the captain, hadn't talked to me much initially. Forwards and backs tended to stay in their groups. Young kids came and went. I was arrogant and naïve, but my ignorance was an advantage. If I had been clued up on rugby, I would have been too much in awe. Because I was ignorant, I just got on with it. Now I look back and think, wow, what an opportunity – me, a nobody, being among these players who were huge, lauded, world-class players. I respected these guys for what I watched them do on the pitch, but I didn't have a clue they came with big reputations in an international context. When I started to play alongside them, and travel with them to other grounds, I started to realise they were absolute legends who had achieved so much. Tim Rodber, captain in the Green Howards infantry regiment, captain of Northampton and a colossus for England and the British and Irish Lions. Justyn Cassell, a member of the England team that won the 1993 World Cup Sevens. Gregor Townsend, of Scotland and the Lions. Martin Bayfield, six foot ten, England and Lions lock. Budge Pountney, the embodiment of absolute determination, Matt Stewart, Nick Beal, Matt Dawson, Ali Hepher, Don Mackinnon, the Western Samoan Shem Tatupu … I was in awe of them as my seniors, without knowing anything about them. Nor did I know anything about Ian McGeechan's history and everything that he had achieved with the British and Irish Lions in 1989 and 1993, or not until the changing-room was buzzing with the news that he'd been invited to lead the Lions in 1997. I was in an incredible position, with the talent and depth of that side – even if I didn't fully realise it at the time.

Geech was laying down foundations, identifying young English players and adding a sprinkling of international super-stars. Through hard work under excellent coaches, I had become part of a group that was on the cusp of something special. On 13 September 1998 – the day before my 20th birthday, I signed my first professional contract: £15,000 for one year. Dad came in with me to sit with Paul Larkin and go through the terms. Dad said, 'Paul, look, I understand football. I don't understand

Dad with me, Jay and Sam. Looks like I'm screaming my head off!

On the beach in Javea with mum.

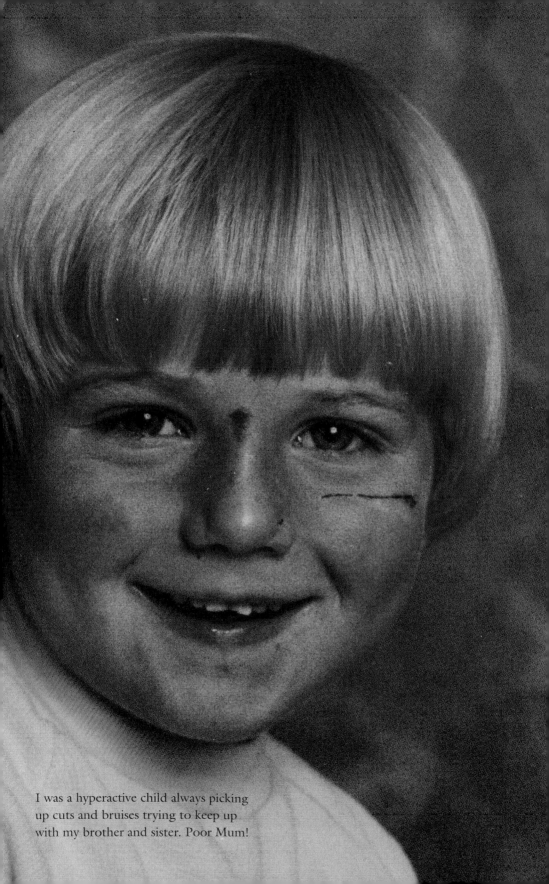

I was a hyperactive child always picking
up cuts and bruises trying to keep up
with my brother and sister. Poor Mum!

Family holidays in Spain. My
very first summer we travelled
down to Javea, all three kids
crammed in a caravanette.

The Cohens are a football family. This is my Uncle George on the left with Bobby Moore celebrating winning the 1966 World Cup.

And me with George's cap and medal. It wasn't until I was older that I really understood what his achievement meant.

Playing out in the back garden with Justin and some of our friends.

Me and Justin posing proudly with a pretty dodgy snowman!

Aged 17 with dad. He always had a cuppa in his hand.

Northampton Old Scouts team photo. I'm in
the middle, standing, Wally – Steve Thompson
– is next to me and Dad's on the far left.

Dad, Uncle Len and Uncle George
on the right, with my cousin
Andrew and his son Lewis.

My and Dad's second trip to
Twickenham, for the East Midlands
Under 19s County Championship final.

rugby. Please don't rip us off.' To which Paul replied that I was much further down the line than anyone else my age. The signature on the bottom of the contract meant I was a professional rugby union player. From that moment I grew up and started to become a lot more independent. I was able to buy a red VW Polo Estate, which cost me £600. I enjoyed saving up and paying for that. Mum and Dad had moved to Moulton; my sister had moved back from Spain and I enjoyed that time. We were happy, things were moving onwards and upwards. I moved into the house Abby shared with her mother as an interim measure while Abby and I looked around for somewhere to buy. Eventually we bought a three-bedroom house, which we refurbished, and moved in with a bit of furniture given us by Abby's mum.

That season I started to feel established as a first-team regular, which meant immersion in tough parallel league and cup campaigns. In his *Chronicle and Echo* match report Terry Morris granted me parity on the pitch with Harvey in a home game against Saracens: 'Ben Cohen on the left wing was Saints' most incisive runner while Harvey Thorneycroft on the other was full of bludgeoning power.' I had taken the left wing from Harvey. From then on, I normally started on the left, though as backs, we could all play centre, full-back or on either wing to cover injuries. The autumn was marked by the failure to progress beyond the pool stages of the European Challenge Cup, the second-tier competition in Europe. I experienced the dirty tactics of French sides Bordeaux-Bègles and Nice, and defeat home and away to Connacht, though I claimed a personal highlight in three tries in Europe against Nice. By early November, Geech was called upon to defend the direction the club was taking as fans became frustrated by league defeats, to which he responded with a rousing 'No Turning Back' argument. We turned things around over Christmas, thanks largely to Paul Grayson's kicking prowess.

In many ways it was a tough school; very male, very aggressive. There was no tip-toeing around. There was a lot of peer pressure, a lot of changing-room chitter-chatter and banter which, if you were weak in that area, meant you could easily fall by the wayside. I always liked to work things out for myself, and I asked a lot of stupid questions and probably made ridiculously dumb comments. I'd be the butt of jokes, but in that very selfish environment my stubbornness – and my deafness – stood me in good stead. I didn't try to ingratiate myself with everyone. I was prepared to scrap my way to the top. The fact that many of these players had played for England or Scotland or the Lions and yet reacted positively to my contribution on the pitch was enough for me. My elders could see I had talent, and that the skills I lacked I was prepared to work tirelessly to improve. I think they respected the way I'd fronted up to Harvey, who was a stalwart and popular. I was completely innocent about the ways of the wider world, but I like to think endearingly so!

On the cusp of professionalism, rugby still had changing-rooms full of educated people who combined their sport with the army or university; there were guys taking sabbaticals from high-flying professions. I am the strongest believer in old-school rugby values. On every level, I learnt everything I needed to know about life from observing the old guard: how to conduct myself, how to build confidence, how to hold a conversation. I had great role models in Tim Rodber, Harvey, Ian Hunter, Grays and Daws; they are people I still look up to. I'd see how they were with people in the bar after a game or in the social side of things, with supporters, with girls. I'd take snippets of their conversation and soak up what I could in order to educate myself.

I spent a lot of time in Paul Larkin's office. I'd make tea for everyone and sit down to analyse my game. Back in the late 1990s we didn't use video analysis as much as we do now. We'd still examine highlights of the game. The coaches would 'code' a video of a match to highlight each individual player's different contributions. If I clicked on my name, I could bring up all the significant moments I'd featured in during the game so I could study various aspects of my play in the context of the backs' moves. What did I do right? What could I have done better? What did I do wrong? I wanted to learn. Everyone did. Sometimes I'd go and see Paul about a positional aspect of our game plan. I was always in there studying.

Under Ian McGeechan the club fostered a very liberating ethos, allowing us to play a brand of rugby that was exciting to watch and to play. 'Go out and express yourself,' he'd say. 'Have fun.' I was never daunted by an opposition. I always gave

100 per cent and I spent a lot of time on analysis. Geech, being an ex-schoolmaster, instinctively picked up different people's learning styles. Without being aware of my hearing issues, he was conscious that I liked to see things. His style of coaching was all about visual reinforcement. If we went through something indoors in diagrams, we'd replicate it on the field. With me, Geech went through every tactic or move physically in person. He would stand out there with the backs ensuring his picture was being effectively communicated. I had good players inside me on the wing, and Geech was brilliant at getting us all to understand how best to use each other. He'd be out there on the field with us, talking through the options, not shouting from 40 or 50 metres away. I'd ask a lot of questions. Is this the best position? Or should I be going there? We had a natural rapport; he could see I benefited from a fairly close player-coach relationship within training, with plenty of chat, to get an understanding of what I could do.

It could be hilarious. When we were working on timing my runs to catch the ball at full flight, he was teaching me to hold back. If you're too enthusiastic and eager, you see the ball two passes away and you're off, and of course by the time it gets to you, you're slowing down. We spent a lot of time with Geech holding me back, so that as the ball was arriving I was accelerating, and by the time I caught it I was at full pace. He would stand right behind me, literally tugging on my shirt while I ran on the spot, and say, 'Wait … Wait … Wait … Here it comes… Two passes away … One pass away … Now you should be accelerating … Now you're at full pace.' We worked out that I could sometimes hit a line from the blind-side, which other wingers didn't do as much. I'd come in off the blind-side wing and do the same – arrive very late into a position, accelerating – and opponents found me difficult to handle.

My visual perception had developed sharply in compensation for my hearing problems. This suited Geech's mental picture of the game, which he called 'three-dimensional'. He expected us to anticipate the shape of moves, the space that would be created, instinctively knowing who we were going to be working on, who was going to pass the ball, where he was coming into the play and where I was going to run off him. It was much more than me being stuck out on a wing, waiting for the ball to come to me. He said it was no good me trying to be Rory Underwood who, small and compact, was the epitome of clinical try-scorers. He tried to relate me to wingers who matched my physical strengths and suited my personality. He said I reminded him very much of Ben Tune, the Australian winger, and showed me video clips advising me to learn from what he and other Australian wingers were doing. 'You're powerful, you have the confidence to take on defenders, you can break tackles, you can be away from 60 or 70 metres out.' Geech was careful to manage the balance of learning with gaining first-team experience, and the established players looked after me in the sense that they didn't give me ball I couldn't use. I developed the confidence to know that if I had a one-on-one with a defender, or a bit of room, I would take off. In my head I had the visual comparisons with the Australian wingers – using space, having power in my running so that others could play off me, tracking where the ball was and arriving late at things to time a run.

My deafness had advantages. I got in a zone. I was difficult to distract and I would built up a strong relationship with the player next to me. It could be verbal, it could be anticipatory. Working so hard on the visual perception of the game – the shapes, the positioning and the timing of when to arrive – took away some of the need for words. I had fun perfecting it, getting later and later with my run, becoming harder and harder for an opponent to pick up. Geech later told me he enjoyed watching me develop my play further for England. He loved the way I looked ten metres off the pace and, the next thing, I was steaming in at full pace, having surprised three defenders. I'd take up positions a lot of wingers wouldn't bother to explore. Traditional wing play meant staying in the outside space and waiting for the game to come to you, but I wanted to be involved. I'd be in play or I'd come late and change directions and give the centres different options. That allowed other players to play more freely too.

In February, all my progress halted when I broke my leg playing against Gloucester in the Cheltenham & Gloucester Cup. I was going in to score a try, and attempting to stay in touch when two players converged on me. 'Snap!' In the three-man pile-up I heard the unmistakeable sound of a breaking bone.

'Uh-oh,' I thought, 'I hope it isn't me.' I literally couldn't tell.

I stood up, tried to carry on, then realised from the pain that it was my bone that had gone. I cried with frustration. A minute beforehand I'd been laughing at a slapstick moment when Martin Bayfield, all six foot ten of him, had been hoisted to an extraordinary height as he jumped in the line-out only for the ball to go straight through his hands – and then I was in tears. I thought that was it for my campaign. It was a nothing break, just the fibula, a muscle bone down the side, not a load-bearing bone, and yet I was out for eight weeks. There is never a good time to get injured, but this was a crucial time for me. I missed out on the England Colts and Under 21 games, and that was absolutely terrible. I wasn't good at sitting on the sidelines. I hated not being part of something, not being able to train. Bored senseless, I spent most of my time on a computer. I came back slowly, but a training collision resulted in torn ankle ligaments and I was out for a further two weeks. But it turned around. I came back at the end of the season, playing in two league games and getting a call-up for the England Under 21 game against France.

I loved attending the England Under 21 fitness sessions, because sometimes the senior England squad was there too. On one such occasion, the two squads combined and we were sent off to do a three-kilometre run. Aerobically, I was naturally very good. I saw another young lad, a little bit younger than me, a little bit overweight, who had already played for England. I thought, tell you what, I'm going to stick with him on this run because he's in the England side. I can't go wrong. I'll run alongside him, he's sort of my level. I must have done one kilometre, matching his pace – barely a jog – and I found that to go that slowly was more energy sapping than running at my standard pace, so I took off and completed the run at my normal speed. The player I left behind was a young Jonny Wilkinson. Soon after that Jonny became the fittest guy in the England camp.

In mid-June I was on holiday in Ibiza when, out of the blue, I was called up by England Under 21s for a five-nation tournament in South Africa the following month. I was so excited. I'd played for England Under 19s in France, but this was my first proper big tour which would take me abroad for a month, staying in different hotels in various locations around South Africa. The call-up meant lots of new kit, but, more significantly, it was confirmation that I'd taken another step up the rugby ladder towards the senior England team. James Bramhall and I were part of a 26-strong party flying out to take on the emerging players from New Zealand, Australia, Argentina and the host nation, players we could be competing against all our careers. It was a great tour, a good feeder for players like Lewis Moody and Joe Worsley, and it was fun to be travelling with friends. South Africa and New Zealand were very strong units. We lost 95–7 to the All Blacks. That was a very long day chasing shadows.

It was a satisfying end, though, to what had been a really bad second half of the season. I achieved my goal after all and it came with pleasing recognition in the universally read end-of-season summary in the local press, where I was referred to as 'the forceful Cohen, aged 19, fast-tracked into the Saints' first team by Ian McGeechan despite tough competition for wing spots'. It's an odd feeling as a sportsman, the first time you realise there is an external perception of your game created by professional observers, and it was a proud moment to see I had been acknowledged for making an impact. The season-long press coverage marked the first time I'd featured in the paper since plucky, have-a-go Ben, the river rescue hero. The accolade felt just as good – and, I felt, a tiny bit more justified.

The goal I set myself for the 1998/99 season was to establish myself in the first team, primed to terrorise defences, and make myself indispensable to the collective club ambition. Northampton Saints wanted emphatically to shrug off the tag of being perennial under-achievers. We wanted to see the fulfilment of Ian McGeechan's philosophy translated into silverware. We wanted to win the league. Having never qualified for the European Cup, the aim was – at the very least – to claim one of England's six places in the big-money Heineken Cup competition for the next season. I say 'we', even as the most junior player, because the nice thing about that squad was that the direction and attitude was set by the whole group. We were sharing in an education. It was a good environment, which just got stronger because we wanted to play a certain type of rugby and we were convinced that, if we cracked it, we would win things, including the league title. The emphasis was on learning together. As Tim Rodber always says, your brain is the most sophisticated body organ and it is important – in sport, business and all human interaction – to keep learning and working hard to improve.

In a further honing of the professional mindset required of all squad members, Tim stated during the 1998 pre-season that the club needed 'a streamlined squad of professionals' who trained professionally and looked after ourselves in the way we ate, drank and slept. The first time I met Garry Pagel, the South African prop who had joined the Saints the year before, I thought, 'Holy shit, I've got a long way to go.' He was chucking 180 kilos on the bench press and I was barely lifting 100. I bumped into him and his wife outside Tesco with their 'weekly shop': three trolleys full of steak, eggs, milk, you name it.

Geech signed what the local paper called the 'Fab Four' – star internationals at the exemplary end of this scale of professionals who would galvanise the remaining squad with their attitude and abilities. Of course I'd never heard of any of them except Pat Lam, of Samoa, who was to be given free rein to practise his exciting brand of flair play. He was known to be a strong Christian who made a point of treating everyone as equals, which made people more considerate to one another and helped younger players integrate with the seasoned old hands. We soon heard that Federico Mendez of Argentina – who was to add wiliness as hooker – was the 18-year-old who had knocked out Paul Ackford with a massive punch to the head back in 1990. David Dantiacq, the French centre, would provide elusiveness, pace and vision, and Richard Metcalfe, as the world's tallest rugby player at seven foot one, would literally add a massive presence at the front of the line-out. He could jump and scoop and still be miles higher than anyone else. The message was clear: Northampton Saints were thinking big.

We experienced an early hiccup in a league defeat to Saracens before getting into our stride. By the end of January, we were second in the league and playing with passion, intensity and belief. Most importantly, we were playing for each other. Of course there were setbacks. On a personal level, I suffered an annoying knuckle break just before I was due to play for England Under 21s against South Africa in November. On 30 January, we came up against a rugged London Irish side in the Tetley's Bitter competition and our cup dream died. This triggered a loss of confidence. The lowest point was losing 22–15 in a key match against Leicester – which prompted Martin Johnson's side to do a lap of honour, brazenly crowing in front of a record crowd of more than 10,000 at Franklin's Gardens – and second place in the league looked very much like a best-case scenario.

We hadn't played well in the wet, muddy winter months, but come the drier end of March we were back to our best, trouncing Newcastle 57–16 on a fast dry pitch which suited our high-tempo style. In scoring the first and last of nine tries in the game, I set another personal milestone: it was the first time I'd ever scored twice in a league game. We duly finished second in the league, achieving our goal of European Cup competition. To celebrate our last home game of a solid season, 30 members of the Saints came down to PC Night Club on Bridge Street, where my brother Jay was manager. He'd billed it to the public as an end-of-season celebration for Saints supporters, and those fans were very surprised when all the players turned up.

The club had changed beyond recognition in three years. And so had I. At 20, I was the youngest member of the team, but I'd won Geech's approbation. In his end-of-season résumé for the fans, he wrote: 'Ben's picked his whole game up and taken it to a new level. He's a local boy who's come through the system and proved himself an outstanding prospect. He knows what to do and when to do it. He has the potential to go all the way and play for England.'

On 7 May, I was thrilled to be named in the England squad for the Paris Sevens, coached by Dick Best. It was a great trip. We reached the quarter-finals, then got thrashed by New Zealand 40–7. We went into the plate competition for beaten quarter-finalists and reached the final of that, only to lose 38–14 to Australia. I had now represented England at Colts, Under 21s and Sevens and I noticed I was starting to be asked a lot about my senior England and World Cup ambitions. 'I've always had this childhood dream of scoring the winning try for my country in the World Cup final,' I said. 'I don't know whether I would have had that dream if it hadn't been for what my uncle achieved, but that was such a fantastic achievement that it's inspired me ever since I started playing the game. There are not many people in this country who can say, "My dad's brother played for England and won a World Cup medal." My uncle takes a keen interest in my rugby. Whenever we talk about the pressure of performing in professional sport, he always advises me to take it with a pinch of salt.'

CHAPTER 6

THE CALL UP

The World Cup dominated planning for the 1999/2000 season. Before he left Northampton to join Scotland coach Jim Telfer, Ian McGeechan had expressed concern that we would be under strength in the autumn games, with more than ten players expected to be away on World Cup duty – the very players who were the backbone of our team. England, he anticipated, would select Tim Rodber, Matt Dawson, Paul Grayson and Nick Beal, in whom I'd noted exemplary mental aggression, and possibly Grant Seely. Scotland would take Budge Pountney and Matt Stewart and possibly Richard Metcalfe and Craig Moir. Wales would call for Allan Bateman; Federico Mendez would join his Argentina compatriots and Pat Lam would meet up with Samoa.

John Steele, a lovely guy, was appointed the new Saints Director of Rugby. A former army officer and fly-half for Northampton and England 'A', Steeley had been Director of Rugby at London Scottish before returning to Franklin's Gardens. We had four crunch league games early in the season to set the tone for our three-pronged campaign in league, Tetley's Bitter Cup and European Cup competition, where we were drawn in a pool with Grenoble, Neath and Edinburgh Reivers. In his long-term plan, Geech had dissected the game to bare bones and made us all understand our individual strengths and weaknesses, and how we should play to each other's strengths. He had created a team culture with a current flowing strongly towards success, and Steeley was now riding that. With Tim, Pat Lam and Daws, the club could run itself. It was coaching made easy. That's not to take anything away from Steeley; he was more of a big-picture guy, a great Director of Rugby more than a nuts-and-bolts coach.

In early September, I signed a new three-year contract. At the age of 20, this signified job security and the opportunity to develop my career without worry. Again Dad came in with me to sit down with Paul Larkin. Paul said he was going to insert a clause that meant I would get a bonus when I was first capped for England. Dad and I liked that. Not if, but when. (And when that moment came, the Director of Rugby came after Paul asking why they were paying me a reward for the honour of playing for someone else! It was the early days of commercialism, and Paul pointed out that it was a win-win situation from a business point of view, owing to the potential number of Ben Cohen Saints shirts sold when every boy in Northampton would want to be wearing one.)

Allan Bateman, the most unassuming, lovely guy, also known as the Welsh Wizard, was Northampton's new signing at centre. He added a lot to the team dynamic. He had a great attitude, great values, and was a rewarding player for me to play alongside.

During pre-season training, a small group of us were filling Allan in about everyone at the club. At that moment, Steve the groundsman, a legendary character, walked out on to the field – which was cue for the Steve stories. One of the boys warned Allan to be careful not to lose his clothes because Steve enjoyed borrowing things from lost property. Nothing stayed lost for long! Once, I had stayed behind to do extra training on the running track when Jim Bramhall emerged from the changing-room saying his expensive new Timberland shoes had just disappeared. In the background we could hear the buzz of Steve's strimmer, and just as we were talking about the missing shoes, Steve edged closer. Jimmy has size 12 feet, and Steve must be size 5, and what did we see but Steve wearing Jimmy's brand new Timberlands packed out with socks and the kitchen sink and covered with fresh grass clippings. While we were regaling Allan with lost property stories, someone spotted a pile of dog crap on the training pitch, which gave us the perfect scenario to show Allan another of Steve's party pieces. Someone called out to ask Steve to get a shovel and take the mess away. He duly came over without a shovel, removed his hat, picked up the dog shit with it, took it to the side of the pitch, and put his hat back on again. We'd seen it umpteen times, but Allan, in his Welsh accent, was going, 'I don't fucking believe it.'

Going into that season, I was an okay player, a good stand-in for the first team. I'd toured Argentina in the summer with England Under 21s and performed satisfactorily, but my body was still misbalanced strength-wise because of the broken fibula. With our star international players away in training for the World Cup and not likely to be back until the end of November, the start of our season was inevitably inconsistent. We thrashed Leicester, and I scored one of the six tries. Then, having studied a video of the game, we noted seven key areas to build on for even greater success – and then got trounced 33–13 by Bath, though I had some recompense in being voted Man of the Match by the Saints supporters. In the end, World Cup selection had taken eight players from us, the backbone of the team. With a depleted squad, I was one of the players used regularly to bridge the gap, but I didn't feel I was having a great start to the year. One week I'd be taking pride in having the highest tackle count; the next week I'd be peeved to fluff an easy tackle.

The broken leg had set me back. We were still in the early days of professionalism, and the club had no infrastructure for intensive physio and recovery programmes. The club gym was in the tin-roofed hut where our hands froze to the metal bars in the winter and where we endured sauna-like conditions in the summer. Playing against Saracens in October, I recall being on our try-line when they scored again – they went on to win 32–8 – and despairing about my game. I'd gone stale. With the vivid realisation that my game had plateau-ed out, I had a nagging fear that my career was stalling. I talked over with Dad about how I could improve my game and, most importantly, find some consistency. I was then named as a substitute against Sale, away, and came on to produce the tackle of the game. It was weird to read in the paper about my 'awesome try-saving tackle' and how 'the game turned on that incident', because I was struggling.

Uncle George had always advocated doing a bit of private extra training. I'd grown up on stories of how he could cover 100 yards in 10.3 seconds and how he'd worked on his fitness away from Fulham by running miles between villages in all weathers. I realised that instead of muddling through on my own, doing a bit more running and throwing around a few more monster weights, I should do what Matt Dawson, Budge Pountney and Paul Grayson did: work in a focused way on a tailored programme. People recommended a local personal trainer called Ron Steel. It would cost me, but I thought: you know what, if I'm going to give it a go, I've got to do it.

England players had been taken to an island off Australia to train for the World Cup. Even though they crashed out in the quarter-finals, losing 44–21 to South Africa, the Northampton boys came back in such incredible shape. They were buzzing, and their energy was contagious. Those of us who'd made up the depleted squad found ourselves buying into their self-belief, and I felt it was rooted in their incredible levels of physical fitness. As a team, their return gave us such a lift. Something clicked; we started to perform so well that we realised we could go and win stuff.

Their return acted as a trigger for me to start work with Ron. I was inspired. Ron was a great chap, a former bobsleigher, who was quiet and reserved and knew the techniques for developing and harnessing explosive power. I asked him to work on all the athletic skills I felt I was missing: footwork, agility, speed, speed endurance, strength, power – the whole package. My power was always going to be my strength. Geech had directed me towards being a new breed of winger, strong, fast, ready to go round or through people, and I wanted to see how far I could push it. Rugby demands all the elements of speed endurance – running at maximum speed, acceleration, sustaining top speed and mastering change-of-direction speed to evade or chase an opponent. It was basically a lot of quads work: repeat springs, weights, biometric exercises. We trained either at Dallington Gym or in the park, where Ron set out ladders and cones to improve my agility and reactions at speed. Ron initially decided I needed to work on my upper body strength, too, to increase potency in breaking through tackles, then we moved on to a Speed, Agility, Quickness programme. We'd dovetail the sessions before and after I went in to train at the Saints, and it soon started to pay off. That extra independent work, tailored to my requirements, made an incredible difference. Within two weeks, I could feel a dynamic improvement. After six or eight weeks, my all-round game had completely changed.

At the time I was earning a goldfish and a balloon. Abby and I had moved house to Barrack Road in October, while the senior players were away at the World Cup. We bought an old Victorian townhouse with three storeys, a kitchen in the cellar and a ground-floor reception room that had been opened up to create a huge room with a balcony that overlooked the back garden. Just beautiful. To buy it, we'd over-stretched ourselves, as you tend to do. My decision to take on Ron at £20 a session, four times a week, with a few extra sessions per month, was like a second mortgage. It worked out around £400 per month. We could live, but we couldn't afford to go out or go on holiday.

However, I took pleasure in the sacrifices because the investment was worth it. Under Ron's supervision, I improved in all areas. The difference he made from the middle of October to the end of November was incredible. And with that physical progress, I felt my confidence soaring. I'd be breaking a tackle and thinking, 'Bloody hell I wouldn't normally do that.' I found myself carrying players three, four or five yards. I was so much harder to stop. Wow, my footwork! I've got the ability and confidence to do that now. I was moving towards what was required of an elite player – and that's what you are when you're a first-team player in a club that's in European competition.

It was all change at Northampton at the beginning of the 1999/2000 season. While John Steele had taken up the reins at the directorial level following Geech's departure, Pat Lam had assumed the captaincy role in place of Tim Rodber. For the greater good, Tim unselfishly gave up his No. 8 position to go to the back row, and he gave up the leadership role to Lammy. That was a signal to the rest of the team. We wanted the best; we'd attracted new world-class players and even a personality with Tim's status was happy to make room. Lammy would sit us down to pray before a game – though I was among those who preferred to think of it as 'focus time' – and he infused the team with quiet self-belief based on mutual respect for players no matter what their age or experience. He introduced a platform for an open forum so that everyone felt like they could say how they felt at the right time. The club was united around him, because at Northampton there were always internationals, superstar players, club players and lots of kids trying to make their mark. In espousing the Samoan cultural ideal of the extended family, he unified feelings on and off the field very effectively. Older players became more approachable to the younger talents. For a few years there had been a divide between the older, former amateur players, who were resistant to new training methods, and us younger players who threw ridiculous power weights around the gym and took to the new regime unquestioningly. Again, I found myself responding well to that inclusivity. Surrounded by excellent players, I started to shine.

Things had changed on the home front too. Jay had been offered the assistant manager job at a club where he DJ'd called The Pelican Cove. The manager soon left, so my brother took over, then drafted in Dad to run the door in charge of security, Mum as receptionist and my sister Sam behind the bar. That was in late summer of 1999. They were excited to have a family 'club' back again, though initially Mum told Dad she didn't want him back in the nightclub game. They had a big row about it. Mum said she had a bad feeling about the venture and she believed that you should never tread on old ground. She later told me the disagreement was so serious that she sat in the bedroom asking herself if she could live without Dad. The answer was no. So she supported him by working there too. No matter how much it's not something you want, she said, you have to support the person you love.

The club was going well, and then, one day, Dad told Justin he'd done a deal with the brewery to take over the lease in November. My brother said, 'Why do that?' Now, of course, he thinks he should have talked him out of taking on the responsibility, but Dad was exuberant. He thought it would be brilliant to have his own place again, which he would co-run with Jay. He was so excited about a new start. He felt it was his last big chance in life to make a go of the club business and be a success. So they gave it a go. The club was shut up completely in November in order to re-style it with an outside sports bar and Eternity nightclub inside. Dad had done a lot of favours for people over the years and he was soon calling in old friends to do the plastering, electrics and decorating. He designed a new back entrance to make it more welcoming. A grand opening was planned for the end of January. The following night the sports bar would be christened with a visit from Uncle George and his family, boosted by a group of Saints players.

The sense of a changing of the guard was heightened when Harvey Thorneycroft was granted a testimonial match to mark his 249-game career. I played for Harvey's XV against his World XV. It was a great occasion, with the crowd chanting 'Har-vee, Har-vee; and the man himself giving a speech to thank those who had always supported him and – rather inspiringly – those who had vocally doubted him, as they had been the spur for him to go on and prove them wrong. I couldn't believe Harvey wanted to retire. He was playing superbly. And we'd miss him on and off the pitch. He was the life and soul – and source of many an anecdote. We were playing in a charity game once and a guy came into the changing-room and said, 'Valuables, guys! Put them in the bag.' We handed in our modest belongings; Harvey put in his Rolex, his pride and joy – and of course the guy just scarpered. At Northampton, we always went on a pre-season tour to Chicago and Ohio. On one of these trips, Harvey was pickpocketed at the airport while on the payphone in arrivals. While we'd gone to settle in the hotel, he went out to sort out a replacement wallet and before he'd even got to a store some guy had him at knifepoint down a side alley. 'You're too late,' he told the guy coolly. 'I've already been done at the airport.'

Training with Ron was just the extra impetus I had needed. I measured my progress in the European Cup pool games. We had beaten Neath in a massive game to give ourselves a winning start, but then lost to Grenoble away. It was a game we threw away, having recovered from a 10–0 deficit to lead 18–10 going into the last 20 minutes, and then had to trudge disconsolately off the pitch with the scoreline reading 20–18. I had scored a try out of nowhere ... Tim Rodber's line-out take was passed on to Allan Bateman who set me up around the halfway line. I hit my stride – saw bodies coming – and kicked a neat floater over them, picked it up and scored. Nevertheless, we lost. In the changing-room, Tim read us the riot act: 'We have got to stop being a bunch of prima donnas and start playing some rugby.' Outside, I was asked by the press about my try and about how I would explain our loss, and I parroted Tim's criticism – thinking I sounded quite clever: 'Yeah, we're a bunch of prima donnas.' I hadn't a clue.

After the setback in Grenoble, we had to win all our remaining European Cup games. With our World Cup players back, our hefty pack winning better and better ball, and great communication becoming our trademark at the coalface, we were evolving into a ruthless side. When we gelled, and got a sequence of play together, we could be devastating. In December we played Edinburgh home and away. I was taking on people on the outside and beating them. Matt Dawson and I were both hailed as match winners and I won my first Star Man accolade from the *Northampton Chronicle & Echo* for my 'blasting runs'. Ian McGeechan, who kept in touch with us all by text and phone, watched the games sitting next to Paul Larkin, thrilled to support the team that was his legacy after five years of his groundwork.

It was hectic over Christmas and I would have to forego the traditional Cohen festivities. We had a crucial match against Newcastle on Boxing Day, and two big games the week afterwards. The schedule was relentless, but exhaustion does not register when results are going the right way. Very gratifyingly, the Saints backline – i.e. Nick Beal, myself, and either Jon Sleightholme or Craig Moir – were billed in *The Sunday Times* as 'the hottest property in the English game, notable for penetrative backline play'. Mum religiously kept every press cutting containing Saints reports, and where she had previously marked with biro a brief sentence or two mentioning my contribution to a game, she was now collecting headlines. BIG BEN STRIKES, COHEN PUTS THE ICING ON THE SAINTS CHRISTMAS CAKE, and all that. We thrashed Newcastle 37–5 and I had the satisfaction of scoring a blistering final-minute try alongside a brilliant Harvey Thorneycroft making his remarkable 250th appearance. I still couldn't believe he wanted to retire.

Keith Barwell hosted a big Millennium Eve party at his house. People came up to me that night and said, 'This will be a good year for you, Ben.' People with perspective. From where I was, I couldn't see it. I didn't take it as more than social chitchat, but at the same time I appreciated their optimism. Senior players always know more about what's going on, while I was just a young player, head down, arse up, getting on with it. Around New Year, I had a couple of storming games, including a hat-trick, which was a game-changer. On 2 January, I was shown a big article in *The Sunday Times* in which Stephen Jones had included me in a list of 'Six players who could improve a jaded England'. I was nominated alongside Mike Tindall, Chris Yates, Josh Lewsey, Jim Brownrigg and Simon Shaw, with the comment: 'Needs more experience to round out his talents but impressive on the move and with the combination of pace and strength perfect for the modern idiom.'

Sure enough, on 6 January, we had just finished a gruelling training session in the build-up to the European Cup home leg against Grenoble, when I saw on Teletext that I'd been called into a 35-strong England Six Nations Championship training squad. I was elated. Ten weeks prior to that, I'd not been playing well and was unable to find improvement, and here, after the work with Ron Steel, I had confirmation that I was once again moving in the right direction. That 'second mortgage' on Ron had proved money well spent. I knew I had only made it into a huge squad, but it felt such an honour to be included. I had everything to prove, and I had the self-belief to do my damnedest to make the most of this opportunity.

I went straight to see Dad at Eternity to tell him. 'All right, son,' he said proudly. The news had come days after we'd learnt George had been awarded the MBE 'for services to football' in the New Year's Honours, prompting the press to speculate about my emulating my uncle. Dad was well chuffed, of course. All those times we'd spent together, going to and from training at the Scouts, travelling in the old Astra to away games or to training at Bedford with East Midlands, me holding his mug of tea while he changed gear and him screaming 'Fuck!' as scalding tea sloshed all over us. Sometimes I'd talk about how the match went and he'd shake his head and say, 'Can't tell you anything, son, because I don't understand the game.' I think what made Dad most proud was the fact that I had achieved this off my own bat. I had discovered rugby for myself; I had asked him to take me down to the Old Scouts Open Day; I had latched on to rugby as the sport for me – and Dad had bought into it, supporting me all the way, sharing my dream.

George had always taught me to do my talking on the pitch, not in company, and to front up to pressure. He had warned me the only way to handle pressure is with your chin stuck out along with your chest. If you want success, you must cope with what it requires to be successful. I'd discovered already that he was right. I had to keep my feet on the ground. It would take a while for my England call-up to sink in, but I had to be sure I turned that notice into selection for an England first team. That night Wally and I went out to an Italian restaurant with Dad, Justin and some of Dad's mates who were helping refurbish Eternity ready for its opening, and celebrated with a few orange juices.

Back to the Heineken Cup, and by 9 January we were playing Grenoble at home and beating them to come top of Pool 6 with ten points. For me, this match was an advertisement for the Ron Steel factor. I had been asked to play my first full game as fullback in the absence of Nick Beal, who had a damaged knee, with Craig Moir and Jon Sleightholme on the wings, and Allan Bateman at centre. I wasn't ruffled; as a team we all helped each other. As soon as the game kicked off, I felt I was operating on a new level. I felt strong, I could run free, I could beat people, step around people. I was playing out of position and I scored a ridiculously satisfying try. I was running up my own arse basically, going nowhere, with someone grabbing hold of my shirt to stop me moving forward. I remember running as hard as I could with my newfound quad strength and, whoever I was dragging suddenly let go, and I shot off – pinged like an elastic band – rounding two players and outsprinting the rest to score in the opposite corner. It was a try from nothing against a very physical side. I did a dying swan in celebration. I knew the England selectors were watching.

CHAPTER 7

NO.11

The day after the Grenoble win I travelled down the M1 with a bottle of champagne for Man of the Match in my kit bag to my first England training camp. It was held at Pennyhill Park, at Bagshot, and I travelled there in Matt Dawson's car. I would be with people I'd looked up to since I had arrived at the Saints Academy, even before I'd signed my first Northampton contract: Paul Grayson, Tim Rodber, Matt Dawson and me in the same England squad. To heighten the sense of a new era, we were meeting in preparation for the inaugural Six Nations Championship following the inclusion of Italy.

Off the field, I was still deep down a shy and awkward lad. I didn't know what to say to anyone, so I looked to Daws. Six years my senior, he was a great mentor. Senior players usually have an input on selection or at least offer an opinion on the line up, the game plan and who can play a key role in that game plan. In the absence of Martin Johnson, who had an Achilles injury which would keep him out of the entire Six Nations tournament, Daws was named England captain. He had the ear of Clive Woodward and I believe he'd been pushing my cause. I was almost like his protégé. I'd ask his advice, pester him with questions and absorb the way he handled himself. As my club mentor, he kept things real for me in the England camp too. He was the best sounding board I could possibly have. You have to have advocates in sport. I've always looked up to Daws and admired the way he works incredibly hard at everything he does. Here, on my England debut, I could ask him whether I was going about things the right way. It wasn't always a two-way conversation. Sometimes he'd just tell me something and I'd just say, 'okay'.

I remember arriving at Pennyhill Park to find bags and bags of new kit allocated to me. In my room I tried it all on, fingering the rose on my chest, looking at myself in the mirror. It was an amazing feeling, knowing my hard work had paid off. Like my uncle, I had gone over and beyond, forking out for a personal trainer to give myself an extra edge. As Dad said, we are a family with a sporting heritage, and I was adding to it. The television was playing *Rugby Special*, replaying the game in which I'd scored the hat-trick that Clive had witnessed. It was surreal. I was thinking, how on earth have I fluked it? How have I managed to get into this England squad that is going out to play in the inaugural Six Nations Championship? Here I was with my new free laptop and O2 phone – and I still have the number from that phone to this day.

The whole week was exciting, but daunting. The cream rises to the top quicker in sport than in everyday life or business. I was around players I'd normally see only on TV, and now I was part of the squad.

It wasn't just an exciting time for me. On the last weekend of January, Dad and Jay opened doors at Eternity and staged the first of two official openings. Dad, the genial club owner, was back in business and in his element.

On 1 February, Clive Woodward was due to announce the team he had selected to take on Ireland in the Six Nations opener the following Saturday. It was an anxious wait, and when I heard the news I could hardly believe it. I was in! Tim Rodber had been dropped, but he still rang to congratulate me and wish me luck. I wasn't just thrilled, I was shocked, because I'd gone straight from the England Under 21 team into the senior team without doing an apprenticeship with the England 'A' side. In front of the rest of the players I allowed myself a massive grin at the news. Once in the privacy of my room, I was jumping for joy as I phoned Abby and my parents. I enjoyed calling Dad to say I wasn't playing for England 'A', but starting for England on Saturday. He said, 'All right, son' in his understated way, but Bill Conisbee and everyone at the Old Scouts were stunned. There was still the thought I shouldn't be there by rights.

I decided there and then, every time England play, I want to be in that shirt. I wanted to make the No. 11 shirt my own. I was the 16th wing capped by Clive in his two and a half years at the helm. Dan Luger had enjoyed a run of ten or more consecutive Tests, but he was hampered by a recurring injury. No one had absolutely made the position their own. In a short period I'd climbed from being a Premiership novice to being one of the most feared finishers in the country and I was fully intent on taking that trajectory to its logical conclusion by establishing myself as a permanent fixture on the wing for England.

While I was taking over from the injured Dan Luger, England's top World Cup try-scorer, it was good to hear Clive emphasise that I and Mike Tindall, who was also making his debut, were there for the right reasons: 'I've been very keen to pick players who are playing well for their clubs and on that criterion Cohen and Tindall deserve their first caps,' he said. 'Both have been playing outstandingly well. They're there on merit, not because we have injuries.'

The first person I wanted to salute was Ron Steel. But I was also very aware that I owed my chance to my team-mates at Northampton. The Saints had been having a great season. We were still chasing the treble and I was benefiting from that. What was odd was to see myself as the focus of newspaper features, with my family being asked for quotes about me. When asked, Mum told the local paper that I'd been a hyperactive child and that I 'had a lovely heart, but he was a little toad and very mischievous …' Thanks, Mum!

Most of the press interest, of course, was focused on Uncle George. So much so that my team-mates had started to take the piss and I had to make a joke of the obsession with the connection in my first press conference. 'It's long been a dream to play for my country,' I said to the assembled media, followed by a dramatic pause … 'just like it was for my uncle.' That prompted a bit of laughter and 'Who's your uncle then, Ben?' Martin Bayfield, who had retired from Northampton just as I was coming into the senior squad, continued the same theme in his column in the local paper: 'Well done you big old unit, what a great piece of news and I promise not to mention your uncle, George …'

It was a great family boost. I'd taken a lot of good-natured ribbing from my family for my love of the wrong form of football. George had kept up his line that it was a strange game to watch, what with all the stoppages and so on, but he also reminisced about how he had shown me his videos of 1966 and brought round his cap and medal and acknowledged he had helped forge my childhood dream to play for my country. And you know what, it was great to be on the path towards emulating what he had done.

As the big day came closer I had nerves, knowing I was going to run out in front of a crowd ten times bigger than for any club rugby event I'd ever been involved in. I didn't want to get shown up. I couldn't eat well. I hadn't slept. I thought shit, this is going to be a challenge. I shared a room with Austin Healey and he was very calming. He puts up this massive façade of being a cheeky chappie but I found him a nice, caring guy. He was very good to room with – except when, to wind me up, he kept taking pictures of me in the bath or shower!

All that week in the run-up to the game, there's nothing on your mind bar playing for England. It was a big week for many reasons, but every detail had been thought through for the new boys. We were given media training at Twickenham, and taught how to embrace media interest and understand how the press works. After a theoretical briefing, they walked me around the ground and then casually took me in the lift to go up to one of the hospitality boxes. When the lift doors opened, there was a camera crew right in my face, and a posse of 'reporters'. It was a test to see how I reacted. That preparation helped massively. It was typical of the details Clive and his team put in place to make sure the players are settled and only have to pull on their shirts and play rugby.

We had a team-bonding dinner out on Wednesday night, the night before our day off. It was really to get us out of the hotel environment and talking about something other than the game. I had to learn the ropes and get to know my team-mates better. I was going out to play for my country alongside them and I didn't want it to be a one-off experience. I wanted my call-up to be a life-changer. The great thing about that group of players was that you could sit next to anyone and have a laugh. There was a lot of comic banter and dry humour from the senior guys, a lot of 'character-building' piss taking of players, silly stuff about going bald – aimed at Lawrence Dallaglio, Austin and Daws – and general, all-inclusive fun.

Before I knew it, it was match day. Dad, Mum, Uncle George, my aunt Daphne, Justin, Abby and her family – they were all there to support me. The morning of your first England game is intensely emotional. I would get used to the rituals and routines, but, on that first day, every tiny detail made an impact. We were driven into the stadium on the bus, the route lined with cheering fans up to the barriers. I felt in a zone, really in the mood to win. I can still see my shirt hanging on the peg, with a label on the corner of the material, upside down with my name on it, and the date – 5/2/2000. Matt Dawson gave a rousing captain's speech: 'This is a new era for England,' he said. 'Let's draw a line in the sand and move forward. This is our time. Express yourselves out there. Don't come off the field with any regrets.'

It was a great time to make my debut; and the day was an initiation for three of us – Mike Tindall, Iain Balshaw and myself. I was too busy preparing myself for the game to see whether they were also nervous. I was determined to perform well. England had under-achieved in the 1999 World Cup. They – we – wanted to make a quick, winning start in 2000 and come out fighting. Ireland were a good side, with the likes of Brian O'Driscoll, Paul Wallace and Malcolm O'Kelly, all these great players. The one thing you know about Ireland is that they always wear their hearts on their sleeves.

In the changing-room, everything we could possibly need was catered for: extra shorts, T-shirts, socks, drinks, supplements, the physios and medics, music playing. Austin Healey was sitting opposite me. 'Take it all in now,' he said, 'because, before you know it, it'll be kick-off.' And he was dead right. Before I knew it, I was out there, thinking … shit. Twickenham was full to the rafters with 75,000 passionate fans and of course there'd be millions watching on television. I had to block that out. I conquered my nerves by belting out the national anthem, which must have been painful for anyone within earshot of my tone-deaf rendering. I'd been brought up on the notion that to represent your country is the ultimate honour, and I was extremely appreciative of the fact that I'd been given that responsibility. I couldn't wait to get stuck into the opposition; I wanted to make the most of every one of the 80 minutes because I didn't think I'd be there for long. Dan Luger would no doubt be back in the reckoning before long.

The first time I got the ball, I went to pass to Mike Tindall and, as I threw the ball, he went back on a switch and the ball went straight into touch. I was thinking, 'I don't fucking believe it. This ain't good, this really ain't good.' Bizarrely, that acknowledgement of nerves relaxed me. I thought I'd messed up, miscommunicated, and then suddenly we hit a rhythm and started playing good rugby. I had a stormer actually. In the 18th minute, Austin Healey passed to Mike Catt, Catt to Matt Perry, Matt to me. I was about 40 metres out and I thought I was going for the corner – well, my thought process had little to do with thinking; I was purely running scared – but, for whatever reason, I cut back inside Malcolm O'Kelly and Conor O'Shea before eluding Tom Tierney's covering tackle. It just happened. Instinct took over 20 metres out. All I could see was the try-line getting closer and closer and closer. No other player. And before I knew it I was there, punching the air as I went over ... and then went nuts, in a manner that wasn't in the tradition of rugby. I'll never forget the moment half of the England team ran up to congratulate me, while a few of the lads quietly pointed out that it is better to score the try before jumping about. I did regret celebrating before I had grounded the ball. I got a hell of a bollocking afterwards – not from my coaches, but from the old guard. The reason why I celebrated was not arrogance, it stemmed purely from disbelief. I could hardly believe I was playing for my country. I thought I'd blagged it, and then I somehow *scored* for my country. I thought I was going to wake up, that it was all a dream. I had crossed the line in my dreams thousands of times since I was a kid.

In the stands Dad and Mum were sitting next to Uncle George and his wife Daphne. George had had to excuse himself from an old boy reunion at Fulham to attend. As I started my run for the first try, Dad was on his feet shouting 'Go on, Ben! GO ON, BEN!' and – as George confessed later – he jumped to his feet too. 'I don't know what I was doing,' he told me in his unperturbable manner. 'I never get excited, but you were so very fast. Though not as fast as me! I was so carried away by the occasion. We were all in tears, to be honest.'

Jonny Wilkinson converted, and after that I made a few breaks, setting up Austin for one of his two tries and scoring another myself, making it a try in each half – 'topping and tailing the England feast' as one reporter wrote. Mike Catt had a field day, Mike Tindall also scored on his debut, and the redoubtable Neil Back: we were slick. We smashed Ireland that day. I loved every minute. The final score was 50–18, a great day; and two tries on my debut at Twickenham. Fantastic! My feet weren't on the ground from the beginning of the match. The occasion meant so much to me I didn't swap my jersey at the end. A few Irish players tried to exchange shirts, but I had to hang on to mine. It meant so much. That shirt symbolised seven years of hard grind on the training pitch. Austin Healey, my room-mate, could see how much the occasion meant to me and gave me the Irish one that he'd swapped, which was a lovely gesture.

We then had the black-tie dinner to look forward to at the Park Lane Hilton, and you'd think there was no better way to celebrate, but I was shitting myself. The ritual for new boys is that you have to stand up and sing on the team bus. I was more terrified about that than running out in front of 75,000 fervent fans. In those days you said hello to your family and guests and then went straight from the game to the dinner. On the bus I sang – if that's the right word – the Righteous Brothers' hit 'You've Lost That Loving Feeling', and predictably got abused and had stuff thrown at me. The torture only lasted a minute. Mike Tindall and Iain Balshaw stood up too and proved surprisingly tuneful. The dinner was a big, formal affair, which incorporated thank-you speeches and presentations to the referee and such. It was also where Tindall, Balshaw and I received our first caps. We also had to play along with the ritual of having a drink with every player on your team and with every member of the opposition too – a drink of their choice. Yes, that means 29 drinks you have to down. Some people are kind and make you have a little sip of beer; some give you a pint of wine. I was completely spannered, but just about held it together, although I reckon Mike, Ian and I were all close to redecorating our tables!

It was an amazing feeling to return home with an England cap in my bag and wake up to read the headlines: BIG BEN STRIKES ... WE'RE COHEN PLACES ... DREAM START FOR COHEN ... COHEN TO BE GREAT. That week was surreal. I had played for England, an incredible side of experienced players, and it was a wonderful feeling. No matter what happened, no one could take that achievement away. Dad had loved the trip to Twickenham with the family and access to the VIP area, but he was the first to urge me to keep the experience in perspective. 'Keep your feet on the ground, son.' In that feeling of euphoria, I have to confess to pondering on the reaction of those who'd had no qualms in expressing their doubts about me. I'd had points to prove, and to two people in particular. The first was Keith Bramhall, one of my early coaches at the Old

Scouts, the one who turned to Bill Conisbee and said, 'As long as Ben Cohen has a hole in his arse he'll never make a rugby player.' The other was Ged Glynn, an England Under 21 coach. He never rated me I think he was convinced I'd never make it. An England kit man watching the Ireland game next to him had the last laugh on my behalf. As I scored my first try, he turned to Ged and said, 'He's doing shit, isn't he?'

The Ireland game kicked off that unmistakable rhythm of alternating early spring weekends that I would come to embrace for the next five or six years – Six Nations, club game, Six Nations, club game. My selection had come off the back of a Saints team playing well, but even so, to go from scoring two tries on my England debut at Twickenham in front of a passionate crowd, to find myself missing a last-gasp tackle playing club rugby at home against Bristol – in open space, and the guy scored, and they won the game, in front of the loyal supporters who'd given me such a lovely reception – was a big dump down to reality. My dad had been right. Returning to play club rugby was always a reality check. What's more I was now a marked man. Other teams planned how to neutralise me. Coping with learning how to protect myself from that was part of the experience of growing up.

Clive Woodward named an unchanged side to take on France, the World Cup finalists, a fortnight later at the Stade de France. Under new coach Bernard Laporte, France had crushed Wales 36–3 in Cardiff, and England hadn't won in Paris for a long time. I must admit, it was the most nervous I've ever been playing rugby. I've never experienced a crowd like it, an environment that can blow so hot and cold. The French home support could be vociferously supportive of their own, and then turn on them in a heartbeat. We played through a steady drizzle. The wet ball on an extremely slippery field cramped both sides' attempts at flair. It was a game for stout defence on both sides. We ran at them from all angles in the first half, but their defence was solid. I had an average game, making a few silly errors in the first half, then making amends with some good tackles and punishing breaks in the second half, but the team was immense, particularly Jonny Wilkinson. He kicked five penalties to raise the winning score of 15–9, and put in a massive tackle on Emile Ntamack, practically cutting him in half. It was a momentous game of attrition to win.

People assume Jonny and I must have known each other well as youth players as there's only a year between us in age, but I'd never encountered him before that run-around at a joint England and England Under 21 fitness session when I overtook him. Even with England Under 19s, I never saw him. Jonny had a meteoric rise through England schools, making his senior debut in April 1998 when he was only 18, whereas I came through the club route. Despite our different routes towards full England recognition, we instantly got on well and became good friends.

Everything was a novelty on my first international game away. For home games, there was a staple pre-match menu: lasagne, spaghetti Bolognese or chicken followed by sticky toffee or bread and butter pudding. I learnt how valued the puddings were when word went out that someone had arranged for bread and butter pudding to be transported out to Paris. The England bus had a police escort and the Champs-Elysées had been cordoned off for our transit. I looked out of the windows to see the police kicking wing mirrors off cars just to move them out of the way and clear a path for us, as if it were a matter of life or death. It was crazy, horrific really, but I set out to absorb every second of the experience. I knew I had to make the most of it.

Because I never thought I'd play for England for long, I encouraged Dad to come out to Paris for the French game. He travelled out with Abby's dad, Rob, in his estate car. There was always a drama with Dad that we'd have a laugh about later, even though this time it wasn't running out of petrol. During the game, he suffered a sudden flare-up of gout in his toe. The pain was excruciating; he couldn't put any weight on it and normal painkillers were giving no relief. It became so bad that I had to ask the England team doctor to have a look at him. Only my second game for England and I had to approach the medical staff on my dad's behalf! Rob had to fold down the back seat so that Dad could stretch out into the boot and lie flat on the drive home. Once he'd recovered, we all found it hilarious of course.

Two games, two wins. Next up, Wales at home. Allan Bateman was winding me up all week, saying he'd told his Welsh team-mates to go hell for leather to slam me, pull me, and take me out of the game. Our side was on a mission to take revenge for the bitter 32–31 defeat at Wembley on the last day of the Championship the previous year, which handed the title to Scotland. It wasn't pretty rugby even though we ran in five tries for our 46–12 victory – four from forwards Phil Greening, Neil Back, Richard Hill and Lawrence Dallaglio and one from me – and we could have scored more. The forwards were immense. I was up against the slight, speedy Neath wing Shane Williams and my try was one I'll always be chuffed to relive. Perry caught a bad kick straight down the middle of the pitch, passed it to Austin Healey, I supported him, he offloaded to me and I scored the try. I made all my tackles and walked off the pitch pretty pleased with my day. My third cap, my third try.

Two things then changed the picture. I'd gone into the changing-room thinking I'd had a good game, scored a try, displayed good work rate, got in all my tackles, set up Phil Greening for a try, and was feeling pretty happy. I was sitting next to Will Greenwood, casually debriefing the game, as you do, when word came round that Clive Woodward was showing around some young lads. Prizewinners being given a tour, I assumed and didn't think anything more. My conversation with Will wound up with him advising me on what I needed to work on, things I should do to improve. As a senior player, I respected his opinion. I took off my top, my shorts and pants, adjusted myself and bent over to get my towel. Between my legs, I saw these two pairs of feet arrive in front of me. 'Ah, fucking hell,'

I thought. 'I'm going to have to meet these lads, completely naked, cupping my nuts.' As I looked up, it was worse than just two lads: I was face to face with a 15-year-old Prince Harry. 'Oh, pleased to meet you,' I said, as he gamely shook the hand that had just been holding my orientals. Unlike me, he wasn't fazed; he loved meeting the players. As a team we later spent some time with him and William – lovely guys, good banter.

After the game, I had a turn with the media. The Welsh were shell-shocked by the result. Their coach Graham Henry said England's performance was the best he'd seen from an international side for a very, very long time. I was asked how I thought Shane played. I said: 'Shane who? Shane Howarth or Shane Williams?' Because there were two Shanes playing that day. The interviewer clarified the question. I gave my answer and thought no more about it. Two weeks later, we were in Rome. Some of the boys on the bus referred to me being a right arrogant bastard. I didn't know what they were on about, and when they explained, I was horrified. The Welsh must have truly resented their 46–12 defeat and my part in it, because when it was aired on Welsh television they deliberately cut my interview short so that I was left looking like I just said, 'Shane who?' – full stop. I'd been set up a treat. It made me look disrespectful and I hated that, but I didn't know the half of it. Later I would get death threats from Welsh Nationalists and the police became involved. I could take the 'Ben who?' jibes. That's when being deaf is quite useful. In any case you have to be thick-skinned. People try all sorts of things to put you off your game. But I hated the idea that people thought I'd be disrespectful of a fellow player.

It was the first year for Italy as the sixth nation in the contest. Their addition broadened rugby. We arrived in Rome, the only team with a 100 per cent record in the championship, looking on course for the title. I fell in love with the place. Visiting that great city, for me, as a Northampton home boy, was incredible. I loved playing in the old Stadio Flaminio, which had been built in the 1950s in a beautiful setting and had hosted the football final in the 1960 Olympic Games. There was a completely different vibe playing in Italy.

The home side proved ruthless tacklers in the first half, and briefly took the lead. With visions of how Scotland had been beaten there only six weeks earlier, we came out in the second half intent on dominating play. Austin Healey claimed a hat-trick of tries in a stunning eight-minute rampage at the start of the second half. Daws scored twice and I scored a couple too, taking my tally to five in four games. The remaining points came courtesy of Jonny Wilkinson's boot. The score was 59–12, but the match felt tougher than the scoreline suggested. We won, which set us up for the Grand Slam against Scotland – and England rugby was front page news.

Victory over the reigning champions would seal England's first Grand Slam since 1995. Rather than elated, the mood was unusually quiet and thoughtful in the visitors' changing-room in Rome after our fourth victory on the trot. You could sense the anticipation that we were on the cusp of something special. As a side, we'd bonded well. After the World Cup, senior players like Matt Dawson wanted to promote a more open and honest team spirit with no cliques in the set-up or splits between senior and junior players, seasoned internationals and young guys like me, Mike Tindall and Iain Balshaw. Once again I appreciated that conscious inclusivity was speeding up my development. I was learning and contributing in parallel. We were all valued for our particular contribution to the team campaign. Alongside Austin Healey and Brian O'Driscoll, I found myself joint leading scorer in the Six Nations.

But there was no danger of it going to my head. I came back from Rome to discover I'd been dropped by the Saints for the home league clash against Sale. Not only that, I was told there would be no easy way back into the squad, still chasing glory in three major competitions. John Steele explained that I simply hadn't done enough in my last club appearance at Gloucester; I hadn't got involved as much as normal, and I'd have to work much harder to get back in. Straight and direct, he said the level at which I was performing on the international stage had no relevance to Northampton, and that I had to perform for the club. They paid my wages, after all. There was no hidden agenda. The club philosophy was that no one had a position by right. Being dropped was galling, but it also gave me time to take stock. There had been a lot to adjust to since making my England debut in an incredible team while trying to fire on all cylinders for my club as well. I was suddenly in the spotlight without being fully prepared for it. Maybe I needed that brief time out to process the experience. I went along to watch the game at Franklin's Gardens in suit and tie.

We travelled to Scotland aiming to secure the Grand Slam at Murrayfield. On paper, it looked promising. We had won all four previous games; Scotland, the defending champions, had lost all theirs. Scotland had not won the Calcutta Cup for ten years, though the previous year they had won the Five Nations crown on points difference on the final day. The build-up week was a funny old time. France played Italy at home, and Wales travelled to take on Ireland on 1 April; and our match was scheduled for the day after. Cocooned in our training camp, we did not fully register the significance of the date. On the Saturday we were told the pitch was going to be painted thistle purple for the TV spectacle. Of course that turned out to be an April fool's hoax. All sorts of strange things happened to put us off our stroke. A girl turned up allegedly to have her picture taken with the players; she put her arm around one and as the photographer said 1, 2, 3, click, she hoicked up her shirt, revealing all – and Clive had to chase the photographer around to prevent it being published and blown up into a distracting scandal. Rain poured down in Edinburgh for the duration of our stay up there. On the day of the match itself, the weather turned Siberian. None of which was any excuse for the fact that, come kick-off, we probably didn't pay due respect to the passion with which Scotland, marshalled of course by Ian McGeechan, came out to play.

It was a classic war of attrition, aggression and intimidation. Under normal circumstances, Wales, Ireland and Scotland up their game by ten to 15 per cent when they play England, wearing their hearts proudly on their sleeves. The home side's pride was at stake and victory over the auld enemy was the best way to reclaim self-esteem. That attitude paid dividends for them. Players on both sides piled into every tackle as if lives depended on it. Tactics-wise, we didn't pay due respect to the weather. We led 10–3 midway through the first half. At half-time, leading 10–9, we based our second-half game plan on a dry ball, but we ran back on in a heavy sleet and snow shower. Then rain came down like stair rods, turning the pitch into a quagmire and the ball into a hostile slippery thing, and an icy chill wind picked up to complete the apocalyptic conditions. We failed to adapt to the changing conditions and that did for us. It was no longer a day for playing pretty rugby. Duncan Hodge was the hero for Scotland with on-song penalty kicking and a triumphant late try. When the final whistle blew, confirming the score at 19–13, several England players slumped on the sodden ground in despair. To lose a second successive Grand Slam was hard to take, especially as odds-on favourites.

We were all massively pissed off and disappointed. We watched Scotland file up to collect the Calcutta Cup, and then walked dejectedly into the changing-room. There was a lot of confusion later about the trophy presentation and an apparent snub to the Princess Royal. Up in the stand too, apparently, was the Six Nations Championship trophy, but Matt Dawson didn't lead us up to receive the silverware. 'Scotland won – it was their day. Let them enjoy it,' was his view. 'We'll pick up the trophy in our own time.' The RFU issued an apology for 'a breakdown in communications'.

So England won the inaugural new Championship and Scotland got the Calcutta Cup, but only one side went away happy. To lose a Grand Slam in successive years on the final day seemed somehow careless. On reflection, though, I couldn't deny the Six Nations had been a fantastic tournament for me: five tries/25 points from five appearances. I was riding a wave with a fantastic England side that had gelled well, and it was all thanks to the Northampton shop window and the amazing initiation it had given me into top-class rugby. How long ago was it that I thought my path had been blocked to the highest level because I didn't go to the right school? How long ago was it that I was driving a white van, hoping to get a job in the print trade? Flipping heck, it was only two seasons ago that I signed my first contract with the Saints. Rugby's a funny sport. A rise to prominence can happen meteorically. I had gone from mid-level professional to first-team regular to playing for my country in the space of six months. For a 21-year-old, there was so much to absorb from each experience. Fantastic though it was, however, that learning curve and adjustment to the media and public attention was hard. I couldn't go out without being stopped for my autograph or a chat. I'd go out to eat with my brother and it would be ages before we could sit down and order a drink or any food. 'Keep your feet on the ground, son,' Dad would say. And I was about to learn the next tough lesson: you have to keep reinventing yourself as a player. I had made an impact because no one knew how to defend against me, but now I had to become a cannier player with a bigger armoury of attacking options.

CHAPTER 8

CHAMPIONS
OF EUROPE

Parallel to the Six Nations Championship, Northampton's 1999/2000 season campaign was marching on. The good news was that we were going into the back end of that season in contention in the league, and still in the mix in the Tetley's Bitter Cup and the Heineken Cup. The bad news was that this meant a major fixture pile-up of one big game after another. From now on, every game was crucial if we were to progress in our chase for the treble.

Saturday, 8 April was a day for low-key celebration as we beat London Irish 24–17 to reach the Tetley's Bitter Cup final against Wasps. The Saints would be going to Twickenham for the first time since 1991. We couldn't afford to let nerves and jitters set in. We still had a lot to play for even though we had now booked a place in one final. As chance would have it, another game against Wasps stood between us and a semi-final berth in the Heineken Cup. We played badly, but not for the first time Paul Grayson's impeccable kicking earned us a nail-chewingly close 25–22 victory with an injury-time penalty to set up a meeting with Llanelli.

We were learning there was a lot of emotional expenditure at the business end of the season. Every game now was crucial. It felt like one after another: a league game against Harlequins midweek, then in-form Bath on Saturday. Tiredness was creeping in, especially for the eight players who'd been involved in the World Cup. John Steele rested Tim Rodber, Paul Grayson, Federico Mendez and Garry Pagel ahead of the Quins game. We lost. Then, up against league title contenders Bath, we were without Matt Dawson and Allan Bateman, both ruled out through injury. At the end of April, we lost a niggly local derby against Leicester, 26–21, with Dean Richards labelling us 'a tired, old outfit'. Commentators suggested we should sacrifice our league ambitions to concentrate on securing the Cup double. We'd been a stand-out side of the season, but the fixture list seemed to be conspiring to leave us with nothing.

We staggered on, boosted by the incredible Northampton supporters. On 7 May the crunch semi-final against Llanelli in the Heineken Cup loomed at the Madejski Stadium in Reading. The atmosphere was magnificent. Both sides have huge, loyal, impassioned followings and the stadium atmosphere was as highly charged as it gets. During the warm-up, they announced the teams player by player. Matt Dawson's name got a boo from the Welsh supporters; and mine got an even more resounding pantomime boo. As we lined up for the kick-off, thousands of posters popped up at the Llanelli end bearing the words, 'Ben who?' – referring to the 'Shane who?' stitch-up after the England v Wales game. Every time I touched the ball, I got booed. If it was designed to put me off, it failed. At the start, my hearing issues shielded me from the impact of the boo boys; I hadn't a clue what was going on. Focused on my game, I was vaguely aware of the Llanelli supporters waving things around, then I read the words, and realised I was the butt of the joke. They were having their bit of fun, I guess, and I didn't have any hard feelings.

In the 70th minute, I scored a decisive try which brought us within two points of winning. It was not a case of having the last laugh, but of making the final. With so much at stake, it was a ridiculously edgy game. Then, in the 81st minute or something stupid, we had a scrum from halfway out and someone stuck their foot out and kicked the ball out of the hands of Dom Malone. Penalty. Yet again, the unflappable Paul Grayson saved the day with an injury-time penalty, just as he did against Wasps in the quarter-final. This time Grays's kick soared magisterially through the posts from 44 metres in the 85th minute. He'd only been on the pitch for seven minutes, having started on the replacements' bench. In dramatic style, we had booked our place in a second final at Twickenham that month.

As a squad, we were weary and wracked by injuries, but enjoying the fun. The last month of a season defines a team. Every game was our last game, potentially. You can't plan. You have to put everything into it. It's what we were all in the game for, pushing ourselves to prove we were the best. It's the logical culmination of all the pre-season, the training in all weathers, the detailed preparation and lifestyle sacrifices: getting to the sharp end of the season with silverware within grasp. And, most particularly, it was the fruition of the long-term plan set in motion by Ian McGeechan back in 1995. Northampton town centre was abuzz with excitement. I couldn't walk anywhere without being stopped. Rugby was part of the banter and festive spirit at Dad and Jay's club. The town spirit was alight and it was great to be a local Northampton lad at the heart of the action.

I loved the headline on the souvenir guide for the Tetley's's Bitter Cup final a week later: ALL SET TO STING THE WASPS! But sadly not. The final took place on a sweltering May day. The game had extra edge as it was the third time we'd met Wasps in a few weeks. We had beaten the side built around Lawrence Dallaglio, Trevor Leota, Josh Lewsey and Kenny Logan with Grays's last-gasp kick in that tense Heineken Cup quarter-final, and they had beaten us triumphantly in a league game. Going into the match, it felt like honours even, and both clubs were equally determined to emerge the winner. The bottom line was that both clubs needed a trophy win to qualify for next year's European competition. The Tetley's Bitter Cup final was Wasps' last chance; we were gearing up for a Heineken Cup final the following week, which we would have to win to secure a place in Europe if we didn't claim this. Talk about pressure. And Northampton's trophy-less history made this pot a serious target, especially for players like Tim Rodber who had given years to the club without a glory scenario.

However, in the midst of this maelstrom of tension, the crucial psychological advantage was handed to Wasps on a plate. The game was as good as over before it started. Saints Chairman Keith Barwell gave an interview predicting Wasps would lose because they weren't as good as us. Well, the London side didn't need any motivation talk from their coach on the day: he just played them the video of the interview. That was it. We went out. We lost. A penalty with only minutes left on the clock would have been enough to take the lead back but, for once, Grays's kick fell short. It was Kenny Logan's conversion following a try by Mark Denney that proved the last kick of the game, leaving Wasps the victors 31–23.

The night we lost the Tetley's Bitter Cup was also the Saints' official end-of-season dinner in the big room upstairs at Franklin's Gardens. I remember earlier that week I had spoken cockily to my dad. It was one of the few times I'll admit I did have my head in the clouds. I was acting a bit arrogantly. I was walking around in sunglasses thinking I was the bee's knees. I was gutted we'd lost the final but I was acting as if we'd won it. From where I am now, I see it was understandable. Things had happened so fast for me. I was a young lad, just 21 years old, and it had been an amazing year. In eight months I'd established myself in the first team, made an England debut, scored five tries in as many international appearances, and throughout the Saints' chase for the treble I'd been scoring tries for fun. I'd also been nominated for the Allied Dunbar Premiership Young Player of the Year. But that was no excuse for cocky behaviour.

Mum and Dad were living with me because they were moving from Moulton to a house in Forfar Street, close to Franklin's Gardens. Before we left for that dinner, Dad made me sit at the lounge table and he perched on the arm of the couch.

'I'm happy for you, son, but also a little bit disappointed in the way you've been carrying yourself,' he said. 'You're not the finished article. Enjoy what you've earned, but never forget the people you pass on the way up are the people you'll meet on the way down.'

It was a good, honest father-son talk, but also a friend-to-friend talk. It's what you need your family for. He didn't want me to get carried away and make a fool of myself. 'Wind your neck in, Benny boy,' was the gist of what he was saying. He drew attention to the way I'd been talking about all the things I'd got, and what I was getting.

'We understand you've worked very hard for it, son, but it comes with a responsibility that you understand that some people don't have that – even if they've worked as hard all their life – and some people just don't have the same level of desire as you and that doesn't make them lesser people.'

He made me see that I needed to be careful about the way I was acting, talking about my remuneration and bonuses. He understood that it was exuberance, that I felt the need to express something because success had come through incredibly hard work, but he told me to be gracious and grateful about everything in life. He was right in every way. I got it straightaway. I understood he was giving me a life lesson, not a lecture I'd ever begrudge. I remember getting to the dinner and telling Wally about it, then realising that Dad and Wally must have had a little chat about the change in me, because Wally just slapped me on the back and said, 'Oh good!' Loyal friends do that. We went on to have a great night.

We were then something like sixth in the league, but it was all very close at the top. If we finished sixth and also lost our Heineken Cup final, we would still not be in the European mix for 2000/01. We had to finish in the top five to secure an automatic qualification into Heineken Cup the following season. The pressure brewing was immense. We travelled up to Newcastle for the last game of the season knowing it was all or nothing to ensure a spot in Europe, or else we'd have to take a lot of negative pressure into the final against Munster. The Falcons were a difficult side to play against, with Va'aiga Tuigamala on the wing, and a great back-line in Jonny Wilkinson, Jamie Noon and Tom May. Ali Hepher scored a try and we were 10–0 up. I was in the sin bin when they levelled, but we took back the initiative and led 13–10 at half-time. The lead went back and forth until I scored a try which, with Grays's conversion, put us 27–17 ahead. I made two try-saving covers in the closing minutes, and we won – which succeeded in taking the pressure off us going into the Heineken Cup final against the Irish side. That security, not a piece of silverware, was our first reward from a season that had promised everything, but threatened to dissipate into nothing. It was about the first time in ten days you'd see smiles in our dressing-room.

The end of the rugby season loomed and, with that, the biggest game in the history of Northampton. It was a hot May. The first-team pitches were rock hard, like concrete. The temporary stands had been removed. Franklin's Gardens was being virtually dismantled ready for redevelopment – and re-opening, everyone hoped, as the home of the 2000 European champions. We had two weeks to train before the Heineken Cup final. Lots of fans watched our preparations from the side of the training pitches. The local press beefed up their coverage. I was photographed presenting Keith Shurville at the Old Scouts with my full England shirt to add to the collection I had donated.

On the day more than 100 coaches – including 82 laid on free by the club – took fans to Twickenham. It was as if the whole of Northampton town had emigrated to Twickenham. Whoever sold the wigs and flags in club colours must have made a mint. And the Munster invasion of London was rumoured to have involved more than 100 flights from Dublin alone. The crowd of 68,441 made for a carnival atmosphere, and was officially declared the biggest club attendance for rugby in the world that season. On the eve of the final Pat Lam, who had just been voted the Rugby Players' Association Players' Player of the Year, called the team together and asked for God to give us strength. What it did above all was focus us collectively in a calm way – which we needed. It was amazing he was there. His wife had been due to give birth on the day of the final, but baby Josiah had conveniently arrived three days early. Lammy promised the rest of us that he would produce a big performance, and because he had already received his prize with the birth of his baby son, he wanted his display to be for the team and the whole town.

As predicted, it was a tight, tense game. I dropped the first ball I received, when I had a clear run to the line. But somehow, through sheer bloody-mindedness and determination, we found the resolve to come out on top in the encounter and bring home to Northampton the first trophy in the club's 120-year history. The points came, as ever, through Grays's penalty kicking. In the dying minutes, Munster fly-half Ronan O'Gara lined up a 30-yard penalty but his effort went wide of an upright and we held on to our one-point lead for glory. It was absolutely incredible. We all piled in together. Pat Lam insisted he and Tim jointly raise the trophy aloft and then we all had a go. The feeling when we hoisted that trophy was fantastic – relief, jubilation, incredulity all together – and just what the doctor ordered after a roller-coaster season. One of the first things Lammy did was call Ian McGeechan. 'Thank you,' he said simply, acknowledging what most of us felt; that it was Geech's foundation work, his philosophy of expansive high-tempo rugby that had propelled the Saints to become champions of Europe.

Peter O'Toole and Richard Harris came into the changing room, drank out of the Cup and got pissed with the lads. Harris had played rugby when he was at school in Munster. I was told it was a classic turn from these old-school swashbuckling actors, but at the time I didn't appreciate how remarkable their presence was in our dressing room.

We became the second English club to achieve European champion status, following Bath in 1998, and our victory seemed to be a very popular one, and not just in Northampton, perhaps partly in sympathy for the run of ten gruelling games in six weeks that nearly broke us, physically and mentally. The town celebrated headily. As the local paper's Cup Special commented:

CHAMPIONS OF EUROPE!
How richly Saints deserve that title at the end of a season of joy and heartache, laughter and tears, anguish and celebration.

To drag their battered and abused bodies through a cruelly-designed and congested season, to blossom, wither and die in the Premiership title race in a few short weeks, lose the Tetley's Bitter Cup final and then, on the very last day of the season, lift rugby's greatest club prize in front of almost 70,000 fans at an electrified Twickenham will put Saints down as one of British sporting history's greatest sides.

It was only my first season as an established first-team player, but I, too, felt a weight had been removed from my shoulders. Northampton Saints could no longer be called under-achievers. All through the season, we tried to adopt a pragmatic approach. We played a lot of games and missed a lot of opportunities, but we always looked ahead to the 'next job'. Nothing without labour.

A few days later, we climbed up onto an open-top double-decker bus and paraded through the town. It was pouring with rain, but the turnout of fans in green, black and gold shirts, waving flags, singing and cheering, was incredible. Roads were closed to traffic as the procession travelled from Franklin's Gardens down St James's Road, Marefair, Gold Street and a teeming Mercer's Row. At Wood Hill, the bells of All Saints' Church rang out. We were ushered along the route by endless renditions of 'When the Saints Go Marching In'. Pat Lam took the microphone and said: 'Thirty million people watched this game on Saturday all around the world and overnight they all pulled out atlases and found a small town called Northampton! Thank you again. This is a classic example – it rains but everyone comes out, you've always been there for us, this trophy belongs to everyone, the whole town, the whole county. Cheers!'

The Millennium ushered in a new status for Northampton – and how good that felt. When you're brought up in a club that you love, that means everything to you, it's a unique relationship. I'd lived and breathed Northampton Saints. It was my work, my life. I was so passionate about my club. After that exceptional season, I wanted to continue the journey onwards and upwards. I didn't consider that season could be the high point in the club's history; I thought we stood on the cusp of a great era.

That summer Mum and Dad moved into a nice house in Forfar Street, not far from the Saints ground – perfect for me to pop over with some mates for a coffee or break from training. I had little time to take stock of an amazing season before I was flying out to Johannesburg for a four-week tour of South Africa with England. The tour featured five matches, including two back-to-back Tests against the Springboks in Pretoria and Bloemfontein. After the damp squib of Murrayfield, and our abject failure to clinch the Grand Slam, it was a chance to prove England had bottle. South Africa always provided tough opposition. On a personal level, I was concerned that Dan Luger, who had recovered from injury and was also in the squad, would reclaim his spot on the wing. When the team was announced for the first Test against South Africa at Loftus Versfeld in Pretoria, I wasn't selected in the starting XV. Dan, who had missed the entire season, was back in the No.

11 shirt. I can't pretend I wasn't gutted, especially after scoring five tries in the Six Nations. Clive explained that I hadn't done anything wrong. He just felt that Dan offered more, and he had reclaimed his position on merit. Mind you, Jonny Wilkinson and I had both picked up food poisoning the night before the game. I'd been throwing up all night, so being on the bench was probably a good thing. I wasn't called upon to play. Jonny had been picked to play, but had to withdraw. (Clive Woodward later appointed an England team chef to prevent such episodes striking the squad.)

Dan Luger played well and scored a try, but looked likely to be out for the second Test with a bruised chest, so it seemed as if through injury I might end up winning my sixth cap after all. It was a lifeline for me, a chance to shine again and get my nose back in front of Dan. Clive wanted me to play half a game against a midweek side so I'd be ready. I had shin splints and was in dreadful pain. I couldn't run comfortably, but I needed to play. I was desperate to push my cause and establish myself in that side. During training we were doing cross-field kicks and I couldn't catch a thing.

Training is famously where all the frustration boils over and fights flare. It's the same with club and country. Each individual player is working on detailed aspects of their own game – getting their run right, perfecting the timing of a pass or the arc of a line-out throw – and other players may not be doing what you need for that particular practice. It's a sharply competitive place which can bring out the worst in people. Everyone wants to show hunger for their place and prove their worth, even if it means playing through injury. Beautifully weighted balls would fly towards me and I just wasn't reliable at receiving them. I could see the coaches were sceptical of me that day and noted this weakness under high balls.

To get through the pain in this midweek game, I was on six painkillers a day. Just before the match, it was suggested I take a suppository pain relief. I'd gone into the toilet before the game to insert the suppository, took a further dose of painkilling pills and filed out onto the field. As the game kicked off, I ran in to make a tackle and as I did, I felt something warm fly out of my back end. Fuck! I thought, I've just shat myself. I don't believe it, I've shat myself on national TV! The pitch was barren, bone-dry, and I was thinking I hope it hasn't gone through my shorts and everyone can see it. No way could it be mistaken for mud. There wasn't any, so I couldn't even 'accidentally' fall into a puddle. I came off gingerly at half-time and sorted myself out. Luckily it turned out it was just the suppository flying out.

I performed okay and was picked as Dan's replacement for the second Test. South Africa had made minimum changes from the side that had beaten us 18–13 in the first Test, six days beforehand. I couldn't have asked for a fairer platform on which to stake my claim for a permanent place in the side, but up against their experienced star winger Chester Williams, I would have to be 100 per cent on my game. The ground in Bloemfontein was a mile above sea level. I'd never played in such high-altitude conditions before. I could kick a ball the length of a flipping field, the air was so thin. The boys had been there in the 1997 Lions tour – we were to play on the same pitch as the one on which Will Greenwood had nearly lost his life, having swallowed his tongue when he was knocked unconscious after falling on to the rock-hard ground head first.

I went out determined to prove myself reliable and solid. I made 13 tackles, put in 100 per cent concentrated effort, and thanks to Jonny Wilkinson, who scored eight penalties and one drop goal, we ended up winning the game. The score read 27–22. With a five-point margin in our favour we had precisely reversed the defeat in the first Test. The result was a huge milestone – the first away win against southern hemisphere opponents of Clive Woodward's term as Head Coach – and hailed as a turning point for England's status in world rugby. That game in Bloemfontein was the long-awaited psychological breakthrough that we could use as a springboard to continued success in the forthcoming Autumn Internationals against Australia, Argentina and South Africa again.

In the last few minutes my leg went completely. All the same I thought I'd demonstrated my abilities well, and this was confirmed when England backs' coach Brian Ashton came up and made a point of telling me I'd proved a lot to them out there: my defence, my attitude, my positional awareness and whatever. That was good to hear, but I could see my game was full of holes: I was weak under high balls and catching above the head; I could improve my passing and what I was like on the turn. I had gone a long way on a raw ability to run through and around people, but I had a thunderbolt realisation that I needed to add more finesse to my game. I had probably sent out a message to Dan Luger that he'd have to fight for the No. 11 jersey, but I was going to have to arm myself for that contest by developing my game. I had to keep battling because, as every rugby commentator opined, it was odds-on that Clive would revert to Dan in the autumn.

I flew home exhausted. I'd played 57 games that year – friendlies, league games, cup games, internationals. I travelled to Cuba on holiday with Abby, and it was the first holiday I'd ever gone on and not done anything active – except getting down on my knee to propose to her. Rested, I began looking forward to the 2000/01 season. Everything was looking good: my rugby was going well and I knew what I had to do to keep up the momentum. I was in love and soon to be married. And the family were enjoying the new nightclub business, which was riding high on the feelgood factor generated by the Saints' rugby success. Eternity had hosted post-European Cup celebrations in which Saints players mingled with fans. Dad and Jay's club was part of the community, both in the town and at large. They had ambitions to grow the business, starting with a sponsorship of the Northampton Balloon Festival, a popular four-day event held at the height of summer at The Racecourse and managed by the Borough Council. It's a big draw in the area, with hot-air balloon lifts and the nightly balloon glow, when balloons are illuminated to create a magical atmosphere for funfair attractions, trade stalls, live music, beer tents and bars. Dad and Jay paid good money to be exclusive suppliers of alcohol over the long weekend. It was a good way to promote the club's name and a sure way to make some money – except that it pissed down every day. To save on paying wages to hired temporary stuff, it was all family hands to the pump – Mum, Dad, Jay, Sam and her husband, with me and Abby working the beer tents. It was crazy, but fun. One night they took £50,000 (before accounting for the cost price of the alcohol) and, despite the atrocious weather, ended up losing only about £1,000.

We began the 2000/01 season as reigning European champions, but we were not playing champion rugby. I hadn't had much of a pre-season training window, and I don't know if it was that sense of under-preparation, or that the atmosphere was flat after so much passion had been spent at Franklin's Gardens at the end of last season. Whatever the reason, we could not find form as a side. We had chased the dream of treble glory to the point of collective exhaustion. No one had considered 'what next'? Before winter had set in, we were out of the Heineken Cup, finishing bottom of a pool which comprised Biarritz, Leinster and Edinburgh Reivers. We were ominously low in the league.

The historic Heineken Cup victory would prove to be the zenith of that team shaped by Ian McGeechan, a fact that infiltrated into our consciousness as news came, in fits and starts, that four of our iconic players would be leaving at the end of the year, namely Tim Rodber, Pat Lam, Allan Bateman and Garry Pagel, all big personalities who had made massive contributions. Their departures would mark an end of an era.

I felt I'd done well in the second Test in South Africa, and that I could establish myself in the England team if I built on the peak physical fitness I'd acquired with Ron Steel by acquiring better skills. I had pace, power and an ability to find the line, but I knew the England coaches were sceptical about the depth and variety of what I could contribute. Being brutal to myself, I'd say I had no skill set. I could run and score tries, but I was patchy under the high ball; I was no good on the turn. My game had not matured. Having identified the weaknesses I needed to eradicate, I decided to analyse all the things I was good at, but not great at, and work on them until I was the best. I was haunted by the idea that I was a player who was going to be maybe second, third or fourth choice, and only used as a stopgap. So I used the beginning of the new season to start my campaign to work on those aspects of my game. Most particularly, I wanted to become one of the best catchers of high balls in the world, especially in receiving cross-field kicks.

England were developing fast as a side under the coaching team Clive had assembled: Andy Robinson, the forwards specialist, Dave Alred, an amazing kicking coach, Phil Larder for defence, and Dave Redding on the fitness side. The attention to detail when we met up for England training camps was incredible. It was a unique time in rugby and I had the best coaches to help me work on the holes in my game. I had to work on passing with both hands, and basics like tackling in certain situations, what I was like with the ball behind me. It's a process you go through. When you're on the wing, you use the touchline as your extra defender. How do I block a player when I'm going through? Do I turn outwards and push him towards the line? All those details that can give you an edge on the pitch. Dave Alred made me re-address the way I dealt with the high ball. He taught me to look for the key factors. Try to read the writing on the ball. Spot one letter as the ball is spinning and focus on it. Put your hands out like this. He made me consider my approach and my body mannerisms for trying to catch a high ball above my head or catching it in traffic. You want to catch it above your head, not in your gut. Soon I was leaping like a salmon to rise above opponents and pluck the ball out of the air, using my knee to defend, getting leverage on people's backs, legs and shoulders to rise above them. We took the cross-field kick from Aussie Rules. With Paul Grayson, at Saints and England – in my view probably the best kicker of the ball in rugby, full stop, who he could kick it off a sixpence any day, any time – we developed this new skill in cross-field kicks. And we got it down to a tee. No one was defending them. I scored God knows how many tries from cross-field kicks. Once we'd perfected it, we were taking teams apart.

I remember telling Matt Dawson that what I found most exciting about playing for my country was the process of learning that came with each camp. I'd look forward to each training session. What am I going to learn today? I loved the feeling that I was becoming a better player for my club and my country. I loved the sense of progress, that we were moving up to a new level. That, for me, is what work should be like.

There was a real buzz brewing ahead of the Autumn Internationals, but our club form was still patchy at best. When we met up going into the forthcoming fixtures against the southern hemisphere sides in early November, Saints players were being picked on reputation not form. I remember travelling to London with Steve Thompson and having one of those flu bugs that prevent you from getting sleep. The nights of 9 and 10 October, I'd tossed and turned restlessly. I felt strangely wired. All the squad got our debrief statistics from the last England game in Bloemfontein. Assessing mine gave me a boost: they were good. I felt reassured that I had proved myself enough, after all. Maybe I would get a place in the starting XV. We were given a £500 voucher to spend in Nike Town as a treat. I caught the train home and later in the week heard I was named in the Saints team to play against Edinburgh Reivers. It was Friday, 13 October, and I went to bed thinking tomorrow was the day Saints would turn things round on the pitch.

CHAPTER 9

INTENSIVE CARE

Friday, 13 October was to be the last truly carefree day of my life for a very, very long time. It had been a routine enough day before a club game right up until nearly midnight. I was at home in Northampton, and had gone to bed early, as always before a big match. I was still awake, though, thinking about the following day's crucial Heineken Cup Pool One game. Earlier, Abby and I had been to my favourite Italian restaurant, Sorrentino's, where I'd eaten like a horse, carb-loading up on my customary vast mound of pasta, followed by steak. After losing our first pool game against Biarritz the previous weekend at the Parc des Sports Aguiléra in Basque country, Saturday was going to be a big day, the game to restore our campaign despite injuries and strangely patchy and indifferent form. I'd trained well, eaten well and gone to bed thinking about the game plan and my role against the opposite number in the red, black and white shirt … when the telephone rang.

I didn't hear it. That's one advantage of being considerably deaf: no need for earplugs when you want to sleep. The phone rang for a bit, stopped, then immediately started up again. It was well after 11.30pm. Abby nudged me. There was something about the caller's insistence that made her think I'd better go and answer it. The phone was down in the lounge, and I caught it just before it rang off a second time. It was my brother. 'Dad's been in a fight at the club,' he said. 'Mum has called an ambulance. You better get down there.' Jay was on his way back from Nuneaton, where he'd gone to check out a nightclub that was for sale, and then for an evening out with a mate called Paul Brown. Dad had asked him not to be late because he was tired, and Jay had agreed to be back by midnight. As he took the call from an Eternity staff member just past 11pm saying that Dad had been in a fight, and wasn't good, the power crashed in the restaurant where he was eating, plunging them ominously into darkness. He quickly paid up, called the local security firm to get some lads round to Eternity to restore order if necessary and made a desperate dash back down the motorway. The concern in my brother's tone of voice told me this was something more than a scrape. Even so, I wasn't over-worried. Physically, Dad was a solid man who could look after himself. He had never, ever shown weakness in any shape or form. I jumped in the car and arrived at the club soon after Jay.

The building that housed Eternity has had several reinventions since 2000. Isolated from the main hub of pubs and clubs in the centre at the downhill end of Bridge Street, it sits on the corner of a long roundabout created by the one-way system in between the town centre and the River Nene, close to Morrison's supermarket. I pulled in, parked and ran straight into the club. The staff were quick to greet me. There wasn't time to take in much beyond the fact that Dad had been taken to hospital by ambulance, Jay had followed in his car, and that what had happened was this: some guys who had been thrown out of the club the week before, and subsequently smashed the window, had come back annoyed that they'd received a police warning following that episode. They trailed one of the club's employees into the building and picked a fight. Dad came down from the office to split up the brawl, and had been attacked in turn. It had spilled outside. The bouncer shut the door, so it was just Dad outside with this bunch of guys. When he heaved himself back inside the club door, they came back after him. One jumped on his back while another rained punches on him. He was being battered so he went in close to protect himself. They pulled him over, and kicked and punched him as he lay on the ground. One member of staff saw him being bitten across his face so that his cheek was ripped open. It was a brutal, cowardly attack: three young guys against a 58-year-old grandfather. Finally Dad had been pushed into a cashpoint machine and whacked his head. Getting unsteadily to his feet, he felt faint, so the staff helped him down to the cellar to cool down in privacy. Mum and Jay were called. As soon as Mum arrived and saw Dad's state, an ambulance was summoned.

It happened at 10.11pm, early for a nightclub on a Friday night, so there weren't many people there other than the staff. I didn't notice masses of blood or signs of a struggle when I arrived. Dad had taken most of the force internally. Mum had arrived before me, and remained there, clearly shocked. When she found him in the cellar, she said, he was severely distressed because his head hurt so much. He was in a real state, covered in blood but still conscious and talking, and he had bite marks on his face. In nearly 29 years of marriage, she'd never known him to cry, and it rattled her. He was not a man to break down. Maybe he realised he had been seriously injured and that scared him? Maybe it was the sheer shock of the brutality, of having his face savaged by another man's teeth? Jay had gone with Dad to hospital. Mum stayed to look after the club, and said she wanted to go with Dad but couldn't just yet. She muttered something about 'not wanting to face things that would hurt her'. What? I'd never heard her say anything like that before.

I drove straight on to Northampton General Hospital. Dad was propped up in bed when I arrived. He'd gone first into a Resus ward, where after vomiting copiously he seemed to have recovered. His face was a bit of a mess, with cuts and bruises and bite marks under both eyes and across the nose, a nasty bloody contusion on his cheek and a big cut/scar along the top of his head. 'I did well, but there were too many of them,' he said wearily. I got him a cup of tea from the vending machine and we chatted. 'There were just too many of them, too many of them,' he repeated, as if apologising for his sorry state. Annoyed that I'd been disturbed on his account, he insisted he was fine and told me to get myself home to sleep because he knew I had a big game at Franklin's Gardens the next day. Bizarrely – given what was about to happen – we had a routine little chat about the game against Edinburgh and then I drove back home, startled by the incident but relieved to know that Dad was as fundamentally indestructible as ever. He had a cuppa in his hand, after all. 'What comes after S?' was his other catchphrase. 'Tea … with milk, and not too hot.'

No sooner was I back in bed, it seemed, than the phone went again. This time the message I received was stark: Dad had sunk into unconsciousness. Mum had been allowed to tiptoe into the four-bed ward where he'd been taken for the night, but she couldn't get a response from him. A nurse heard her repeating his name, trying to wake him, came in immediately and conducted a simple neurological test. She pressed a pen over his finger nail. A normal reaction would be to recoil from the pain; Dad pushed back towards the nurse. He was rushed away and taken for CT scans, which revealed that the trauma he'd suffered to his brain had caused an aneurysm that had ruptured with the equivalent of six strokes. Within an hour I was back at the hospital again – and Dad's bed was now empty. Already our rugby chat over a polystyrene cup of tea seemed a whole world away. I found him in a critical care room around the corner.

I never went to bed that night. It did not look good at all. I sat there trying to understand how my dad, who'd seemed so chipper as I'd chatted to him over a cup of tea a few hours earlier, could now be lying here, surrounded by monitors and wires and machines that bleeped. What kind of state would he be in, if and when he woke up? Jesus Christ, how was this even possible? Mum was there, with Justin and his wife Michelle, my sister Sam and her husband Jason, Abby too, and we were all pretty raw and tearful. Mum insisted we all have our partners with us. She wanted us all to have a shoulder to cry on. And I sat by Dad's bed, waiting to see how the situation was going to play out.

As morning slowly broke, I rang John Steele at the Saints and told him what had happened, that I wasn't going to be able to play against Edinburgh. The doctors had organised a transfer to the Intensive Care Unit at Queen's Medical Centre in Nottingham, which specialises in neurological injuries. Dad was on life support, having been prepped for the journey, and lay in another critical care room in the transport area in readiness for the specialist ambulance. Mum was allowed to take one person in with her and she asked me. The room was a big space, as sterile as an operating theatre, and in the bed in the middle was Dad, lying unresponsive, in a coma, with a pipe coming out of just about every hole. The doctors said he had loads of head injuries and a bruised brain. He had been put on a ventilator to help him breathe. He looked as helpless as can be. We didn't stay there longer than a minute; neither of us could handle it.

My Dad never showed personal frailty to anyone in his life. Even in the shit times, when his businesses went bankrupt, when we had no money and life was tough, he remained robust, confident that something better was around the corner if he carried on working hard. Mum always describes him as Del Boy, with a finger in every pie. He was a do-er, a trier and pretty happy-go-lucky; he wasn't a man to burden others with his worries. If anyone asked how things were, he'd move the conversation on quickly. He had his pride. He never let anyone buy him a drink; he'd always put his hand in his pocket and buy a round. Work hard, try your best, never give up – that was his mantra for making everything come good. But what help is that when you're lying in a coma fighting for your life? He was powerless. And so were we. It was excruciating to see him lying there that long night, so exposed and defenceless.

The next day dawned. The whole family followed Dad up to Nottingham. Jay had phoned Uncle George, who was with his wife Daphne on a rare reunion cruise with the 1966 World Cup squad. On hearing the news in Madeira, they flew home and jumped straight into a car at the airport driven by their son Anthony to join us at the bedside vigil. When the hospital staff showed us a room with beds allocated for our use while Dad was receiving round-the-clock treatment, it became clear this was a long-term scenario with no evident outcome. We were all in a state of suspense, loitering around the hospital bed, unable to do anything but wait. And wait for what? We were told Dad had a 50-50 chance of survival. An ICU is a tough, tense environment. Medical opinions verge towards pessimism. No one wants to raise false hopes. That's what I found so hard. It was in total contrast to my world of sport, where a positive attitude is the driving force. 'Hoping' to do well is negative: you *expect* to do well, you practise to improve, you plan around anticipated challenges and enter the fray with a can-do, we've-trained-for-this attitude. For Dad, unconscious, there were no controllable factors to control and no game plan to follow.

Dad remained in a coma in the ICU for ten days. It's difficult to talk to an inanimate person – you talk to the wall, basically – but I kind of chatted to him about how the Saints were doing. Paul Grayson, Steve Thompson and Matt Dawson came to visit him as well. Early on, we noticed he twitched and grew restless when I alluded to the fact that I wasn't training or playing at the moment. Somewhere in the dark recesses of his impaired consciousness, that bothered him.

So, as it became clear that he might be there for a while, I booked a hotel and started travelling up and down, alternating training with time spent at his bedside, waiting for him to wake up, and returning to the Saints to train and play at weekends. I talked to him about how my rugby was going, what was going on at the club, and he never twitched in agitation again.

Wherever his mind was, he seemed to be at peace knowing I was maintaining my side of our rugby dialogue.

All of us – my mum, my brother, sister and me – felt rootless, our thoughts remarkably similar in the Get Well Soon cards we wrote individually for Dad. My card showed a little cartoon mouse – me! – with sweat beads flying as he tries to push a big poorly tortoise along on his upturned shell. Inside, the little mouse stands triumphant and happy on the back of a happy and fit tortoise. Under the printed message – 'Hope you'll be back on your feet very soon!' – I wrote, 'To the BEST DAD in the world. Get better soon because we need you back. Love you lots, Ben'. In his card Jay inscribed: 'I need you so much. Hurry up and get better. We want you home.' And the heartfelt message from Sam was, 'You have a very important role in our lives because you're my dad and my hero and we need you for a good pair of ears for listening.' *Need* was the operative word. Dad was the person we looked to for affirmation about what we were doing and how we were living our lives. Mum too. We all needed him back.

It was a slow-drip limbo, but I was lucky. I had an escape. In a rugby changing-room, you don't expose your personal life. Everyone leaves that at the door. It's a tough place, full of focus, full of banter, and you need your wits about you to survive. You have to stand up and not be afraid to be part of it. But team spirit is an embrace too. Us against the world and all that. Camaraderie is forged from resilience on every level, on and off the pitch. I could walk in there and normal life resumed. Everyone knew of the incident in the club, but no one imagined for a moment that Dad would die. They probably just thought, 'That's awful. Give Ben some space. Speak to him direct. Give him as much support as possible.' People would ask how Dad was doing and I'd say, 'Yeah, he's a little bit better.' I was quite pragmatic. I didn't like to dwell on it.

The game was a fantastic distraction and I began playing incredible rugby. I wasn't consciously thinking about what Dad would expect of me, or using the injustice of his circumstances to motivate me. At that stage I was simply making a superhuman effort to block out the horror, channelling my emotions into one thing in the one place where I could forget about reality, and that turned me into a man possessed.

On one occasion I couldn't help myself. We were playing touch rugby in training and Ali Hepher had a right go at me for not stopping. It's difficult to slow down where you're running at full speed. I lost my temper and hit him. He was momentarily knocked out. Everyone was saying to him, 'Wrong person, wrong time to have a go.' We both felt ashamed afterwards.

Driving between training pitch and hospital occupied a lot of time, and gave me a way of coping with the situation. I used to mind too much about my rugby and let little things bother me, but I was beginning to gain a better perspective on its daily trials. It was just a game, which happened to be my livelihood. Something clicked. I had a better perspective on life. Our European Cup defence, for example, was shockingly poor.

A week after Dad's incident, we played Leinster at Franklin's Gardens and lost 14–8; on the return fixture in Ireland, a week later, we got hammered 40–31, with Budge Pountney collecting a red card in the first five minutes. A few weeks earlier, I'd have been eaten up by those results, but I came to see I couldn't do much about them individually other than try my utmost. On match days at Franklin's Gardens, I'd receive a lot of sympathy and good wishes from fans and families of my team-mates. The number of supportive emails from fans sent through to the club for my attention was incredible.

Back in Nottingham, we were becoming friends with other families sitting next to their unconscious loved ones in the ICU. We became close to the parents of one young lad who was in a bad way after a motorbike accident. He loved rugby – and that gave our families a bond – so I got him an England shirt signed by all the players. It was the least I could do. I knew as a sportsman, and I was coming to realise as a hospital visitor, there is nothing like a tide of goodwill to make the world seem a more positive place. Dad's bed was surrounded by cards and flowers. Messages arrived every day from old friends, local businesses, suppliers, from all at Northants TV, all at Northampton Old Scouts Colts rugby team, the Millennium Volunteers, former neighbours, the Saints, from the 'fit U16s NOSRFC', a former next-door neighbour who'd had brain surgery and was 'walking proof that miracles do happen'; a card addressed to 'Our Pete', another from a man who 34 years earlier had been cheered by

Dad when they were both in the old Fulham Hospital. Every single card or note was a fillip. Some made us chuckle, bringing back to life the mischievous Dad we could no longer see beneath the hospital paraphernalia. One old friend wrote:

> Dear Lana, Sam, Justin, Ben,
>
> I spent a lot of time with Pete when we were young, and it was very sad to read about him in the paper. He was always a loyal mate and was there if any of us had problems, which was quite often. He has never been a quitter and this will see him through this ordeal ... Keep your heads up as he would. See you all soon. Forgive hand writing and spelling. It was only Secondary Modern School and we played truant a lot ...

Others came from ordinary people he'd encountered in his working life, running the Grand Hotel car park by day and working as a nightclub doorman by night.

> To Pete,
>
> I hope you remember me because I certainly could never forget you. I've known you for 30 years back to the times when you used to run the Grand Hotel Car Park. You were always there with a welcoming chat and a hot cup of tea on those cold winter mornings. You've had a few knocks in your time and I know you'll get

over this one. All the best from an old ex foot plodding Bobby on the beat ...

The flow of supportive words seemed to have an effect. Dad regained consciousness and after ten days was transferred back to Northampton General Hospital to save us all the daily flog up and down the motorway. More flowers arrived and cards full of encouraging lines – 'pleased to hear he's getting better' and so on – with offers of help and support for Mum in the long-term rehabilitation programme that lay ahead. I'd taken him my Man of the Match champagne. I'd talked to him about the dream of being in the starting XV for the game against world champions Australia.

On Sunday, 12 November, I travelled to Pennyhill Park to meet up with England. Once there, I spent less time thinking about the hospital where so many patients lay suspended in life, where tiny incremental improvements are plotted on patients' notes. A sense of stagnation gave way to the electrifying buzz I found so addictive about an England camp. I travelled up and down to see my Dad in hospital; I would leave Pennyhill Park fired up and arrive at Northampton General praying Dad was making progress. As a patient, he was officially stable, but as my Dad, he didn't look to me as if he was doing great. Mum saw it too but we didn't say anything, even to each other. Neither of us wanted to acknowledge our instinct, but I could glean something from his eyes. He couldn't speak or make himself understood easily. He looked so sad and frustrated, unable to do anything for himself. Maybe he knew his end was near; maybe he couldn't bear to live in the state he would be in. Maybe I was just imagining it, because we had never seen him this way before. But I knew he would have loathed the indignity of it all. There was no getting away from the fact that he'd been left with brain damage, epilepsy, partial paralysis, vision problems – the list went on.

On the morning of 14 November – at the very moment I was talking to journalists about my excitement at facing Australia at Twickenham and the honour of winning my seventh cap – Dad was at a washbasin in his wheelchair, determined to wash himself, when he was struck by a massive heart attack brought on by a pulmonary embolism. Apparently a clot that had formed on the back of his head probably as a result of the attack had travelled to his lung. Poor Dad; such a lonely, pitiable end.

The hospital staff summoned Mum. She and Jay arrived to find a team of medical staff working on his chest, desperately trying to keep him alive. They shut the doors on them, not wanting next of kin to witness their urgent efforts. And it was hopeless. He could not be revived. After a further 15 minutes Mum had to give her written approval for them to stop working on him.

That's when she called Clive and asked him, please, to tell me the news that my dad had passed on and send me home to say goodbye.

*

I appreciated Daws being there for me, although it was a pretty silent journey in his car back to Northampton. What was there to say? I knew my dad was dead, but I couldn't take it in. I would need to see him lying in hospital before I could understand what those words meant. We stopped at Toddington Services on the M1 and queued up for a Burger King, still in our England kit. We'd missed lunch at Pennyhill Park and there was no need to rush. Dad had gone.

I don't know what Daws was thinking, but I was trying to get my head around the last four weeks or so. The strangeness of the situation also felt faintly familiar and I realised it was the second time I'd been sent reeling by a thunderbolt from a blueish sky concerning my dad. Just a month ago I had gone to bed early to rest up before that big European game for the Saints against Edinburgh, but ended up not getting a wink of sleep.

We arrived at Northampton General and the thought of seeing Dad in that state was … unthinkable. Daws asked if I wanted him to come in. I said I did. 'Are you sure?' he repeated. I reassured him I was. Part of him was obviously worried he was intruding, but it was comforting to have him there. Rugby was family, mine and Dad's. We'd been embraced together by Northampton since Old Scouts days. Dad, me, rugby, Northampton, East Midlands, Midlands, England – that was our life as father and son. Daws and I walked through the hospital corridors on this unseasonably hot day, sun streaming in through the windows, and found the door of the room where Dad lay. He had died at 10.30am, but

Mum would not let them move him until I had been in to say my farewells. No one else was in the room. Just me and Daws and Dad. Neither of us had seen a lifeless body before. I went round the far side of the bed. I kissed my dad on the forehead. I held his hand. I could feel emotions stacking up inside me. There he was as I'd never seen him before, all that energy and passionate spirit gone. I don't recall how long I spent there with him. What can I say?

Abby appeared in the doorway and Daws left. We hugged. It was a unique moment to share with someone. I look back now still perplexed by the extremes of emotion I experienced in that couple of hours. Talk about highs and lows. One minute I had been euphoric. I'd been publicly confirmed in the England line-up to face the world champions at Twickenham. I had proved myself against evident doubts about my all-round game. I'd been congratulated by reporters and asked about my thoughts ahead of the encounter. And with Dad –– on the mend, turning the corner – punching the air with his good arm, our rugby companionship was intact. Then Clive, breaking the news that he had gone. Me, seeing his unmistakeable physical form for the last time. My world crashing down, while the last autumn sun shone unsympathetically on the scene. Now the two things that meant most in the world to me – family and rugby – would be inextricably linked for ever more.

I sat with Abby outside the room where Dad had died, both of us weeping. I was still in my rose-crested England tracksuit and trainers. Mum says I cried and cried in that room when I went to say goodbye and came out a different, stronger man. That's not how I felt. I didn't feel strong at all. Lost, confused, reeling, numb; I was experiencing all sorts of feelings I didn't have words for. I looked out of the hospital window on that gorgeous autumn day and saw the bustle of people outside, walking along pavements, driving their cars, arriving, leaving, chatting, laughing, doing their thing. My world had just come to an end, but everyone else's was still going on. That didn't seem right. I wanted theirs to halt too, and the sun to go behind a cloud. I wanted the whole world to stop to recognise the moment.

CHAPTER 10

AFTERMATH

How do you say a final good bye to your dad? How do you walk away from his physical prescence forever? Even when we'd been told in Queen's Medical Centre that he had a 50-50 chance of survival after he had fallen into a coma, I had never imagined he would really die.

I don't know how long I stood at the hospital window in my England kit, with the unnatural November sunshine cascading in, bathing me in a warmth I didn't feel. To this day – 15 years on – I can't drive past the hospital in my home town without that image forcing its way into my mind. The view from that window. A bustle of people. Life going on. A road leading where, now, for us as a family? For me?

In the short term, there were formalities to attend to with the rest of the family and condolences to receive. The RFU issued a press release extending its deepest sympathy. John Steele, the Director of Rugby at Northampton, said, 'Everyone at the club is deeply saddened by the news of Peter's death. We will do everything we can to support in the next couple of months.' The Old Scouts offered their sympathies and thoughts and said Dad was 'well respected by the boys he put through their paces and will be sadly missed'. Keith Barwell, Saints' owner, said: 'I have known Ben and his family for years. They were always tremendously supportive and fantastically proud of him. Our thoughts are with Ben and his family at this time.' I was humbled by some of the words of support. Bereavement is a lonely place. You speak to your peers; people say lovely, kind things, but no one could really guide me. Only I truly knew what my loss meant to me. I had to find a way of coming to terms with it myself.

Harvey Thorneycroft, my old rival and role model, was quick to wish us the best and share a confidence. For the first time, I learnt that Harvey had lost his mother from a heart attack when he was 21 – exactly the same age as I was now – and a week later he'd played in the Pilkington Cup final. 'I understand exactly what you are going through,' he said as he described how he'd found solace in rugby. 'It is early days,' he said, 'but it will be possible to channel your grief through rugby. The first few months might be traumatic but I am on hand to help you if you want to talk.'

Coroner Anne Pember opened an inquest. The official cause of death was given as a blood clot to the lungs which had travelled from Dad's right leg. The inquest was adjourned.

Uncle George and his family arrived in Northampton to say farewell to Dad. George said he was just grateful his parents had already passed away, because the death of their youngest son would have upset them terribly. Peter was the darling. My uncle and I had the first of quite a few little conversations we would have over the next few weeks and months. Should I play against Australia in a few days' time? Or not? Would it affect my future selection? Would I cope under the media glare? I was adamant at first that I was not going to not play for my country, but then I saw that in the rawness of the situation I wouldn't do myself justice. George gave me advice that could only have come from someone who knew my father well and who had performed at the highest level of sport himself. He said that my father would want me to do my best for England, and that just now I couldn't be sure of how all the different pressures would affect me. I might suddenly find myself unable to meet my responsibilities to my coach, my team-mates and, ultimately, to my country. My father wouldn't want me simply to make an emotional response. There was a stronger way to deal with the situation. He would have wanted me to think it through. George ultimately advised me not to play. 'What will happen to you is that you will go out there for about 15 minutes and then it will all fall apart,' he suggested. 'But it is your decision, Ben. You have to work it out for yourself.'

I called Clive and we agreed it was best if I sat out the game on Saturday. I thought I'd be focused on the game, but I couldn't trust myself not to break down during the national anthem. The

Australia team wrote me a lovely letter of condolence, signed by every single member of their squad and backroom staff. What was reassuring was that Clive was clearly going to be keeping me as involved as I wanted to be. On match day, the England team wore black armbands. As I watched the game in the stadium, sitting next to Jayne Woodward, I felt overwhelmed by the capacity crowd's observation of a minute's silence in honour of Dad and couldn't help thinking how proud he would be to know he was the centre of attention for more than 73,000 in the stadium and a global television audience of millions – especially as England proceeded to assert superiority over the world champions on home soil for the first time in five years. The final score was 22–19, and it was, of course, a try from Dan Luger in the 87th minute that clinched the victory, after a nail-biting consultation with the video referee to make sure the ball had been touched down correctly.

Twickenham went crazy. This proved that this England side was the business. We had not won back-to-back Tests against southern hemisphere sides for six years. Had I been sitting it out through injury, I would have felt a tinge of regret at not being part of it. As it was, I could genuinely feel part of the triumph as it was our summer win against the Springboks in Bloemfontein which had truly built up the necessary bank of self-belief for this encounter.

The police continued to talk to legal experts to establish what charges could be brought in connection with Dad's death, and four arrests were made. Meanwhile I was picked to play against

Argentina on 25 November, and decided I was ready. George reckoned that now the initial shock was over, there was no benefit in not playing. I had my own life to lead as well. He told me I was good at channelling my emotions. I shouldn't stop, I had to earn a living and support the family. And remembering how Dad, in a coma, had twitched and flinched when I wasn't playing, I agreed. Even unconscious, his mind became restless at the thought that I'd taken time out of playing rugby because of him. My place was on the field.

At the time, senior England players like captain Martin Johnson, Lawrence Dallaglio and Matt Dawson were in the process of trying to negotiate a better pay deal with the RFU. They wanted a larger guaranteed match fee and a smaller win bonus, and to force the issue the players were prepared to go on strike and not play against Argentina that weekend or South Africa the following week. As one of the youngest and newest squad members, I didn't really know the details and kept a low profile, wanting to show solidarity with my peers without jeopardising my future. Privately, I was desperate for the match to go ahead. I wanted to go out there against Argentina for Dad. I wanted to score a try for him. To lose that opportunity for a strike over pay would have been very lowering, however much I was behind the efforts for the greater good of the team. The drama was a massive situation, and a good distraction for me in that my grief was caught up in the politics. The issue reinforced the unity of the team, the trust we had in the leadership of the group and the 'one for all and all for one' mentality that would become our trademark.

There was a pre-scheduled charity event at the Café Royal, at which players and coaches were segregated and everyone wandered around on their mobile phones. We didn't get what we wanted. On 21 November, a strike was called. The player reps told us to vacate Pennyhill Park; the RFU told us that those who failed to turn up to training at 11am would not be considered for Saturday's Test against Argentina. We were made to understand that we might never play for England again. I went back with Jonny Wilkinson to his parents' house in Farnham. We had two nights there and spent the days doing kicking practice all day, Jonny putting up cross-field kicks, me catching, bored shitless. Jonny was good to me. We sat around his house and talked.

On the Wednesday morning we were told we had to get to a players' meeting at Wentworth Golf Club because we had a decision to make. The route there from Jonny's house – Farnham, Camberley, Bagshot, Wentworth – took us past Pennyhill Park, and by the time we were driving through Camberley we received the news that the meeting was off, an agreement on a pay package had been reached, and we should make our way back to the team hotel. We were practically there, so we turned in. Of course, all the press were waiting and they didn't yet know that the players had settled on a package. When they saw Jonny and me randomly turn up they would think we'd reneged, that we were turning up behind our team-mates' backs. How would we handle it? We parked and I could see it was going to be difficult to dodge past the journalists. I said to Jonny, 'What do you reckon?' But Jonny had pegged it. 'Sorry, Benny, got to go' was his parting shot. I eventually made my way up to the physios' room and there he was, watching the live coverage, having hysterics about darting off and leaving me to face the media like that. Thanks for that, mate.

On the day of the match, the weather turned to classic rugby conditions. Torrential rain fell at the start, which led to sloppy play and lots of spills, but in a way it was exactly the sort of game I needed to focus and fully apply myself. Eleven days had passed since my dad died and I was determined to go out and do him justice. The scoreboard ticked over courtesy of Jonny's kicking, but it was slow progress. The game needed a try. Twelve minutes from the end, a grubber kick from Jonny bounced off the post and on instinct I slid in and touched down. I looked up to the sky: 'That's for you, Dad.'

Mum came to the game and, quite coincidentally, had an empty seat next to her. She took it as a sign that Dad was there in spirit, and found it comforting. The same thing happened when I played against South Africa a week later, and thereafter. Mum said she and Abby noticed a solitary empty seat close to them at every match they came to support me in. It became a game: spot Pete's seat.

Dad was well-known and his death attracted the full glare of the media. It would have made headlines anyway, but with the

Uncle George connection and me playing for England, the case was reported on assiduously, but thankfully never intrusively. In retrospect, I can see it was probably helpful in that it confirmed how loved and respected Dad was, and encouraged us to articulate our feelings. Justin gave a statement to the press on behalf of all of us. He said, '[Dad] was our mentor and encouraged us in whatever we decided to do. Everybody will miss him. We are trying to come to terms with the loss, which has been made even more difficult due to the circumstances surrounding his death. This is a very difficult time for our family, who are naturally hurting. My father was a well-known and respected member of the Northamptonshire community who would do anything for anyone.'

I anticipated a bleak Christmas. We all tried to stay strong, but Mum couldn't accept Dad's death. Two weeks after he'd gone, she went to the police station and reported him missing. She couldn't let go. She would wake up every morning thinking he'd come home. She left a separate bedroom, the one Dad used when working late at Eternity, untouched from the night he was attacked. She put a red rose and a rugby ball I'd given him on the pillow and arranged framed family photos around the room. She went to the bedroom every night to wish him a good sleep and tell him she'd see him in the morning. Months after his last minutes in hospital, she went to the police station again and handed herself in for murder. She felt such terrible guilt over signing permission for the hospital doctors to stop working on him. Each of us was trying to get through the waves of grief that each day brought us and it was difficult in those first few weeks and months to stop and consider the different effects the traumatic loss of Dad might have on us individually. For Mum, it became clear that the security of Dad's love and larger-than-life personality had enabled her to lock away elements of her past. To have Dad snatched from her by violence triggered a flood of haunting memories. The brutal circumstances under which her rock and saviour was lost to her unleashed all the demons of her unhappy childhood. A funeral, arranged in the traditional ten-day timeframe, might have helped her accept her loss. It would be a chance to say goodbye with respect and help her find closure, but that was not to be.

You could not have scripted a more painful scenario. By mid December, four weeks after his death, it was still not clear when Dad's body would be released for burial. The nature of the criminal charges had not yet been established, and lawyers might need samples from the body for any ongoing forensic tests prior to a trial. The police were in contact with the Crown Prosecution Service to ascertain what charges could be brought. They were not expected until the New Year. Until then, we couldn't announce a date for a funeral or even plan one; every element of a ceremony – the church, the venue for a reception, catering, the hearse and cars, the vicar, flowers, the choice of music – depended on booking dates and times and availability. Mum was all over the place. We all were. She didn't want to move the cards of condolence that were displayed on the mantelpiece and all around the lounge. To do so would be an acknowledgement of moving on, and she couldn't do that before a funeral had even taken place. She was a very long way from moving on. It was awful. We existed in a state of limbo, dreading Christmas because it was a time of year Dad loved. He was always the first on the phone to ring all the family and wish them Happy Christmas and everyone had memories of him dressing up as Father Christmas. Mum refused to put up decorations at all. She said it didn't seem right.

On 23 December, I came home to the house I shared with Abby and I could tell before I'd got to the front door that something weird was going on inside. I couldn't get in the front door; it had been latched from the inside – the tell-tale sign that burglars had got in. I bolted round to the next-door neighbour's and approached from the back, but that had given the thieves long enough to escape. Sure enough, there was a panel lying on the ground which they'd pushed out of the back door. I wandered around the house, numbly surveying the damage. They'd ransacked the house and stolen, among other things, more than £3,000 in cash I had saved for Dad's funeral and stashed in the bottom drawer in the lounge. They'd got away with computers, DVD players, cash and jewellery. They'd used pillow cases as bags and pulled a sock out of the drawer to carry Abby's jewellery. Fortunately, they'd grabbed a sock with a hole in it, so some of the jewellery, including Abby's nan's pearls, had fallen through onto the floor and been left behind. They'd got away with about £13,000 worth of goods. The whole thing was horrible. In one really weird touch, they had carefully laid my England shirts out on the bed – and they were only in there for 11 minutes. It was all on the CCTV.

I came back from training another day to find pellet holes in the front door and strange objects that had been thrown at the house. I remember being on the phone to Clive Woodward, walking around my lounge as we chatted, and spotting someone lighting matches in my hedge. I was shouting out and Clive was saying, 'Are you alright, Ben?'

'Yeah, yeah, someone's just trying to set fire to my hedge.'

Not long after, I was in the car parked outside my house in the wintry dark, talking to Clive again, and I could see some guy shamelessly trying to break into the car next to me. The light reflecting off my windscreen from the street lamp above meant I couldn't be seen. I opened the door and shouted, 'What the fuck are you doing?' – and on the phone I heard Clive again saying, 'Ben, BEN, are you alright?' He must have thought I lived in some hellhole.

On 31 January, three men were charged with my dad's murder. Gavin Kerr, aged 32, of Clinton Road, Far Cotton, his younger brother Colin, aged 31, of Elderstump House, Rothersthorpe, and Robert Evans of Thorn Hill, Briar Hill, all denied the charge when they appeared in court. A few days later, I was due to play in the first Six Nations game of 2001, against Wales. I was still opening thoughtful letters of condolence but, increasingly, these were now interspersed with poisonous letters from Wales fans. It went back to the 'Shane who?' scenario, which I had explained a zillion times. I was getting fed up with the number of abusive letters that kept on arriving, some containing death threats.

When we played Wales in Cardiff I expected animosity and the usual 'Ben who?' barracking, but inwardly I knew it would simply sharpen my focus on rugby. The death of my father had put everything into perspective. I certainly wasn't going to get wound up by a bit of verbal abuse at a sports ground. My only aim was to help England win and, hopefully, create some tries. On the day we won 44–15, and I did score a try. It was important we set out our stall for the 2001 Six Nations Championship, and the BBC match report was gratifying to read:

Clive Woodward's backs have often been criticised for not finishing off the work of their forwards, but they stole the show. Will Greenwood justified his inclusion with a hat-trick which was completed soon after the interval. And Iain Balshaw added an extra dimension with his pace from full-back which exploited any gaps in the Welsh defence. As the game petered out as a contest in the second half, Ben Cohen breezed beyond two isolated Welsh props to round off an exhibition of back play. The difference in pace between Cohen and his front-row pursuers was just the last of many examples in the match when Englishmen left their opponents grasping at thin air.

The weekend of the Wales game coincided with the closure of Eternity. It was heart-rending for the family, as it had been the business Dad had viewed as his last chance to make a success of a business in life, and he'd invested in it heart and soul. Jay and Mum came to the decision together. Ultimately, neither of them could bear to be there any longer. The car park, the entrance, the bar, the cellar, the upstairs office – every square foot of the place held reminders of that harrowing night in October. So Eternity didn't live up to its name and closed down. This meant the family no longer had a source of livelihood, or a daily schedule to get out of the bed for in the morning for. I was the lucky one: rugby gave me a rigid daily and weekly structure, and a distinct sense of purpose. Dad's burial looked a long way off. We were in limbo in so many ways now. That cowardly brutal assault on a much-loved family man had so many devastating knock-on effects. Inside, I was churning with anger, raging at the injustice of it all, even if I wasn't showing it outwardly.

During training – that Dad so often used to come and watch – and on the field for games, I did all I could to make him, wherever he was, proud of me. I was playing fantastic rugby because I was trying my very hardest for myself and for my dad. The game had become a vehicle to channel my fury and, surprisingly perhaps, I enjoyed it a lot more than I had done. Except that I missed the dialogue I had with Dad. I no longer had anyone to share it with. I no longer had a sounding board. I was winning England caps but had no Dad to call.

It was a weird old time. At the Saints, the management and back-room staff had discussed plans A, B and C for how I was to be handled should I break down or implode, but they were never needed. I was the number one pick on the team sheet.

The regular rhythm of the Six Nations fixtures was disrupted by a serious outbreak of foot and mouth disease in Britain, which led to severe restrictions on travel, especially between Britain and Ireland. Ireland's three fixtures against the home nations were postponed until the outbreak of the livestock infection was contained. (The games were then played in September and October.) For the third consecutive year England would be left on the cusp of a Grand Slam approaching the final game – but would have to wait until the autumn to play it. At Northampton, we turned our form around enough to finish fourth in the league and I had the welcome accolade of being voted the *Northampton Chronicle & Echo*'s Player of the Year, ahead of Garry Pagel and our departing skipper Pat Lam. I collected the award on the pitch, mobbed by fans after a seven-try win over Saracens. I hadn't shed tears since I'd said goodbye to Dad in the hospital, but I had tears in my eyes when I received the award. It had been a long, hard season and to be appreciated by the fans meant so much. I'd scored 20-odd tries for the Saints that season, and I found it moving to be praised for my resilience, given all that happened off the pitch.

The greatest vindication for my pain-fuelled form came a few days earlier when Mum rang me while I was training at Franklin's Gardens to say I'd made the touring party for the British and Irish Lions, and that I had become the Saints' youngest ever Lion. I'd been listening to the news, hoping to hear my name, but had to leave mid-announcement in order to make a doctor's appointment, so Mum called to let me know I was in. She knew it was a dream I'd shared with Dad. I was over the moon – I thought this was going to be one of the best experiences ever. I watched a video of the 1997 Lions. I spoke to Nick Beal, Daws, Tim Rodber and Austin Healey, and they all said it would be fantastic. Dad's body had finally been released and a funeral date set for Friday, 4 May – nearly six months after he had died – and Mum said she wanted to bury Dad with a framed cutting of the local paper's report on my Lions selection. She knew he'd have been proud that I'd won the highest accolade for an England player and she saw it as a way of still including him on the rugby journey we'd set out on together.

At last we could bury Dad and let him rest in peace. He'd been in the freezer in the mortuary for six months. Initially, Mum had just had him embalmed, and for three weeks she went every day to spend time with him. She used to talk to him and play music, all the songs they both loved. She'd dress up to go and visit him; she found it so hard to let him go. None of the rest of us wanted to go, and she respected our decision. Jay and I both said we wanted to remember him alive, not dead on a slate.

None of us had ever been to a family funeral so we hadn't a clue where to start organising one. The finality of it, after the delays, made us all obsessive about the occasion. Mum set to work, intent on getting every detail right for the funeral and the burial, to the extent of stipulating that when she died, she wanted to be buried face down, so she and Dad could lie down at last to cuddle. Poor Dad had suffered all sorts of indignities in the post mortem and forensic procedures. His body was left unsewn and returned to the undertakers in that condition; the undertakers were fuming. Cue letters to and from Mum, the mortuary and the undertakers, and another sense of injustice we could have done without. On the day before the funeral, the accused men's defence rang and said they needed hair samples for another forensic test. We could scarcely believe the tactlessness of the timing; they'd had nearly six months to think about that. Dad's brains had been removed and could not be buried with his body, because they hadn't been returned to us.

The aim was simple. We wanted to give him the best funeral imaginable. Mum buried him like an Egyptian pharaoh with all his prized possessions and things to bring him good luck in his next life. 'Peter is going to be well prepared,' she said to sympathisers. 'We have all made sure that he is going to be comfortable.' She bought a huge American burial casket, eight foot long and made of brass and copper. The casket alone weighed 14 stone. She bought him Italian cashmere socks and a decent Crombie coat. He wore a Midlands rugby tie and jacket, and we folded an England tie and put it in his pocket. A lot of England memorabilia went down with him, including one of my Man of the Match magnums of champagne. Mum jests about worrying about the cork exploding – it'll either go up his arse or make a hole in the casket. There's no doubt he's well catered for in the afterlife, right down to his favourite beverage. He's got a tea cup in there, with tea bags, dried milk and a teaspoon. He would have laughed to see it all.

The day of the funeral was a beautiful sunny day. Mum had ordered six silver Rolls-Royces from London to take the coffin, close family and the dozens of floral tributes sent by well wishers. There was a reason for every aspect of the day. Dad loved Rolls-Royces. More than 200 mourners joined us to pay their last respects to Dad. The procession set off at 11am from the Sturtridge Pavilion at Franklin's Gardens as a gesture to both Dad's and my passion for rugby. Mum, Jay, Sam and me considered getting out and walking too. 'We've paid for the flipping cars,' Jay said. 'We ain't walking!' So we sat in comfort, marvelling at the long line of people, soberly dressed in black, accompanying the cortege on foot, including the whole of the Saints squad. The procession walked for 45 minutes through streets that had been closed by the police. Outriders accompanied the cortege. Bells rang out from churches as we passed on the way to the Roman Catholic Cathedral of Our Lady and St Thomas in Kingsthorpe Road.

I was one of the eight pallbearers who carried the casket into the cathedral. My brother-in-law said he could hear the teaspoon tinkling inside the tea cup with our every step. I particularly wanted to share that last journey with Dad.

Justin paid a sincere tribute during the service. His intention was to make everybody cry, and I'm pretty sure he succeeded. 'I am not here to just say goodbye to my dad, but to remember him as well,' he started. 'He was a distinctive man, with his bald head and beard. I always wanted to be like Dad. Whenever we went into town we would always have to leave home early because he would always want to stop and say hello to everyone. During the first 14 months after we opened the Eternity nightclub, I spent more time with my dad than with my own wife and son. He was my mentor and my teacher in life. I remember that when Dad died, my son asked me if we would see him again. I looked up in the sky and pointed to the brightest star, and said, "That is Pap." I now look up to that star myself.'

Dad considered the Saints as extended family, so it was poignant that Pat Lam agreed to read the 23rd Psalm. To reflect his love of life, Mum had chosen a playlist of Dad's favourite songs for the hour-long service, including 'On the Night We Were Wed' and 'San Francisco'. We had 'Unchained Melody', the Righteous Brothers' song that was used as the theme tune for the film *Ghost*. I'd been to a few funerals with Dad and he'd always mess around. He'd see the absurd in them – gallows humour, I suppose. There was one moment in the funeral service when Dad's friend stood up to sing 'Autumn Leaves' at the piano. Halfway through, he broke down all croaky voiced and couldn't continue. It's very English to find overt emotion embarrassing, isn't it? I had my head in my hands, thinking, 'This is too much. I'm going to get such a ribbing from the boys about this... ' and I know that's what Dad would have thought too.

After the service the Saints very generously allowed us to host a 'Cup of Tea' buffet back at the Sturtridge Pavilion for all Dad's friends to toast his life. It was a long, exhausting day, culminating in a private family interment in Moulton parish cemetery. It was a sad moment, putting him in the ground, but a relief, too, because the casket was so flipping heavy – and Dad would have laughed at that too. Mum brought Dad's favourite blood-red roses and her own favourite flowers, freesias, to throw on the casket when it was lowered in the ground. She didn't like the idea of dirt being thrown on the casket, no matter what the traditional symbolism is. The floral tributes were incredible. My own was a rugby ball in a huge floral tea cup and the message, To Dad, WHO LOVES YA! And that line – his catchphrase – is what I was adamant we'd have inscribed on the gravestone, though Mum had to argue with the parish council for approval because of the spelling. After the interment we milled quietly around the grave. I had bought all the plots around Dad's in the cemetery so that one day we could all be together again.

CHAPTER 11

A LONG WAY FROM HOME

An end-of-era feeling prevailed at Northampton, with Pat Lam moving back to Newcastle and Tim Rodber retiring. The colossus Tim – hands on hips and mouth open barking a command – was the figure on a poster I had once received in a goodie bag when I'd attended an RFU Open Day at Franklin's Gardens with the Old Scouts. I hadn't a clue who he was then, but he was authoritative and inspiring, a fantastic person for me to look up to and learn from. He had been at the club for 13 years, five as captain in his military style, a role he relinquished selflessly when Pat Lam arrived. It had been a great moment for everyone when, at the end of last season, after he had been toiling away at lock for months, he was beckoned forward by Lammy to receive the

Heineken Cup at Twickenham. There was no way he would have left the Saints until we'd won our elusive first trophy.

In mid May I signed on at Northampton for two more years. I was 22, and it was strange to think I had now racked up 100 appearances for the club. I didn't have Dad to discuss the deal with, or to talk to about the upcoming Lions tour. Mum and my sister would go to the cemetery to talk to Dad, but neither Jay nor I could 'go there' in any sense of that phrase. I'd see him again one day, I reasoned. I did make one special little visit in the first week of June though. I wanted to share my excitement about the Lions adventure with him. Like him re-establishing himself with a nightclub, the Lions had always been my fantasy. I put flowers on his grave with a card saying, 'Dad. The day is here. I am going on the Lions tour. Something we always talked about. The drive and ambition I have comes from you. It's what you lived on. See you soon, Love Ben xx PS: Keep an eye on me.'

After leaving Northampton, Ian McGeechan would still text some of his former players, and he now wished me luck. Geech was so good to me. He related to me, not just on coming into rugby from a state school background, but also now that I'd lost my father when I was coming into my prime in the sport. His father had also died just before he was first capped, and never saw him play for Scotland. I can't remember when exactly he shared this with me, but what stuck in my mind was the way he believed his father still knew about everything that he had gone on to achieve. He was excited for me heading off Down Under with the Lions. As a coach whose name was synonymous with Lions success, he used to talk about it as the ultimate challenge. We had to see the Lions as an eight-week challenge, from the first training week to the flight home, he said. It is very different to any other rugby tour and certain players thrive on that. He said he had found as a coach that on every Lions tour players came through who he hadn't expected to be part of the team. Players from disparate clubs and nations have to learn quickly to adopt the mindset of a Lions collective. Some players adapted better than others and forged the chemistry necessary to go out and perform as a team greater than the sum of its parts. I could not wait to go on that tour and experience it at first hand.

Graham Henry, the New Zealand coach of Wales, had a lot to live up to. For many reasons – not least that he was the first Lions coach from outside the Home Nations – his appointment had raised eyebrows. I wasn't troubled by big-picture questions like whether or not he was familiar with the needs and requirements of the Lions. What excited me was the opportunity to test myself among the cream of the world's players and wear the famous red shirt. Three days in, Henry told us younger players we had everything to play for. He said he was looking for form on tour, not reputation, so selection was wide open. The first week was all about merging the four nations into a united party and Henry giving us a crash course in organisation on the rugby field. This seemed rudimentary, and a lot of the experienced Lions didn't feel they needed that. Then there were team-bonding gimmicks. To speed up bonding, for example, every player and member of the management staff was given a percussion instrument and told to go away and practise for an hour. We all trooped back, clutching our tambourines and sticks, and performed as a 50-piece samba band. This sounds laughable now, but I bought into it. I was so excited to be selected for the Lions – the best of the best, and all that – and I knew I had a short space of time to make the most of it.

Very early on, I'd hear rumblings of criticisms about the management style from the older players. I had nothing to compare it to. Matt Dawson later got into trouble for writing an honest Lions Tour Diary which was published in instalments throughout the tour, and didn't go down well with Graham Henry and tour manager Donal Lenihan. Austin Healey was critical in the press, too. For me, everything was novel, and I was always up for learning, but the main disappointment was that right from the beginning, despite Henry's words about Test selection being 'wide open', there was a clear divide between first team and second team.

I played in the opening match against Western Australia. The Lions won 116–10. I didn't have a great game. I made two mistakes, but it was the kind of one-sided encounter when mistakes happen. But that was it for me. I was immediately written off and would remain in the Wilderness XV, as Daws put it, for the rest of a very long tour. I wasn't getting another chance.

It had been a horrible six months and now in my rugby, the place where there had at least been order, I felt like an unwanted spare part. The 'second stringers' were not treated well. We were not given the opportunity to go out and play and fight for a place in the Test side. However much you wanted to, you couldn't show your form because there weren't enough opportunities. I knew we weren't there to win midweek games, but to win Tests, and as a player, you want time and good preparation to be able to show your worth to play on a Saturday. I was deeply disappointed with the tour. I felt my form got better and better as the weeks went by, but they didn't want to know. It was like I was invisible.

It's a long tour and the worst point actually came when I met up in Melbourne with Mum and Abby, who'd come out to support me. In a lovely generous touch, Matt Dawson donated his all-expenses-paid trip courtesy of Lucozade to my mum and girlfriend, but it turned out to be a nightmare. Mum was not herself at all; she kept going missing at night and Abby would have to go and find her. Though Abby tried to shield me from Mum's antics, it was upsetting. It's difficult enough to entertain family and friends when you're in a tour bubble, let alone deal with a worrying situation.

On a scheduled day off I arranged to visit the Blue Mountains with them, which required an early-morning departure from the hotel. That day the management changed their plans and called the players for an extra training session. Having already left, I knew nothing about that summons and was the only player who failed to turn up. I had a huge black mark against me.

I did enjoy playing against big teams like ACT Bumbies, but generally I was miserable. I couldn't see that I'd gained anything out of the tour experience. I felt thoroughly lost. It made me hate Australia and I didn't want to experience anything like that again. I could feel my confidence ebbing away day by day, and there was no way to turn it around before the long flight home. Was I depressed? No, I was lost, confronted by questions I'd never thought I'd have to answer at that young an age. I've always done my talking on the pitch and, after that one early mistake, I didn't get the opportunity to put it right. As an over-analytical perfectionist, that was more than I could bear.

After the tour I kept my Lions blazer and a couple of jerseys, but eventually got rid of every single other bit of kit. For a while, I'd occasionally find something from that tour at the back of a drawer and it would bring it all back – the horrible, aching feeling. Even now I hate to think of my Lions time. In one of the hospitality suites at Franklin's Garden there is a huge wall-size picture of me, in Lions regalia, running with the ball on that tour. Others might see Ben Cohen, Saints' youngest ever Lion. I look at it and see a lost soul. I was in a lot of pain. How the hell did I get through it? I was very fragile. My brother and sister were grieving privately, but I was on a national stage. I was vulnerable. I felt guilty if I laughed or had fun or did well. I couldn't work out how to handle myself.

Back at Northampton, the Saints were not performing well. As September turned into October, I was dreading the anniversaries:

first of the attack on Dad, and then, four weeks later, of his death. In sport, 'storylines' become attached to you in terms of ongoing media interest, and now the tragedy of what happened to my dad had replaced the Uncle George connection.

On 13 October 2001, we played Leicester, a horrible, error-strewn game which we lost. Franklin's Garden was dressed up for a party to celebrate the official opening of two new stands – a huge fanfare with music and fireworks – but I was not in the mood to share the jubilation. It was a hard day on the pitch and off it. I was trying to inspire the team on the field and to make my mum and family happy and proud of me, but I couldn't perform. It was no surprise, a week later, when England played the postponed Six Nations game against Ireland, that I wasn't selected. Nor did I make the side for the clash with world champions Australia. Jason Robinson, who'd made his name in rugby league, had been picked for the Lions tour, too, and had dazzled. He was a phenomenal player, electric; no opponent could deal with him. He was one of the outstanding players in the side that won the first Test in Brisbane, where he side-stepped brilliantly past Australian full-back Chris Latham. He went on to score another spectacular try in the final Test. I realised I needed to re-establish myself, because Jason Robinson needed to be in there; he was brilliant. He was brought in on the wing but in the eventual shuffle-around he went to full-back.

That autumn I had to wait until the strange mismatch of Romania v England to get the chance to prove my worth again.

We won 134–0 – England's highest ever points tally. I scored a hat-trick – one of them turning the score into triple figures which felt bizarre; Jason Robinson notched up four, Dan Luger three, Mike Tindall two, Charlie Hodgson two – practically everyone had a go.

In December John Steele moved sideways to become Director of Rugby and Wayne Smith, the former All Blacks coach, was appointed Saints' Head Coach. His arrival gave us all a lift. We had good players; we needed a new voice to direct us. And he was inspiring. We won three out of three from the moment he took over until Christmas. The appeal of the job for Wayne was the club's history, the great new facilities and the ambition in the board to keep striving for success. Everything was in place, but we, as a squad, had stagnated. We were bottom of the Premiership and, after an initial visit, Wayne felt he could help us out of the hole. The way he transformed the club in five months was partly a response to a shocking first impression of the changing-room. When he was shown around, he was taken into the team room and it was in its usual absolute mess with banana skins and dirty cups all over the place. Visibly appalled, he asked his guide why it was in such a revolting state. 'Because the apprentices haven't picked up the stuff yet,' he was told. 'They haven't cleared up.' In that cameo, Wayne instantly identified the root of our problem: the lowest paid players were expected to do most of the work. He was determined when he took over officially to make sure there was more equity. Everyone had to work hard and show good character. No player would be feted because of past achievements or reputation. It was a simple philosophy. 'There are good people here,' he concluded. 'They just have to feel a bit more uncomfortable and put in a bit more. They have to show more pride for the club and respect the jersey.'

Wayne had obviously seen a lot of us in international games, but he didn't know us well individually. He made it clear that reputation and record would count for nothing; he had no bias or preconceptions. He was looking at what we were like on the inside, whether we had the right attitude to fulfil our talent. We were told we had to be ready to go and prove ourselves to him quickly. He came up to Newcastle to watch us in November. Everyone went on to the field determined to give a good account of themselves to him. As a team, we weren't performing well at all, but we won. Afterwards, I was pleased to hear he'd described me as 'the jewel in the crown of this side', not for any particular attacking move or try, but because he saw I was still determined to play at my highest level in a team that weren't going well. He praised me for maintaining my standards. For the first time since Dad's death and that demoralising Lions tour, I could feel my confidence start to trickle back.

One of the first things he did was conduct interviews with each squad member individually to get a feel for our personalities. He asked us all the same question: 'If you were hanging over the edge of a cliff on the end of a rope, who would you want on the other end of the rope at the top?' My name kept coming up as the player my team-mates would want on the end of the rope to stop them sliding down the cliff. Wayne decided I was 'a solid character who a lot of the guys trusted', 'a good bugger' with the character he was after. I shocked him too at one point. He was the kind of coach who is visibly excited to be doing his job, and one day he stood up and said, 'Isn't this great, boys, we're playing the game that we love and we all love what we're doing, and we're getting paid for it.' I put up my hand up and said, 'Well, I didn't really grow up loving the sport. We're a football family. I'm doing this because I'm good at it.' It was a different mindset from what he was used to in New Zealand, where kids want to be All Blacks from the minute they start crawling.

Wayne was a great coach – talismanic, in fact, to several of us – because he was interested in our development as people as well as players. In order to make us more versatile as players he wanted us to explore our motivation, so that we could be more adaptable, reliable and useful to a coach. He taught us it was good to have another string to our bow – and tried me at outside centre for a few games. He tried to identify our mojos. On another occasion, he asked us to muse on the reasons why we played rugby, why we were prepared to put ourselves in this tough competitive arena week in, week out. He was going to give us all a glass jar, and we had to think about what we'd put in the jar to symbolise to the rest of the squad our motives for being in professional rugby, and then we'd meet in a pub and share our reasons. I'm always honest and direct. I had a picture of my dad in there and I had money, because I viewed rugby as a job, and a job I loved and was good at. I wasn't good at anything else. And you know what? I was the only player who put money in the jar. I remember everyone sitting there, going 'Whooooaaah, his motivation is money …' I thought it was untruthful to hide the fact that I was proud to earn a living as a professional rugby player. I was proud to represent my town and community but I came from a background where money had sometimes been scarce and I knew its importance and value.

CHAPTER 12

THE TRIAL

On Monday, 14 January 2002, shortly after Wayne took over and two days after our rousing Heineken Cup win over Cardiff in which I'd scored my ninth try of the season, the trial of the men accused of attacking Dad opened at Birmingham Crown Court. The charge against the three men had been reduced from murder to manslaughter. All three defendants pleaded not guilty. They were also charged with violent disorder, which is defined under section 2(1) of the Public Order Act 1986 – I looked it up. It means a public order offence that is committed by three or more people gathered in the same place, who 'use or threaten unlawful violence' to make others 'fearful of their personal safety'. The threat or act of violent disorder may be committed in private as well as in public places, and it doesn't matter whether or not the people use or threaten violence together or separately.

I was given time off training sessions to attend the trial. I wanted to go and see justice done for Dad, and to support Mum, who was not in a good place, but it was going to be an ordeal sitting there impassively, listening to every detail, seeing the faces of the defendants, who had shown no remorse. They had torn the heart of our family from us and now they were attempting to wriggle out of taking any responsibility for their actions. Fifteen months after the assault, 14 months after Dad's death and eight months after his funeral, the duration of the criminal trial just brought all the pain and anger back again.

At least one member of the family was there every day, but we didn't all go all the time. Jay went a few times, I went several times, and Uncle George attended too. Mum and Sam went most days. It was difficult listening to the excruciating details of the horror of the night again as the prosecution called the witnesses. Kim Fieldwick, head of the door staff at Eternity, described how she was pelted with beer glasses as she tried to telephone police after Dad had been attacked. She said one of the three men had attempted to grab the phone from her hand and that Colin Kerr had tried to rip the phone wires from the wall. She told how she was extremely scared, but managed to pull the phone back off him. Four other members of staff gave accounts of how Dad suffered serious head injuries. All confirmed they had seen the three defendants at the club.

Another member of the door staff, Richard Umney, told how he was punched on the nose in the club's foyer after going to the main entrance where Dad was involved in a confrontation with a small blond-haired man. He'd been grabbed around the neck by another man, who had a scar on his face, before a third man hit him, breaking his nose. Part-time bar attendant Mary Browne also witnessed the ensuing brawl. She said Dad was returning from the foyer into the main bar when another man ran in and jumped on his back. A fight broke out in the bar area with two men attacking Dad. 'As the fight was happening, I was screaming, "Don't hurt him, get off him, somebody help",' she recalled. She remarked that one of the men ended up with his trousers and underpants around his ankles. Clarke Timson, a cellarman at the club, had gone to Eternity on a night off when Dad was injured. He told the jury he saw the Kerr brothers and Evans punching and kicking Dad when he fell to the floor in the bar.

It was extremely stressful for the witnesses. On the fourth day of evidence, Clarke twice had to leave the witness stand with chest pains, and a female jury member felt faint, which delayed proceedings while she was treated.

Justin was called next as a witness. It must have been horrendous for him to relive the events, as he naturally felt a bit of retrospective guilt about being away in Nuneaton that night, and enjoying a meal out with his mate when he had received the call from a frightened Mary Browne telling him there had been a 'serious fight'. He went through the facts: how he caught a lift with his friend back to Northampton, how he'd called Maurice Young, who ran the security firm, to take charge of the club, how he found Dad, injured, in the upstairs office: 'I arrived at the club and went upstairs. As soon as I entered the kitchen I saw a police officer at the office door, I went through the door and saw my dad on the floor in the emergency recovery position. He was slipping out of consciousness. He spoke to me and then went silent.'

The defence lawyers took issue with the club's security video tapes. They said a tape had gone missing, but what actually happened was that the camera – which recorded on a 24-hour loop – had not been set. There was no recording. The previous night, 12 October, the club had hosted a private party for a police officer's daughter. Everyone at the club had their different little jobs of a night, and one of Jay's was to switch on the surveillance camera at 10pm. He had done that the night before, but of course when he'd gone to Nuneaton, no one else remembered to switch them on. The tape had rewound from the previous night, but not been re-set and so nothing was recorded on the night of 13 October. The assault on Dad was at 22.11pm. The defence team tried to make it sound like Jay had taken away a tape to hide something. It was ridiculous. Besides, the footage would only have shown the exterior of the club, and not the inside where Dad was most savagely attacked.

On Friday, 18 January, it was Mum's turn. I felt for her so much. She clutched a framed photograph of Dad in the witness box and broke down in tears as she took the oath. She had to give evidence for more than an hour, and managed to stay composed throughout, even when she described finding Dad in the cellar in an extremely distressed state. Mum confirmed she had been at home in Forfar Street when Jay called to tell her Dad had been hurt. She'd arrived at Bridge Street about 11.30pm and found Dad downstairs, where he'd been taken to remain cool after complaining of feeling faint. When asked what she saw by David Farrell, prosecuting, she said: 'It was tragic. He was leaning against some boxes. He looked awful. I was standing in the middle of the steps when I first saw him and I said, "Oh my god, what's happened?" He had a serious contusion to his cheek, and a gouge on his right temple about three inches long. He was hurt, and he cried. I have never seen him sob like that.' She went through it minute by minute. She helped him to an upstairs office with Liz Roberts, a member of bar staff. Minutes later he collapsed and an ambulance was called. She said she stayed to look after the venue while Justin went with Dad to Northampton General Hospital, where I joined them. She concluded by saying she had taken on the running of Eternity with Justin after Dad's death until they decided to close the club early the following February.

The first week of evidence was over; next week would be the turn of the medical experts. I had a heavy heart whether I was attending court or not, sitting through the procedures or knowing it was going on 60 miles up the motorway. Wayne Smith had a lot of conversations with me during that period. He could see I had always played rugby for a reason – I'd found something I was good at, that I wanted to be the best at, and that I could earn a living from – and he could sense that the court case and my family difficulties were shaping me in the manner I was playing the game. He encouraged me to see rugby as my escape from what was going on in the courtroom and in my family. He suggested the more you connect with a cause or a source of strong emotion, the more resilient you can become. And it was true. As things got tougher, I seemed to go up a level on the field. I put something extra into my game. The easy part of my life was playing rugby. I could go and get my mind off everything.

My mum had tried to take her life a couple of times, which were really cries for help. She'd taken an overdose. She was getting up in the middle of the night and blasting Pavarotti. My dad had rescued her from anguish in her youth and buried the past for her. The misery stirred by the fatal assault on him re-opened old wounds. She was crying out for help and it was beyond her children to be able to deal with it, though my sister Sam was fantastic and took the brunt of helping her gradually to recover.

I was up and down the motorway to Birmingham attending the trial. Northampton stuck by me. I had time off training during the week but played matches at weekends. I felt so indebted to Wayne and my team-mates, I gave as much as I could on the pitch. For 80 glorious minutes, I could escape the reality of my life and go out on a pitch among equals. I didn't have to worry about Mum, the family, Abby, bills, my house, nothing. My

Playing for Saints aged 19.

Celebrating our Heineken Cup win in 2000, Saint's first major trophy. Tim Rodber and Pat Lam hold the cup.

Playing against Ulster in 2002.

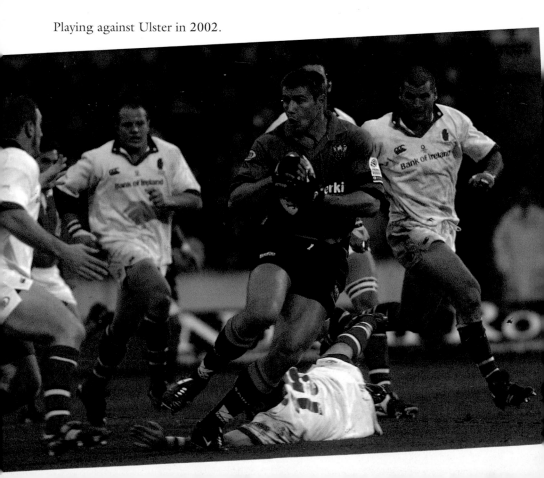

Scoring a last-minute try against
London Irish at a packed Franklin's
Gardens in 2005.

Ian McGeechan, Clive
Woodward and Wayne
Smith. Three inspiring
coaches who made all
the difference.

Looking incredibly young in my first photocall for England with Mike Tindall.

Celebrating my second try against Ireland in my England debut.

Making it over the line despite the best efforts of Australia's Chris Latham at Twickenham in 2005.

With Saints teamates Wally, Daws and Paul Grayson celebrating our Six Nations Grand Slam in 2003.

Sydney, 22 November 2003. The looks on our faces as we watch that kick sail between the posts says it all.

Jason Robinson and I holding the cup as we do our lap of honour.

With Laurence Dallaglio on the plane home.

Our reception in London. That such a huge crowd turned out to see us was both amazing and humbling.

With my beautiful girls Harriette and Isabelle.

It's great having Sir Elton John's support to promote StandUp, my anti-bullying foundation.

worry was catching the ball, making my tackles and winning the game. It took me away from everything, and acted like a tonic to keep me level and straight off the pitch. Every aspect of the trial was tough: the lead-up in the press, hearing the excruciating details of the attack and Dad's medical condition, scrutinising the faces of the jury and hoping they were going to concentrate and give a just verdict. They had been selected to assess fairly what happened to my Dad, a man who meant everything to his family, and we needed their full attention. I worried one or two of them might be drifting off, or looking at their watches, hoping to get out of there sharp-ish. And this is my dad, our world. The defendants' character witnesses included their own relatives, who of course said nice things about them.

In the second week, medical experts were called for the prosecution. Dr David Hope, a consultant neurosurgeon at The Queen's Medical Centre, Nottingham, said Dad's condition had rapidly deteriorated after he was taken to Northampton General Hospital before being transferred. When he arrived, 'he was extremely ill, and fighting for his life in virtue of what had happened to his brain'. The jury heard that CT scans had been taken at both hospitals, and the later ones show serious swelling, putting pressure on the brain. Dr Hope said the condition could not be attributed to natural causes, and had been caused by the head injuries Dad had suffered. Dr Andrew Jeffrey, a consultant physician at Northampton General, confirmed that Dad had begun to make a little progress after he was transferred back from Nottingham and had attempted to communicate, although he still did not have any movement down the right side of his body. He described how, on 14 November, Dad had suddenly collapsed after suffering a cardiac arrest.

Mum had already told the court that Dad did not drink but smoked between 10 and 15 cigarettes a day. He was fit for his age and regularly trained at the Old Scouts rugby club where he coached. The cause of death was given as a pulmonary embolism, or a blood clot travelling to the lungs. Dr Jeffrey's statement concluded: 'Had Mr Cohen not been unable to move, it would have been highly unlikely that the clot would have formed.'

It was unrelentingly awful. And seeing those guys who had shown no remorse. How did they get to the point where they beat people viciously? I wondered about their upbringing. In another case, Evans had pleaded guilty of beating up another club's bouncer, who subsequently needed part of his leg amputating. One of them had scars down his face, another the pronounced eyebrows and flat nose of someone who's been in a lot of fights. Kerr and Evans had criminal records as long as a book. What I couldn't understand was that these guys had kids and partners, and they worked for a wage during the week. Their dependants were sitting there, too, hoping they wouldn't go to prison. And yet their idea of weekend fun seemed to be to go out and beat someone up. I still struggle with that. I came from a loving family. I kissed Mum and Dad after every rugby game even as a senior. When these guys put their kids to bed at night, did they kiss them?

Hearing the defendants provoked a lot of anger inside me. By Wednesday of the second week of the trial, the court heard that Colin Kerr had three convictions, including one for assault at a pub. On Friday, his brother, labourer Gavin Kerr, was accused of lying in court after his prolific criminal past was revealed to the jury. It emerged that Kerr's long history of offending dated back to when he was convicted of dishonesty at the age of 14, since when he'd had convictions almost every year for two decades. His criminal record included assault, burglary, criminal damage, theft, taking a vehicle without consent, threatening behaviour, resisting arrest and assaulting a police officer. He had served several prison terms, the longest for three years in May 1995 for burglary and assault. In 1987 he was convicted of burglary and assault with intent to resist arrest, and given two years' youth custody. He had appeared in court every year, sometimes on more than one occasion, up until 1995. The only 12-month period where he was not involved in criminal proceedings was 1988. Prosecutor David Farrell said: 'You are a thoroughly dishonest person and it was you who was doing the fighting, not a 58-year-old man.' Kerr replied, 'I did not assault Pete Cohen in any shape or form.'

It was extremely uncomfortable hearing the exchange as Farrell claimed Gavin Kerr's word could not be trusted and Kerr argued that he'd tried to make a new start after being released from prison in 1996. His lawyer, Stephen Coward, said his client had 'only two' convictions since 1996. Only two in four years!

Kerr told the jury the charges he was facing were the first he had ever pleaded not guilty to. The third defendant, Robert Evans, opted not to take the witness stand. Judge Michael Morris told jurors to make up their own minds about why he had not given evidence. The prosecution summed up, and the following week began with the defendants' barristers outlining their version, which was always going to be the most difficult to sit through. The only new thing we learnt was that the fourth man was Evans's cousin, Steve Martin, and the evening began for them as a group of eight who had between £400 and £500 on them after being given the cash by Lionverge, the railway maintenance company where they worked. They maintained that despite the sum of money at their disposal, and the fact they had visited several pubs before heading to Eternity, they were not drunk.

Each of the charged men had his own barrister, and each of them said the prosecution case was littered with holes. Tim Spencer, representing Colin Kerr, branded it a 'complete shambles'. The three barristers argued that there were seven prosecution witnesses from the nightclub, but none of them agreed with one another about how the fight started. They made ridiculous allegations of a cover-up, referring to the surveillance tapes and the failure to record any footage inside the club. Stephen Coward, defending Gavin Kerr, said, 'If the defendants are right, Mr Cohen went berserk (and attacked them). If they are right, there would be clear evidence on the video of what he was doing.' This was preposterous and contrary to all the evidence.

Medical evidence presented by the prosecution was also called into question. Where David Farrell said Dad died from a blood clot caused by immobility, which had in turn been brought about by brain damage he had suffered from head injuries, all three defence barristers pointed to their medical evidence, which claimed his injuries were not serious enough to bring about the stroke that caused the brain damage. They claimed other possible causes of the stroke included the use of illegal drugs, after the jury had heard that traces were found in a fibre of Dad's chest hair. We sat there thinking, are you kidding? A 58-year-old man? A man who was always militantly anti-drugs in his clubs? The only credible explanation was that a tiny amount of something must have entered his bloodstream when he'd counted the money. Every night he'd lick his fingers to get through the wads of notes; and it must have been off them. The defence summing-up concluded: 'The hallmark of truth is consistency, which the defence have in abundance. But the prosecution is in disarray.'

The jury retired to consider the verdict and we were convinced we would see justice for Dad. But then we had noticed that a lot of the evidence seemed to pass over the jury without appearing to register. It was difficult to stomach. Inside, I was incandescent with rage, boiling over with the frustration, but I was lucky. In rugby, I had my outlet.

Following ten hours and 20 minutes of deliberation the jury of seven men and five women at Birmingham Crown Court found the three men not guilty of manslaughter. Instead they were found unanimously guilty of 'violent disorder with others unknown'. George was present; Mum and Jay sat outside as the verdict was returned because the emotion became too much to bear. Family and friends burst into tears. It seemed so unjust. The sentences they were handed were so light it made me inwardly boil with rage. We saw it as a huge miscarriage of justice, and George was so angry that he made an appointment with his local MP and even called the police to have his say.

Privately, I fantasised about revenge. You'd have to be a saint not to think of it, wouldn't you? Someone very important to us had been taken away through these men's depravity. Of course I imagined how I could get revenge. We didn't get justice in the court system. But what would we do? Get a gun and shoot them? Run them over? I would get a tougher sentence than they got, and anyway two wrongs don't make a right. With the benefit of hindsight, now I'm a parent, I know that Dad wouldn't want me and Jay to do anything like that. He would say, 'Get on with the rest of your life. Don't dwell on it. Look after your mother. Always look forwards, not backwards.' I know I've done the right thing, but it is very hard not to harbour bitterness and hate. Do you get over it? Never. There is not a day when I don't think of Dad. You just learn to live with it. You get on with life. There's no other option, nothing else to say.

Mum and George wanted to press for a civil prosecution, but the rest of us could not bear any more turmoil. We'd had enough. Jay said to George, 'Let's finish it. It has dragged on too

long. We can't get Dad back. We have to get on with our lives.'
And so we dropped all further legal proceedings. The whole
painful saga made all of Dad's kids reassess our lives. Sam said
that after everything she'd gone through, she'd thought hard
about what to do with her life and thought she might go back to
college to study midwifery. Jay, having been unemployed after
he shut the club, wanted to rebuild his life and make a career in
the police. He'd initially opened a shop dedicated to his love of
motocross, but he'd had to close within three months because
the foot and mouth restrictions prevented free movement in the
countryside. That was bad luck, but now he was motivated to do
something to help other people who might have to live through
what we'd been through. Some people thought it was a knee-
jerk reaction, but I really admired him. He believed he could
do some good, keeping peace on the streets and working in the
family liaison field.

For Mum, it was much more difficult. She'd lost her husband,
her life partner and her saviour. It would take her a long, long
time to accept that loss, but we all rallied around her as best
we could and tried to help her see she had kids and wonderful
grand-kids to live for.

CHAPTER 13

THINKING CORRECTLY UNDER PRESSURE

Yet again rugby gave me an escape. That same day that the jury retired to consider their verdict I was told I'd been selected to play against Scotland in the Six Nations campaign. After the confidence-sapping Lions tour I had been passed over for England's autumn matches in spite of my record of 11 tries in 13 Tests. I'd returned for the November game against Romania. Rugby, more than ever, was my extended family and I felt an embrace of sympathy even from the press. I was one of five changes made to the side Clive had fielded which beat South Africa in November and this was reported with lovely little comments like, 'and none is more deserving'. It would be my 14th cap. Momentarily my mind turned to my phone ... but, no, I had no one to share my news with, no one to give me a gruff, proud 'All right, son'. That left me feeling empty – and even more determined to add to my 11-try haul for England and make Dad proud.

I had worked hard to improve all aspects of my game, and it was strange that in enduring the pain of what happened to Dad I had become a much better player. I had always played with passion; now I played with added purpose. I was running in tries for my club, helping Northampton storm up the Premiership table. Guided by pep talks from Wayne Smith, I took a consciously professional attitude to my rugby. He made us all respect the jersey and play to a higher standard. He'd got the whole Northampton back-line on the move again and scoring tries. He'd given us direction. At the same time I'd matured and acquired a better perspective on all fronts. When I was at the club, I focused on rugby. When I showered and went home, I switched off. What happened to Dad changed my approach to life. Two years beforehand, when I made my debut for England, I could not see life beyond rugby. I ate, slept and drank the sport. Now I had to support my family. I'd learnt that rugby is the best job in the world and something I love, but I'd also learnt to chill out. I'd matured as a person and this made me operate better on the pitch.

With a line drawn under the court case, my rugby life could resume its normal full rhythm. Right off the back of the devastating verdict, the game against Scotland proved a good, honest focus. It was a huge game, as we looked to exorcise the ghost of that Grand Slam loss at Murrayfield, and because Wally was making his debut, which was cue for a lot of stick from me. 'How the hell did you blag this, eh?' He'd had a tougher route than me in gaining recognition because he'd had to change position, from back row to hooker, and dog his way through. It came harder for him, and it was great to have him around. We might bicker and snipe away, but we were as thick as thieves. Dad had been a father figure to Wally on many occasions, like the time he had idiotically filled his nasty beige VW Polo Estate up to the brim with oil. It was spewing out all over the engine, making a terrible smell, and he took it to Dad to sort out. Dad had to get under the car and remove the excess oil via the sump cap.

The Murrayfield scoreline of 29–3 reflected a memorable job well done all round. Jason Robinson was electric, scoring two tries, one of which I helped set up, and I was pleased to respond to a horrendous week with a try of my own. Another for Dad. I couldn't think of anything else when I crossed the line now. The triumph in scoring would always be bittersweet. Two weeks later, it was yet again a case of erasing negative memories, this time against Ireland who had snatched the Grand Slam from England in the final postponed game in the autumn, a game I'd missed out on. Again, we produced a great win, notable for a try in the 25th minute for which the ball must have gone through every player's hands and went the length of the pitch. The move started in our 22, I just tracked the ball, worked hard and ended up going over. It was amazing, and my tally was now up to 13 tries in 15 Tests. We were described as 'the form team in world rugby', but that accolade didn't stick permanently. Up against the French, we lost, a painful 20–15 defeat at the Stade de France, and yet again the elusive Grand Slam had evaded us.

Three weeks later, against Wales, the championship campaign was back on track with a stirring 50–10 victory. Wayne Smith had urged me to focus wider than on scoring. His attitude was, if you chase tries, they won't come. If you play your heart out, and play well, the tries will come. In working on my all-round game, I was taking just as much pride in not missing any tackles as I was in scoring tries. In the Wales game, I put in a hefty tackle on Scott Quinnell, which was picked up as significant by Terry Morris in the *Chronicle*. 'It was the tackle that defined the growing gulf between England and Wales,' he wrote. 'With the Welsh well beaten, No. 8 Scott Quinnell gathered the ball in broken play only to be stopped dead in his tracks by Saints wing Ben Cohen, who then drove the Llanelli forward backwards. There was a collective gasp from the Twickenham crowd – wingers aren't meant to do that. But England are bigger, meaner and fitter than ever.'

6 April 2002 would have been Dad's 60th birthday. We would have had a hell of a party for him, that's for sure. I was trying to face up to the fact that there would be no more birthdays or anniversaries. There were so many things I'd have liked to talk to him about, or shown curiosity in. For instance, I worked out

he had lost his own father when he was 20, pretty much the same age as me, and he'd never talked about that, never let on how that had affected him. It was the first of quite a few parallels I found in his story and mine that somehow kept him bound up in everything I did. Another resonant family story was the fact that although my grandfather knew George was playing at England Under 23 level, he died four years before he could see him run out at Wembley in the 1966 World Cup final. I made the dreaded visit to the cemetery – I hardly ever went because I hated the finality it represented – to put flowers on Dad's grave before I left for Italy. The best present I could give him, though, was to figure in Clive Woodward's plans for next year's World Cup. It was the big dream we'd dared to talk about together, and to fulfil it I had to keep giving my utmost on the pitch.

In Rome, we had a rousing 45–9 victory and in the 24th minute I drove through fly-half Diego Dominguez's tackle and scored another. It was my 15th for England, and I phoned Mum back home and told her, 'That was for Dad.' I'd had a solid enough Six Nations campaign, scoring four times in five appearances, always responding defensively, but at the back of my mind I feared I was there partly on reputation. I wasn't consistent, and even for the Saints I wasn't always an automatic pick towards the end of the season. The coaches knew I had it in me, they also knew I'd been through the mill; and they thought I needed time. But the 2003 World Cup was looming closer and something had to change.

The biggest turning point in my rugby career came from a conversation I had with Wayne Smith. A kind, gentle man in demeanour, he doesn't strike you immediately as a dominant rugby authority, but his knowledge of the game and canny psychology quickly comes to light. He knows what makes players tick and teams perform and club structures work. He is the ultimate conscientious professional. So much so, he aged in that role at the Saints. It really took it out of him. He'd helped a lot already with his slightly New Age-ish emphasis on learning about yourself to better learn how to express yourself on the pitch. This time he sat me down and helped me start from a clean slate. He made me re-define my goals. We talked about how I would approach my game, how I could work at my attitude and my dedication, and I left that room with two clear goals: I wanted to be the best winger in the world, and I wanted to win the World Cup. Wayne put my current state in context. He said he had a huge regard for what I'd been going through. He was the only person, really, to see from the inside the pressures of how, at the age of 22, I'd had to help lead the family through an ongoing traumatic situation while trying to rationalise how I could put all my effort into top-level rugby. He said the club needed me badly and I realised the need was mutual.

Wayne likes coaching people's strengths. His view is that if you are very good at something, you can get even better at it, and if you dedicate yourself to that process, you can be a champion. It chimed exactly with Dad's little mantra – Take something you're good at, and be the best at it. I had a renewed sense of purpose. Wayne told me I already had the tools and encouraged me to work harder on my strengths. Be even quicker, get even stronger, become even better in the air. That was pretty much the attitude. He made it sound like a question of re-directing my focus, and I knew I had the drive and resolve to carry it through. He showed me that my resilience and toughness came from an emotional connection with my family difficulties, and that love of my family could give huge personal meaning to what I went on to do. He gave me confidence, assuring me it said something about me as a character that I'd gone through this awful time without dropping my standards; that inner strength, he said, could help me become a better player.

Wayne was great for me, and for Northampton as a whole. Instead of looking at roles and results, he liked to focus on the process behind a team culture. Like Ian McGeechan, he dissected the game, going back to basics in a way that was quite novel at the time. The pitch would be split into three areas – A, B and C. Previously, you might have a repertoire of set-piece moves and then you'd carry on and play the game – you know, the backs would be backs and the forwards would be forwards. Wayne started to say, right, if the scrum is on the left-hand side it is in A, let's have different patterns of play. Daws would turn around to his fly-half and say B, C, A, so everyone knew we were going to attack in B, then C, then A, and we'd know people would be in certain areas. It was chaos to begin with! And perhaps a mentality that aligned itself more with international play, but the result was we were able to show off our skills a bit more and create more space for try-scoring – which was good news for me. I remember Wayne teaching me how to do a scissor – when one player gets the ball and runs across and another player comes the other way on lines similar to an open pair of scissors. It relies on split-second timing to outwit the defender. Wayne coached me in this fine little detail: standing close to the fly-half, timing the switch, and soon we were ripping people apart in tiny spaces. He is very straight and direct, which I like. He would tell you straight if you were under-performing, but he would praise you straight and make you feel very good when things were going well.

Wayne was building towards a long-term campaign based on attitude and spirit, and the irony was that we were to get a masterclass in his philosophy in a hard-to-stomach defeat in the Powergen Cup final. On Saturday, 20 April, we lined up as favourites against London Irish, a team that had been written off as relegation fodder at the season's start, who had few internationals and specialised in a physical game. At the end of December we'd played them in a typically robust encounter which ended with their player-coach, Brendan Venter, accusing several of us of foul play. We were cleared of any offences, but there was a bit of needle there. The final – a rare chance for Northampton to collect some silverware – was bitterly disappointing. They overwhelmed us from the start and we never regained our composure. Nothing gelled for us. We were crushed by all the qualities Wayne had been trying to drill into us: energy, enthusiasm and a real desire for work. His post-match verdict was that we could use London Irish as a role model. It was gutting.

In sport, you are always taught to look for the positives to take from a defeat, and there was one stand-out cameo moment from which Saints and England would gain in the future. The only points we earned in the 38–7 drubbing came from a combination of Paul Grayson and myself. We'd been practising a move we had come to call the DA – after Dave Alred, the England kicking coach – and we executed it perfectly that day at Twickenham. I leapt high to catch a beautifully flighted cross-field penalty kick from Grays, and ran on to score. It was a devastating piece of play because no one knew how to defend against it. It was like an NFL American football move, but instead of passing, Grays kicked it. It became so potent that Wayne Smith later took it back to the All Blacks when he left Northampton in 2004.

Saints fans endured the usual end-of-season thriller, with us needing to win the last few games to ensure Heineken Cup qualification. We got there and, bizarrely, given the emotional backdrop to my season, I could say hand on heart I was playing some of the best rugby of my career.

I wanted to move up a gear in preparation for the big Autumn Internationals, but I'd played so much rugby, I was completely broken. My groin was so inflamed on both sides I had to have cortisone injections. The procedure meant I had to pull out of the summer tour, but it had to be done. My adductors were just about hanging on to a load of cracked bone. The doctor inserted a hollow tube right through the pubic bone and injected cortisone. It was excruciating. When the injection went in, I could feel the pressure all the way down my leg. I eventually had three of those during my career, sometimes under anaesthetic, sometimes without. I knew it was going to hurt, but the effect was always brilliant. Once it's done, it makes you feel like you're 18 again, though that sensation only lasts three to four months.

In the summer, Abby and I got married. We'd put if off because of all the dreadful events which had happened – Dad's death, the trial, the burglary and, on top of that, the death of Abby's grandfather. On 13 July we tied the knot at the village church in Spratton and went on honeymoon to Jamaica. There had to be the beginning of a new chapter, and it was a lovely occasion with my Saints and England team-mates among the guests and the Clem Curtis song 'Build Me Up Buttercup' playing all afternoon. We wanted a wedding where we could walk from home to the church and back to the reception, and we wanted everyone to wear what they liked to keep it fun and informal. Some people took that to extremes, with one guest turning up in sumo wrestling kit.

The only problem was that I went into the autumn with virtually no preparation at all. My pre-season consisted of the warm-up friendlies, and when I was selected to join England's Autumn Internationals training squad, I was still 20–30 per cent off full fitness. I was still looking for more speed when on 9 November we took on the ultimate challenge: the All Blacks. Arriving at Twickenham we knew that, as always, playing New Zealand would be a special occasion. To go out and compete and win, though, would be something that would give us immense self-belief to carry forward. All the statistics in the build-up focused on how England had only beaten the All Blacks four times in 97 years.

I was among the backs Clive chose for the start along with Jason Robinson, Will Greenwood, Mike Tindall and a Gloucester wing called James Simpson-Daniel who was making his England debut. Jason was very driven and professional. Having switched codes, he wanted to make his mark. Away from games, he wasn't someone you'd ever have a cup of coffee with because he always had his family in tow. Will was the brains in the back line. Very vocal, he called the shots and had a cerebral approach to each game. Like me, Tinds was a young lad in the team, and we both tended to shut up and get on with it. James was a revelation. He was playing great rugby and set me up for some good tries, and it was a shame that after the following Test against Australia he was diagnosed with glandular fever, missed the South Africa game, and then developed a back problem which kept him out of contention for the World Cup.

Going in against the All Blacks, Clive emphasised his T-CUP mantra: Thinking Correctly Under Pressure. Clive was great at teaching us how to soak up pressure with his go-to plans, what-if scenarios and coping mantras like T-CUP. They marked a fine-tuning process of a fairly settled team. We knew that when we went behind by 10 points in a game, we could nearly always trace that back to a bad five or ten minutes caused by a mistake or a not so clever bit of play. That can prey on your mind, so we were becoming drilled in mechanisms which encouraged us to think calmly, 'okay, let's start again', so that we could take back the momentum.

I have to say that you only learn to think correctly under pressure when you've experienced a great deal of pressure, and England certainly had – with the miserable 1999 World Cup campaign and the last-gasp failures to land the Six Nations Grand Slam in three successive years and so on. With Martin Johnson, Lawrence Dallaglio, Jason Leonard, Trevor Woodman, Phil Vickery, Matt Dawson, Steve Thompson, Danny Grewcock, Lewis Moody and Richard Hill on the pitch that day in front of the backs, we had a mixture of youth and age, although they still called us Dad's Army. We had a good balance in that side. As players, we knew and respected the hierarchy within the squad – which had nothing to do with rank, but with experience, commitment, bonding and emotional intelligence about the game. A lot of the older players had been smashed by international opposition in Clive's regime. When you start winning, and winning with style, the internal dynamic changes. No one bitches or moans. No one wants to hear negative chirps. Everyone wants to be a part of a successful side. All those world-class players wanted to stay in a team that was performing. With chemistry growing between the developing young talents and the people who had long established themselves, we were starting to create something special. This squad did not allow for energy-sappers. It didn't matter how good you are, if you didn't buy into the mindset, you wouldn't be included. Success was breeding success, but none of us had an inkling that it would prove to be the golden era of English rugby.

Inspired by Jonny Wilkinson, we led all the way through the game, but then let them back in, so that in the closing moments they weren't far away from achieving an incredible claw-back victory.

Lewis Moody scored the first of our three tries, followed by a solo effort from Jonny. I scored early in the second half from quite a long range. I didn't think I'd make it. Doug Howlett was a lot quicker than me. As I neared the line, I was thinking 'I have to get airborne, I have to get the ball over the line. Any second now, there'll a cover tackle coming across...' So I flew across the line with a big swallow dive. I know, I know, technically it wasn't the safest way to ground the ball, but all the emotions came flooding through at once and I lost it for a bit. It was incredible to be able to score against the All Blacks like that. It was the defining moment in that game. It showed the character and inner belief we had as a team.

A further 16 points came from Jonny's boot so we were 31-14 up, but they came back on the hour, first with a storming try from Jonah Lomu, which was followed, ten minutes later, by a try from Danny Lee. New Zealand had seized the momentum; the clock was ticking down. I'll never forget seeing Howlett launch a last-minute counter-attack. He was an incredible player, a nightmare to play against. He'd pop up and have the ability to beat you in half a metre of space. He drew Jason Robinson, and sent Ben Blair sprinting with nobody between him and the line. I had to scramble from the opposite wing, holding off in case Blair tried to step back inside. I had to show him the outside, and he took it, and I smashed him into touch a few feet from the corner. It was a long way for me to go, but that's the way we worked, covering for each other. Then Ben Kay stole the ball from their line-out and the whistle blew. We'd actually done it, we'd beaten the All Blacks!

The primary emotion was relief. Imagine if we'd surrendered a 17-point lead. Imagine if I'd missed that tackle on Blair. Last-ditch tackles were part of my job description in the back-three unit. It was a job-saving tackle. I said at the time that if I'd missed it I would have gone and packed my bags, got into my car and never played for England again.

In the changing-room afterwards, Martin Johnson – usually a man of few words – emphasised how crucial a win it was, the first against the All Blacks since 1993, but there weren't scenes of raucous jubilation. It wasn't the statistic that was important – satisfying though it was. Johnno wanted to mark the milestone. The victory was another step forward. We'd put our marker down, but it wasn't a perfect display. We'd played 30 good minutes and he said we'd have to work hard on the other 50 minutes. After all, we had let them score four good tries. We'd lost far too much ball at the breakdown; we needed to play more go-forward rugby.

Two years ago we'd have been happy just to win. The measure of this team was that we had become more self-critical. If we missed a tackle, made a mistake, we were tough on ourselves. We went away and we worked and we practised and we tried to expand our game. But that result made it three consecutive wins now over southern hemisphere sides – and that set us on our way.

Next up, world champions Australia, in a match which again was relentless pressure from beginning to end. I had a stormer, scoring a brace of tries, and raising my scoring tally to 18 tries from 19 appearances, but the game was anything but straightforward. We played a great initial 25 minutes and final 20 minutes, but in between managed to concede 22 points including two soft tries.

I'd scored the first try after nine minutes, finishing off a move which began with Richard Hill winning a line-out and the ball passing through ten players before I finished. It's always satisfying to score when so many players have contributed to the build-up, but then Australia came back in ten minutes of madness either side of the interval with a try from Wendell Sailor and two from Elton Flatley. Going into the final quarter, we had to fight back from a 12-point deficit before producing a thrilling winning scoreline of 32–31 for the crowd. It was back to T-CUP

big time. The message was Don't Panic, and we didn't. When
they scored their second runaway try to go 31–19 up, Johnno
stood us around in a circle and told us we had to show character
and we had to dig deep. It was a big message. That is what great
teams are made of. We could have gone down by 30 or 40 points
then. But we wanted it and we went out and got it. The good
thing about Johnno was that he never spoke any bullshit. He
was a man of few words and he said it like it was. So when he
did speak, we listened and got on with it. It was him, Daws,
Dallaglio, Leonard, Back, Greenwood, Jonny, all seasoned internationals, saying this is what we have to do: whenever we get into
their half, we have to come away with points. They would give
a penalty away from 40 yards out and Jonny would kick it. We
gradually built the score, and then I popped up to score a try. A
ruck had formed, James Simpson-Daniel moved to first receiver
and I could see this gaping hole. I had to get myself in there.
James and I were trying to communicate. Me deaf, of course,
and the stadium roaring. He was telling me to come short, and
I was trying to read his lips. At the same time I was shouting,
'I'm coming short off your shoulder! I'm coming short!' I took
the bull by the horns and went for it, got past George Gregan
and then veered outwards to dive over the line and round off
our comeback.

I got up and there was a simultaneous pat on my back and
words in my ear. 'Well done, mate, but you could have got it
nearer the posts.' That was Will Greenwood. The try took us

to 30–31, and Jonny converted it with ease. That try was a very satisfying way to reclaim the lead. James and I had both acted on instinct. We loved that moment. Afterwards he said, 'When I looked up you were right there on my shoulder – and I thought, oh shit, take it, it's yours. And you were gone!' James was amazing; he'd only played two internationals, and that was the third try he'd set up. Matthew Burke missed a penalty and we held on to win the game. That was a watershed moment. England had been coming close to winning games, and now we were turning narrow losses into narrow wins. This was sending a signal to the world that England did have bottle enough to come back from behind to win these games.

I found myself the main focus of front-page pictures and big headlines: BOMBER BEN … BIG BEN STRIKES TWICE … and a hilarious headline in the *Sunday People*: COH, WHAT A BEN-SATION! WING WIZARD'S MAGIC SPELL PUTS OUT THE BLIZZARD OF OZ.

After two classic Tests in eight days, I was asked whether I could up my scoring rate to a hat-trick for the third Test against South Africa. 'Yeah, that would be nice.' In the record books, the 53–3 scoreline suggests it was a walk in the park for England – and it was the Springboks' biggest ever defeat – but it was a tough, niggly encounter. South Africa were in disarray and the opposition they produced was not pretty. This was a violent game – actually a sad game, because they were nasty off the ball, deliberately trying to injure players. Jonny was targeted with much of the physical intimidation and had to be taken off with a shoulder injury. Afterwards Clive criticised South Africa for 'unacceptable brutality' and commended his players for staying composed and the referee for handling it well.

I managed one more try, so my ratio stood at 19 from 21 matches. My scoring rate had become a bit of a media obsession. In one press conference I was asked if I knew how many Rory Underwood had scored in his first 20 internationals. Fifteen, 16? I guessed. No. Eighteen? The answer was three! I did know he was England's all-time highest try-scorer with 49 from 85 international appearances, and that I was a long way off getting close to that, but it was interesting to hear he was slow to start. I always liked to insist that I didn't go out just to score. Scoring a try at Twickenham is a big, big sensation, but my main concern was not letting anyone down. I was far more worried about missing a tackle. Do that, and you could be out of the side. I had an amazing tournament; I felt energised by playing in this England side. I loved it. I went back into club rugby for six weeks before it would be back to England for the next Six Nations campaign.

When I got back to Northampton, Wayne Smith congratulated me. He could not believe how much I had come on. Nothing had de-railed my drive to become the best winger in the world and to win the World Cup with England. I was still hurting inside, and that dedication to practice was my way of channelling my aggression and anger into developing my skill set and pushing on towards my goals. Yes, I was paying attention to detail, but mostly it was about focusing my mind. Practice occupied my mind for large chunks of time. It distracted me from my grief. My mum, sister and brother cried a lot; I didn't shed a tear, but grief was my driving force. I didn't go through a traditional mourning process. Instead I let my emotions flood out on the pitch. It helped me find a balance because I never had time to sit and let my thoughts fester. I cracked on with it. When I thought of my dad, I thought of him laughing and smiling. I had no regrets about our relationship. Every day I'd told him I loved him. I'd kiss him goodbye. We shared stuff. We had fun together, despite the financial hardships. I didn't have a single bad memory. He was loving and giving, a grafter, an underdog, and I admired his spirit. I just missed him.

CHAPTER 14

THE COUNTDOWN

The elation I experienced from those wins in an England shirt, during that special time, will never leave me; nor will the memory of what it meant to people all over the country and what privately it meant to me. The England rugby team was simply an incredible phenomenon to be part of and, in my heart, I was commemorating my dad's spirit with every try, every crunching tackle and every ounce of effort expended. I needed to find a way to keep going. I was flying and I didn't want to stop. My emotions were still swinging from grief to anger and depression and back again. I have never seen a grief counsellor, but it is said that four years is the typical length of time it takes before you accept the loss of a close family member, and that it can take seven years or more if the loss is sudden or traumatic.

Dad's way was to keep problems to himself and to look forward not backwards; and I knew he would want me to immerse myself in rugby.

That wasn't difficult, heading into World Cup year. As conscious as I was of the significance of the tournament scheduled for 10 October to 22 November 2003, I was on the treadmill of club games (Premiership and cup competitions) as well as internationals, and my focus had to switch week to week. It's a cliché, but as a team and as an individual you can't look too far ahead; you have to concentrate on doing your absolute best in your every next game. We'd just beaten the top three sides in the world, we'd come from behind twice, so let's go and try to win the Grand Slam. Next up would be a summer tour to New Zealand and Australia, an opportunity to travel with a full-strength squad and mean business. Only then would we allow ourselves to talk about the World Cup. You have to play your way into it. Quite literally, in the case of Josh Lewsey, who made his England comeback in the 2003 Six Nations and played himself into contention for World Cup selection.

I always looked on my rugby as an education, and to be a member of Clive Woodward's squad was to be a student in an all-consuming masterclass in how to be successful. The superb and innovatory preparation that was put in behind the scenes, all orchestrated by Clive Woodward, made an indelible impression. 'Winning the Rugby World Cup was not about doing one thing 100 per cent better, but about doing 100 things one per cent better,' he famously said later. The drive for perfection, based in science, innovation and analysis, and managed by a carefully chosen support team, was the key to our success. 'I want sponges, not rocks,' Clive would say. 'I want sponges thirsty for knowledge and understanding, receptive minds not know-it-alls.' As an international coach, Clive oversaw us for maybe 13 or 14 games a year, so in his view part of his role was to introduce ideas that might add something novel to our game, something the opposition hadn't planned tactically to neutralise.

I found the buzz of an England camp addictive. The emphasis was always on progress and learning new ways of playing and looking at the game and, like my dad's attitude to business, the mindset was definitely not risk-averse. That group of players led by Martin Johnson was full of big, robust characters – it was no bunch of angels, as the strike of 2000 had proved – and they'd let Clive and the coaches know if they hadn't delivered a good session. There were leaders in the scrum, leaders in the line-out, leaders in the backs. It wasn't so much about being outspoken, it was more about knowing what they wanted to achieve. Past disappointments fuelled an intense desire for success. Will Greenwood, for example, had first played for England in 1997. He'd lost his place, worked hard to get it back. Many of the players who'd had six years with Clive had unfinished business. Pushed to our limits during England training sessions, different elements made different players speak their mind. There might have been too much of the mind games and sports psycho-babble stuff for some. Personally, I thought the visual awareness was a load of bollocks. We had a specialist coach to exercise our eye muscles to enhance our visuals skills in order to make better decisions on the sporting field. But what it all did was to make us generally more aware of the importance of details. The fact that we did it all together made us more in tune as a group. We were given so many ideas; it was up to us to decide what to make our own.

Off the pitch, every little detail concerning our fitness, nutrition, hotel facilities, transport, guest ticketing and so on was in place so that we never had to worry about anything logistical. On the pitch, every one of us knew our role inside out and had the tools we needed to perform at our best. We had a game plan, but we were given confidence to make correct decisions on the pitch. Dave Alred would make sure that we backs knew our key roles and our communication codes; we'd know what the first line-out and first scrum moves in their half would be; we'd have counter-attack options. A lot of our options had become second nature. During the World Cup, for instance, Clive allocated a room to be the analysis room, manned by an IT team. We could ask for information on the opposition or our particular opponent to be downloaded on to our laptops. It was all about finding tiny elements that would help individuals to be in prime state to perform and give the team a collective edge. We had our own chef and a kit technician; we had personalised strength and conditioning programmes. Sir Steve Redgrave, whose five consecutive Olympic gold medals made him the embodiment of motivation, came in to talk to us. There was no sitting back. Clive wanted quick learners who would keep developing and be able to follow his mantra of Thinking Correctly Under Pressure.

The general consensus was that we were on the cusp of a period of significant achievement. As an individual, I had the bizarre experience of being 'scouted' as a potential recruit to the big-money world of American football. It was all down to my trademark cross-field catch, apparently, and I found my physique and attributes as a rugby wing being measured for a transition to playing in a wide receiver position, or even as a linebacker. It was amusing to pose in the bulky shoulder pads and helmet, but I was contracted to Northampton until May 2005 and anyway had plenty of pressing business to see to in an England rugby jersey.

By the end of January 2003, I'd chalked up 150 appearances (and 63 tries) for Northampton. I was keeping my eye firmly on my goals of winning the World Cup and becoming the best winger in the world – and I did all I could to eat, sleep and recover well while on the club fixture treadmill.

We'd made the quarter-finals of the two cups and a top-three finish in the league was still on. England's first game in the Six Nations was a good test against the reigning champions France at home, which we comfortably won 25–17. Looking at the game now, you can see the clear hallmarks that would win us the World Cup nine months down the line. The pack were dominant, Jonny Wilkinson kept the scoreboard ticking over with five penalty kicks and a drop goal, and Jason Robinson scored with a scorching try after leaving three French tacklers grasping air. In the final quarter, the French scored two tries, sparking the usual late nerves, but we didn't panic and held out. In the changing-room, you'd have thought we'd lost. There were no celebrations. We'd won, but not played well according to our high standards, and everyone was disappointed – we'd trained all week to go out and perform well. Still, it was the first game of the campaign and we had something to build on.

Against Wales, the panic was mine, in that I tore my thigh muscle by four centimetres and couldn't come off because there was no one to come on. We'd gone down to 14 men early on with Phil Christophers being sent to the sin bin, and we'd lost a couple of other players. I ended up playing full-back, in pain, worried about exacerbating the injury. The last thing I needed was an injury. We beat Wales, though, and I had a couple of weeks off to heal. I travelled to Lanzarote with a friend, chilled out, did light fitness work and came back to pass all my fitness tests with Pasky.

I'd missed the Italy game, but returned for the Calcutta Cup battle with Scotland at Twickenham. As usual, Scotland played with tremendous spirit but they never looked likely to dominate at a venue where they had not scored a try in four years. Jonny collected a haul of 18 points from his boot, while Jason Robinson scored twice, Josh Lewsey registered another and I got probably one of the easiest tries I've ever scored. When Bryan Redpath made a mess of an attempted clearance, I just caught it and put it down. We were not 'on song' as a team, but we were winning the matches. The 40–9 victory may not have been particularly rousing to watch but it set up a Grand Slam decider against Ireland in Dublin.

I had never played at Lansdowne Road before, but I was well aware that it was a tough place to come away from with a win. The ground had hosted Test rugby since March 1878. It looked dated, but the relatively small spectator capacity of 48,000 could still generate a hell of an atmosphere. For the fourth year running, we set out to win the Grand Slam, which was an enormous pressure and challenge. Ireland had been playing really well and we travelled to the game knowing it would be unforgivable to fall at the final hurdle again. The city provided a great atmosphere. The old stadium itself had the quirk of its own train station running through under one stand. I remember being on the pitch and hearing a station announcement, 'The next train is the so-and-so from Lansdowne Road to Malahide ...' That was a novelty.

The game started with – and was arguably won by – a diplomatic incident. We ran out first and took up our place on the T-shaped red carpet that had been set out for Mary McAleese, the President of the Republic, to greet the players. Martin Johnson led us to the side of the T shape where we were going to kick off from. Then Ireland came out and asked Johnno to move: 'This is our side, our lucky side.' But Johnno stood his ground. 'We ain't moving. Lads, we ain't moving.' Even I could hear him bark through my deafness. You normally line up in the half that you warmed up in, and that was what we did. We stood there defiant and, across the field, the Irish team were refusing to get in line on the other side of the carpet, incensed that we had been directed to their place to the left of the tunnel as you face the main stand. It was hilarious. 'None of us are going to move, and if anyone does move, I'll kill them,' was the message that came down the line from Johnno. None of us dared move. As Wally would say, 'If Martin Johnson said "Jump", we'd say "How high?"' We were more scared of him than of them, so we stayed put. Johnno could command immense respect with very few words. In game mode, he was the personification of T-CUP. He knew what he wanted from a game, and from his players, and heaven help anyone would stood in his way.

Finally, the Irish decided to line up as a continuation of our line – on their lucky side, but on the grass – so the poor president had to muddy her shoes. Afterwards, Johnno said to the press, 'President McAleese walked on to the red carpet in front of us. I never made President McAleese stand on the grass. If the Ireland boys had stayed where they were to the right, then she would have been on the red carpet for them, too.'

It seems so trivial, but we saw something similar in 2015 when Chris Robshaw refused to lead the England rugby team onto the pitch at Cardiff's Millenium Stadium before their Welsh opponents. England would have had to stand in the cold, exposed to the febrile atmosphere generated by the home fans, possibly for several minutes, and they were not going to subject themselves to such a blatant form of intimidation. The captain's decision to show uncompromising will again paid dividends, as they too won their Six Nations meeting.

We won our Slam decider in 2003 by holding ground. Rugby is a game of conquest, about occupying more and more territory until you break through and score. In standing firm in our half, we out-psyched them from the start. We went on to win emphatically with a 36-point margin. Having let people down in the past, we stood up when it counted. We'd stuttered and spluttered in the Six Nations, but we progressively got better, kept our feet on the ground and finished with our best performance. At last we had won the Grand Slam. We could rightfully now be called a big-match team. It had been a long time coming. And Dublin was a great place to celebrate.

We had acquired a reputation for being a special team, and the reason we functioned so well was that, in terms of our strengths and weaknesses, we complemented each other extremely well. There were many flaws in our individual games, but we knew each other so well that someone else always picked up. Jonny was brilliant at kicking off either foot for dropped goals and penalties, but for kicking out of hand, we had lots of options with Mike Tindall, Matt Dawson, Mike Catt and Paul Grayson who could come on. One reason we would do so well in the World Cup final was that the Australians did not know that Mike Tindall could kick, and we shifted every kick out to him because they hadn't trained to defend that move. While Jonny was peerless at keeping the scoreboard ticking over and building the score, we relied on Will Greenwood's distribution and decision making. It was all about the balance.

Tindall and Greenwood were two very different kinds of players but rock solid in defence, with Will also being a great thinker and director of the back-line. I was a great communicator, because I'm deaf so I commentated loudly, and the back three combined well. What made us a devastating team, however, was our phenomenal pack. We had youth and experience with Wally, a big, athletic, powerful scrummager, and Phil Vickery and Trevor Woodman, both of them agile, ball-handling props. The second row, Ben Kay and Martin Johnson, supremely fit, great ball handlers. Ben Kay ran that line out. The back row: Richard Hill – his unseen work was indescribable; Dallaglio – charismatic, heart-on-sleeve player; Neil Back – everywhere and a right pest to the opposition. The prevailing spirit of the squad was utterly selfless, like that of the Musketeers – 'all for one and one for all'.

We set off at the beginning of June with a full-strength England squad for the summer tour to New Zealand and Australia, to play one midweeker and two Tests. It was clear our individual performance levels here would make an impression towards selection. Beating the All Blacks and the Wallabies at Twickenham at the end of their season is one thing, but playing them on their home soil, early into their season, was another thing altogether. With all key players fit, available and determined to shine, this tour had an edge to it. We had to dig deep and we did.

It wasn't all rugby. Richard Hill's cousin is Peter Jackson, the filmmaker who directed *The Lord of the Rings*. As a result of his family connection, we were taken on a tour of the set of the final part of the trilogy and got to meet the cast and watch scenes being filmed. While we there, the lads who weren't involved on the Saturday night went out for a few drinks. They ended up in a bar called Mermaids with some of the crew from *The Lord of the Rings*. One of the players could not work out who this friendly little lad was who kept coming up to them, offering to bring more drinks and involving himself in the banter. He was getting more and more offhand with the uninvited guest until the other guys laughed and pointed out that it was Frodo, the Hobbit, or rather the actor Elijah Wood.

New Zealand expected to win at home in Wellington. It was their winter season and the weather was blustery, rainy and grey. Everything you can imagine bar snow and sleet hit the Westpac stadium, which is like a bowl – and also known as the 'Cake Tin' thanks to its low silver external walls – so when the wind hits, it just whips around. You expect hostility over there, but I picked up something else through sheer animal instinct. There was a shiftiness in the air, an extra edge, because people just knew that this England side was special. The midweek team won against New Zealand Maoris, 23–9, at the Yarrow Stadium in New Plymouth – and the Maoris don't get beaten. Our 'midweek' side was a world-class line-up. The England squad was a hotbed of players over-performing, putting their hands up for selection. The first team was flying because the rest of the squad were after their places – wanting to get themselves into a side that would be going to the World Cup with a very good chance of winning it. For Clive Woodward, that was a fantastic scenario – guys playing out of their skin, playing through injury, setting out their stalls for selection. For me, it was unsettling. My mind played games with me, running through every scenario except the one when I was picked to play in the World Cup side.

The New Zealand side featured the tricksy Carlos Spencer and the formidable Doug Howlett. Joe Rokocoko made his debut on the left wing. After the Six Nations Grand Slam, we had the self-belief to beat the All Blacks on their home soil for the first time in 30 years. Our resolution would be tested against a team like them and in the difficult conditions, but our desire to win was almost tangible. We had a poor first half, and went down to 13 men through yellow cards for Dallaglio and Back mid-way through the second half, but Jonny's long-distance kicking was immense despite the wind. Every one of our 15 points came from him, including a delicate drop goal. Josh Lewsey took all the high balls. Doug Howlett scored a soft try towards the end but we held on through sheer gritty determination to maintain our reputation as the world's number one ranked team with the scoreline reading a momentous New Zealand 13, England 15 – and the next day's headlines sending shockwaves throughout the rugby world.

I was as moody as hell at the prospect of flying to Australia next. And I was no more cheerful when we arrived.

'What's wrong with you?' asked Matt Dawson when we'd been in Melbourne a few days. 'You're really crabby.'

Bad memories of the Lions tour was the problem. 'I hate Australia, that's what,' I replied. 'I've got nothing but shit memories of this place and I want to put them right.'

We were to play against Australia in Melbourne under a closed roof in the Telstra Dome. It would be the first time I'd played indoors. The stadium felt ginormous in every way with a crowd of almost 55,000 anti-Pommie spectators. We trained at a private school's facilities and it pissed with rain, as it can do in Melbourne. Bizarrely, we didn't drop a ball in training. It was the perfect session, in fact worryingly so. Clive looked perturbed because normally training is a bit wayward and you get your focus from that and the subsequent de-brief. The Australian media followed the trading of psychological banter between Clive and his counterpart, Eddie Jones. The papers were full of jibes. Boring England. England can't win away from home. England bottle the big games. They also criticised England for having 'little inclination to play expansive rugby' and over-reliance on our pack. We didn't let it rile us, but the game came with more nerves than the New Zealand Test. As it turned out, we overpowered them up front and outplayed them in the backs. Scoring three tries to their one was the best possible riposte.

We started that game off really well. It was intense. Will Greenwood and Mike Tindall scored early, Jonny kicking his kicks. We were battering them, taking the game to them. They scored a try in reply. We knew exactly what we were doing to a nod and a wink. We knew all our go-to's and get-outs. We knew how to shove it up our jumper and keep it tight.

In the second half I remember speaking to Jonny and calling for a move called Drifter which involved Nos. 10, 12, 13 and the wingers. The blind-side would come off 10 and the open-side would come off 12, so you had various options. I turned to Jonny and said, 'Let me come short off 12, like Drifter A, B and C.' I came off my open wing, hit the line, broke the line – Jonny had timed his pass to perfection – and rampaged up the middle, stood up Latham and went round him to score under the posts. It was a brilliant try, probably one of the best I've scored, and then we kicked another penalty to win the game. It was a great way to end a remarkable season. All the players loved my try, making a fool of Latham, and we watched the video over and over again. Everyone had thought of England as a slow team, and that try forged a different image. England's performance made the whole world think we could go on and win the World Cup. We looked unbeatable. I couldn't have dreamt of a better way to erase my bad memories of Australia 2001. Our last night in Melbourne was the last time I saw Jonny pissed. He changed after that. He's such a humble, nice guy, and he was soon having to cope with national-hero status. I think he struggled with that; he wasn't ready for Jonny-mania.

Before we flew home, we travelled to Perth for a five-day stay to train and familiarise ourselves with the facilities of what would be England's World Cup base. It was another example of the management's impeccable planning strategy. We didn't want any shocks when we arrived in the autumn. We would land there to do a job. We flew home trumpeted as likely favourites to win the World Cup in four months' time. It didn't add to the pressure. Part of the management strategy was to give us time to switch off when we landed back in England – and we could do so from a comfortable position. We had to admit the statistics looked good. That was our first win over Australia on their soil in 40 years. We had beaten two of the best teams of the world on consecutive weekends, making ten wins from ten matches this year, 13 on the bounce. It may not have a significant bearing on our World Cup prospects, but England had emerged with a stronger reputation. Best of all for us players, Clive seemed to be sticking with us as a unit notable for our harmony and understanding. The only question our critics could pose was, had we peaked too soon?

You're doing something we all used to dream about as lads and still do. You're living the dream. Go out and do us proud.

I received this touching message from a former Northampton colleague whose career had ended with a broken leg. It matched my own thoughts exactly. I wanted to go and emulate what my uncle did by winning the World Cup – I wanted to change the pain I felt whenever I thought about Dad into a huge show of pride that he could share wherever he was up there. We had three weeks or so off before we met up for pre-World Cup training at Pennyhill Park. Everything was beautifully set up. A massive marquee had been erected in the grounds, fitted out with three lanes of weights. Our routine was planned to the hour. Train early. Sleep in the afternoon. Practice in unit groups. Video analysis. The focus was on strength and power and we trained our flipping nuts off and ended up in incredible shape. It was an amazing time, not surprisingly. You are free to live and breathe rugby. You have the chance to go to a World Cup and be part of something special.

I went go-karting in Northampton on our long weekend off. It was some sort of stag do or birthday event, and at one point I took a call from Clive.

'Ben, you'll be playing against France. Make sure you're there mentally. Get focused, okay?

'Yes, Clive.'

I was massively pissed off. I'd been selected to play for England against France, but not for the game against Wales in Cardiff. I feared there was significance in this. It looked like Clive was sending a stronger team to Wales than France, though the people who had been selected to play Wales thought the stronger line-up had been picked for France. 'Shit, that ain't good,' I thought. 'I'm not going to make the squad here.' I watched the team play Wales and they were *phenomenal*. I had an opportunity to shine. It was torture. Honestly, England could have sent three teams to that World Cup.

We lost the night game against France in Marseille 17–16. We were wearing our radical new shirts, the skintight non-grip ones, and all the numbers kept falling off – we walked off at the end in blank shirts, leaving random numbers scattered all over the pitch. I got knee'd in the head and was left with a cut right down the middle. The medics shaved my hair and some wise guy said it looked like I had a vagina on my head. I'd been a bit lacklustre in the game and that worried me. I didn't want a question mark next to my name as we approached final selection for the travelling squad.

The next game against France at Twickenham was the last warm-up game before the World Cup. If ever there was a game in which I wanted to put my hand up for selection to travel to Australia, this was it. And I did. Two tries set up by wonderful passes from Jonny and Will Greenwood earned me the Man of the Match award, but there was pain in the process. Of three last-ditch, try-saving tackles I had to pull off – on Aurélien Rougerie, who always flipping beat me with his inside step; on the monolithic Sébastien Chabal; and on Raphaël Ibanez a yard from the line – the last earned me a right smack in the mouth. With my teeth slammed inwards, I couldn't get my gum shield out and had to go off. I was in the middle of being treated when the team radio crackled: 'We've lost another player, we have to get Ben back on the pitch.' So with teeth yanked forward, my gumshield back in, I returned to the fray. (The teeth had to be shaved and straightened by Bill Treadwell, the England dentist, the following week.)

I never took my seat on the plane to Australia for granted. I didn't want to go out and breeze through that game. I felt I had to go out and give it full bore to give the management food for thought. And that attitude earned me an unexpected commendation from Jeremy Guscott. 'Ben Cohen was inspirational,' he said. 'He scored tries, he made last-ditch tackles. He played like a top-class wing, a top-class centre and a top-class back-row forward. He was as good as I've seen him and is clearly one of the best wings in the world, if not the best. He probably felt that he needed a top game, not to secure a place already his, but because the truly great players always bring themselves to a peak for the great matches. Cohen is in devastating form.'

Had one of my two goals become reality?

After the game, we trooped back to the training camp where they were going to announce the final selection for the tour party to go to Australia. I have to say I didn't think I would get on that plane, because the strength and depth of the squad was incredible. Even when I heard that I'd been picked, I could hardly believe it. The people that were left behind – your Austin Healeys, your Graham Rowntrees – I never in a million years thought those guys wouldn't make the plane. Clive had had some tough decisions to make. I felt desperately sorry for those not picked.

Four of us from Northampton were named in the travelling squad: Matt Dawson, Steve Thompson, Paul Grayson and myself. I was chuffed for Wally and Daws, but above all for Grays. Before Wayne Smith arrived at the club, he had been told to give up rugby and find another career. He put on a tracksuit and moved into coaching, but Wayne – sitting him down to re-set his goals, like he did with all of us – showed faith in him to prove he still had plenty to offer. He re-galvanised him, as he had me. And here was Grays, effectively Jonny Wilkinson's understudy, with a chance to win a World Cup winner's medal.

How I wished we had Dad back to come on this trip to Australia. My grief was still raw, still my driving force. When I climbed down the steps of the British Airways flight at Perth, wearing my England suit, blue shirt and tie, ready to prepare for the opening game against Georgia in nine days' time, it was not the exultant try I'd scored in Melbourne in the summer that I recalled; it was still that bloody miserable Lions tour. I'd been using those bad memories to wind myself up before matches. And now, on the biggest stage of the rugby world, I was determined to make my family proud. I asked George whether he'd come down to Sydney for the final if we reached that stage and I was selected to play.

'Imagine if we win,' I said. 'There'll be two World Cup winners in the family! What do you think of that?'

'Well, after years and years of being wined and dined and feted for my accomplishment, I'll be totally pissed off,' said George.

CHAPTER 15

22 NOVEMBER 2003

All Black legend Grant Fox nominated four key England players that apparently all other nations feared. To find he'd included my name alongside Jonny, Johnno and Wally was hugely gratifying: 'Potent, particularly in one-on-one situations, big, fast and a natural finisher, which is so important now defences are so tight. And he has a point to prove Down Under after the Lions.'

Our first pool game, against Georgia, fell on 12 October – the eve of the three-year anniversary of the assault on Dad. A scoreline of 84–6 did not reflect what must rank as probably the toughest game of rugby I ever played. Georgia was a physically abrasive side. They defended their line with their lives and battered us through sheer force, not rugby nous. We had to graft all the way to the final whistle: nothing without labour, and all that. Despite the bumps and bruises, it was a vigorous run-out and a fantastic collective effort on the scoring front. Twelve players contributed towards the points total, and I was delighted with my two tries: Grays, who'd come on as a sub, placed a perfect cross-field kick for me to catch for the first one, and for the second I used my footwork to get past my opposite number.

'Why didn't Danny Grewcock come on?' I asked casually at the end of the match, having seen all the other subs come off the bench. To my horror I learnt that, during the warm-up, I'd trodden on Danny's toe while he was holding a tackle bag. A scan revealed a hairline fracture; he would miss at least two games and he hated me for it.

Six days later, we faced our biggest threat in group C: South Africa. This meant a distinct change in the atmosphere. After the Georgia game, their players had flooded into our dressing-room asking to have their pictures taken with us. We see-sawed from that kind of rugby kinship to the ferocity that was in-built in our rivalry with the Springboks. I always went out looking for new ways to keep opponents guessing, and I was getting a lot of media coverage, with previews of the game describing me as England's 'pocket Lomu' and so on. It was flattering, but I hated the fact that so much attention was focused on me rather than on my team-mates, great players like Richard Hill, who you'd never hear a squeak from in the press, but who would go out there and do a world-class job, week in, week out.

We defeated South Africa 25–6 after a predictably heavy physical encounter, but we came nowhere near reaching the level of performance we'd shown against Australia in Melbourne and then France at home.

We played Samoa in Melbourne under cover. It was one of those days when everything stuck for Samoa. They could have passed to nobody and still somebody would have caught it. We missed a couple of kicks and there was drama at the end when our fitness coach Dave Reddin, who was in charge of the substitutes' bench, accidentally sent Dan Luger on before the injured Mike Tindall was off – so for 30 seconds we had 16 players on the pitch – which prompted a row between the fourth official, New Zealander Steve Walsh, and Dave Reddin. It was all kicking off for us. We came out with a 35–22 win but it was a scare. We'd had two games now when we hadn't performed.

I missed the Uruguay fixture and the incredible scoreline, 111–13, because I'd twinged my calf on an organised fun day out at a water park, but was back for the quarter-final against Wales in Brisbane, where it was hot and humid, and monumentally tough. We'd moved from Perth to Melbourne and flown on to the Gold Coast capital and we weren't acclimatised to the humidity. Coming off the field, we were all falling asleep. Wales were up for it and it was a close game, just the wake-up call we needed. They led 10–3 after 43 minutes. We had our backs against the wall and put it right. Mike Catt had come on for Dan Luger in the second half and we started to play a bit of rugby. Mike fed the ball out to

Jason Robinson, who tore through the Welsh midfield, beating five men and drawing a sixth, and put Will Greenwood away. It was a moment of brilliance that turned our campaign around and we got through to the semi-final against France. We had struggled so far to dispose of South Africa, Wales and Samoa; we'd let them get too much of a good start. The question was whether we could raise our game to the effectiveness we displayed in defeating New Zealand and Australia six months previously? Right now our game had plateaued.

George called before the semi-final to wish us luck. He didn't tell me then, but he was planning to fly to Australia as soon as we'd booked our place in the final.

France, we knew, could turn up in Sydney on fire. They would always either come out and give a good performance or else come out and give an absolutely awful display. Whenever we played them, we were on guard for anything. They didn't have an identifiable rhythm to their play. It was off-the-cuff stuff, especially on counter-attack. We just had to expect the unexpected. We got a reminder from Johnno in the dressing-room about the significance of the game and our plan to counter them. I also liked to take a bit of time to myself to concentrate on bits of my game, ticking off mental notes of things I'd jotted down during the week.

We woke up on the morning of the game to rain. That was promising. The French never enjoy shit weather, and conditions were appalling: high winds and torrential rain. The game was

as tense and nervous as you'd expect with a place in the World
Cup final at stake. The French went ahead with a try from Serge
Betsen against the run of play. That gave them momentum even
though they were down on men after Christophe Dominici
was sin-binned for deliberately tripping Jason Robinson. We
regained the lead just before half-time following a classic, calm
Jonny period when he slotted two penalties either side of a drop
goal. Jonny was magnificent, kicking five penalties and three
drop goals for all our 24 points. Frédéric Michalak, on the other
hand, who'd been magisterial all tournament, managed just one
kick from five attempts. Jonny added two more penalties and a
drop goal to earn us a place in the World Cup final.

The only World Cup Final I'd ever watched was the 1991 game
in which Australia, captained by Nick Farr-Jones, beat England
12–6 at Twickenham. I was 13 years old then and had just taken
up rugby. I can't pretend the match made any lasting impression
on me at all. I had no context of World Cup finals in which to
place my own experience.

As we had progressed through the tournament, it felt
increasingly like being back home. The England supporters were
incredible. We couldn't go out for being mobbed by an army of
supporters in red-and-white face paint, clothes and wigs, waving
flags and banners. Posses of fans dressed up as medieval crusaders
with chainmail, shields and swords, or redcoat soldiers, or
blazers and boaters, you name it. Our hotel was surrounded by

fans singing the traditional rugby anthems, and when we heard loud renditions of 'Swing Low, Sweet Chariot' while we were watching the New Zealand v Australia semi-final on television inside the Manly Pacific hotel in Sydney, we thought at first it must be coming from the fans cordoned off outside our hotel. But we were gobsmacked to spot a sea of white in the stadium for the all-antipodean decider and realised the sound was actually coming from the TV. Fans had obviously bought tickets for two semi-finals, hopeful we'd get through but not banking on our taking route one to the big day on 22 November in the Telstra Stadium. We could have been in the other semi-final if we'd not won our group. We couldn't go anywhere without being besieged by fans. And none of us particularly wanted to remove ourselves from the team bubble. I did go out with Abby and her family one night but it felt wrong to leave the camp. We were such a tight group.

Mum also flew out as a surprise to cheer me on. I'd got tickets for friends and family and met up with Uncle George on the eve of the final. We were tired, but it didn't matter if we were on our hands and knees. We were acutely aware we had the opportunity to go and do something special. I wasn't nervous for the final itself. The bigger the game, the less nervous I was. It was the little games I'd always been wary of, because some little shit would go out to show me up! What was so nerve-racking was the anticipation. The build-up gives you time to contemplate the 'what ifs'. I was excited and determined to win it, but simultaneously fearful of failure, picking up on the collective nerves and tension. I wanted more than anything to win it and I had all those positive emotions as well as their polar opposite.

There had been a couple of surprises in selection on the way to the final. In the semis, for example, Mike Catt played while Mike Tindall was on the bench. We were all shitting ourselves over selection. They don't read the team out to the assembled squad beforehand. It's written up on the board in the meeting room when you arrive. Was my name on the list? Thank God, it was. That was a whole new experience of anxiety – but then this was the biggest game in professional rugby. The day before, we went and had a little walk-around and throw-around, feeling clammy, stomach churning.

On the day, our pre-match rituals were just the same. Holed up in the Manly Pacific Hotel, it was essentially a matter of keeping occupied until the evening kick off. Breakfast, a walk, physio treatment, lunch, an afternoon sleep, more food, and eventually time for the rousing pre-match talks. The forwards had gone off into a group and the rest of us were sitting around, sunk in deep bucket armchairs. I was looking over the high side of my chair trying to read the headlines on a pile of newspapers fanned out on the floor beside me – 'Dad's Army', all that stuff – and when I looked up, Clive had all the backs on the far side of the room, giving each man his last rallying call. I hadn't heard everyone make a move. My bloody hearing! I bolted over to Clive and said, 'Sorry, can you go over that bit for me again?'

'Don't worry, Ben,' he said. 'Just get the ball and run!'

We were on our way to make history, but the pre-match routine was the same as ever – music playing on the bus, hydrating, weeing every five minutes, going out on the pitch to take in the surroundings. Flashing up on the giant screens were highlights from the previous World Cup finals. I hadn't seen half of it, like in 1995 when South African Airlines flew a jumbo jet over the stadium with a good luck message to the Boks painted on the undercarriage. How had I not seen any of these iconic images? It proved to me how focused I'd always been on myself and my career. George came and spoke to a few of us. 'You can play a game of rugby every week,' he said. 'But if you win this game of rugby, it will change your life forever.' I remember going out for the warm-up speaking to Josh Lewsey, Will Greenwood, Jason Robinson and Jonny Wilkinson, talking about communication and moves.

Johnno's team talk was brief. 'We've taken some shit, we've been through some shit, but there is no other band of lads I'd rather walk out into a World Cup final with than you lot ...' That was pretty much all he said, and it struck me he wasn't just talking about rugby defeats or missed Grand Slams or the hostility of the Australian press in their ridicule of our combined age of 423. Several of us had suffered family-shattering tragedies that had given us extra drive to succeed and bring everyone together. Will Greenwood and his wife had sadly lost a baby. Lawrence Dallaglio's sister had died in the *Marchioness* disaster.

We were all men on personal missions wrapped up in our rugby ambition. We may even have become better players because of the brutal things that had happened in our lives.

Before we knew it, we were singing the national anthem in front of a red-and-white sea of swaying fans – talk about surround sound – who we wanted to win it for as much as for ourselves. Then the biggest game of our lives kicked off. The momentum of the game is stored indelibly in the memory of every rugby fan. We went behind. They beat us at our own game with Lote Tuqiri scoring a try, then we dominated the first half. There had been a few close calls, with Ben Kay dropping the ball by the try-line after a great move in the 25th minute – and Jason Robinson scoring eight minutes later when actually if Jonny had passed to me I'd have been under the sticks. I had a clear line. I could have walked it. I was calling to Jonny but he passed it to Jase … Are you joking? In the second half, they came back to level. It was boiling down to a contest that would be won by the side that made fewest mistakes. We gave away penalties. Elton Flatley had the kicking game of his life. We never scored a point. Extra time. Both teams were tired. Clive was flapping like you would as a coach, calling Jonny over to talk to him, but Jonny wanted to be left alone to go and practise kicks because he'd missed quite a few that day. Johnno called us together and said, 'If someone had said to us before the tournament that we would get to the final and would be level with Australia we would have bitten their hand off.' It was time to remember T-CUP.

Our in-built confidence continued as we went into extra time with neither side seemingly being able to nail the match. The clock stood at 18:54 in the second half of extra time when Wally took the line-out, Lewis Moody received the ball at the back and Mike Catt charged at Australia's defence. Daws darted through a gap and gained 15 yards but became trapped at the bottom of a ruck. Johnno carried to allow Daws to take up position again at the back of the ruck to feed Jonny. 'Please, please don't pass it to me,' I was praying. If that ball came back to me I didn't know what I'd do with it. And then the quick pass from Daws to Jonny, poised within kicking range. I was standing behind Jonny after the ball left his weaker right foot. It wasn't one of his most powerful kicks, but it was heading the right way. It was going to do the business and get over the bar and through the sticks. And then the surreal moment that has been replayed a million times: 'He's done it. It's over. Jonny Wilkinson on target. England in the lead with only 20 seconds remaining ...'

'Get back,' everyone screamed. 'Get back.' There were still 20 seconds for Australia to answer ... until Mike Catt booted the ball out of play. We'd spent years working on how to think clearly in tense situations, how to keep the scoreboard ticking over, how to create a platform to conjure three points when we'd needed them – and we'd done it. We'd won.

No one tells you how to celebrate or prepares you for what it's going to be like. I recall a whirl of hugs and celebrations, a lot of jumping up and down, a backdrop of raucous jubilation, a red-and-white riot in the stands, an incredible time. Up in the stands opposite the tunnel we ran out from, our family and friends were a visibly ecstatic party. I looked up to where Mum was and saw an empty seat next to her. Dad's seat. Did I imagine that? My eyes filled. 'This is for you, Dad. This is 100 per cent for you. I would not be standing here on this pitch without you as my driving force.'

We had our medals practically thrown round our necks by the disappointed Australian Prime Minister John Howard, and enjoyed a lap of honour, breathing in the sights and sounds of our faithful fans. In the changing-room, Prince Harry joined the party. A gracious John Howard came along (it turned out the TV scheduling meant he'd had to rush through the medal ceremony) and Tessa Jowell, the Minister of Culture, Media and Sport. Everyone was having a celebratory drink, taking pictures. An oversized pallet of beer cases had been delivered to the dressing-room – enough to last a team a week, and it had all been necked within an hour.

Up in the stands, George, who had been sitting with my cousin Antony, was quite spooked by the dynamic of the match. The scoring mirrored the pattern of the 1966 football World Cup final, with England's no. 10, Geoff Hurst, scoring the winning goal. In Sydney, Antony leant across to George towards the end of extra time and said, 'We've been here before...' And we had, courtesy of a winning drop goal from our no. 10, Jonny Wilkinson.

It was extraordinary to think that there had been two great moments in English sport in 37 years and the Cohen family had been involved in both. That experience is something that I hold very close to my heart. If ever there was a game I wanted to dedicate to Dad, it was this one. Every match I played, I'd wish Dad was there. I always played for him. It was my way of feeling he was still with me. I liked to pause and integrate him in all my big moments in life. It was nice to have Mum there too, of course, but again there was an empty seat close to her … I imagined Dad was bursting with pride watching from wherever he was.

The *Sydney Morning Herald* published a public notice which summed up the impact of the win.

To England and its sports fans. Regarding your magnificent football team's 20–17 triumph in the Rugby World Cup final on November 22, on behalf of all Australians, we would like to admit the following:

You were not too old (although we hoped you would be when the game went to extra time).

You were not too slow.

You scored as many tries as we did.

You kicked no more penalty goals than we did.

You ran the ball as much as we did.

You entertained as much as we did.

You did it with one of your own as coach (even though he did spend some formative years playing at Manly).

You are better singers than we are (and just quietly, Swing Low, Sweet Chariot is growing on us, as is Jonny without an 'h').

You played with class, toughness and grace.

You were bloody superior ... and

You are, for the first time in 37 years, winners of a football World Cup.

The spirit was great, full of humour. Being on the other side of the world, and ten hours ahead of GMT, we had no concept of what our achievement meant to people in England. The flight home via Singapore was a continuation of the after-match party. The surprisingly small Webb Ellis Cup was taken around the entire plane; everyone was on their feet. Passengers had their pictures taken with it and with the players. Martin Corry, Mike Catt and me got smashed. All the players were celebrating with drinking games; we were all trolleyed – safely and not obnoxiously, I hasten to add. When we landed at Singapore, the travelling RFU legal counsel Richard Smith QC, turned around and said, 'Ben, you've been cited in the World Cup final. It looks like you and I are going back to Sydney.' Fuck, really? I couldn't believe it. I recalled the incident. I'd been taken off the ball by Stephen Larkham, and as I went down he caught my heel in his face, getting cut in the process, and after that was on and off the pitch.

Apparently I was getting cited for deliberately kicking him in the face. I was trying to get my head around having to turn around in Singapore and fly back when news came in that Australia had dropped it. So I hit the Duty Free mall and bought myself a nice watch. I don't wear watches, but I wanted to mark the occasion with something special – as well as with a World Cup winner's medal of course.

I would have been so pissed off to have missed out on the arrival at Heathrow with the rest of the guys. What a reception! It was something like 4am and, after the long flight, we expected to follow the procedures we'd been told. We'd land at Heathrow, collect our bags and travel to Pennyhill Park. We were about to pass through Customs when the message went out, 'Guys, we've got to wait for security, because the terminal is packed to the rafters. We can't take you through; it's absolutely mental out there. If anyone can get on it, sit on it, stand on it or hang from it, they're on it.' The police approached us and said it was probably safest if they escorted us through in ones and twos. What? When those automatic doors opened to let a few of us through at a time, a crazy noise erupted. 'Swing Low, Sweet Chariot' ... 'Rule, Britannia!'... 'England, England', all at a level that was deafening even to me. There truly were several thousand people crammed into the arrivals hall to greet us, cheering, applauding, singing. Hundreds more lined viewpoints from the different levels of the multi-storey car park across the slip road.

It was very humbling. We'd set off as a large travelling party focused on going about our business as rugby players to achieve a long-set goal, and we'd come back to a rapturous, national show of appreciation. It was out of this world. We fought our way through the crowds, savouring every surreal moment in our jet-lagged states, and clambered onto the black team coach to return to Pennyhill Park. Following a bacon sandwich at a media breakfast, I prepared to go home and face reality – my mind turning to what awaited me after so long away: the mountain of post, unpaid bills, utilities cut off, all those administrative hiccups I'd have to sort out.

The euphoric reception went on and on. Thirteen days later, we re-assembled for the open-top bus parade that was scheduled to take us from Marble Arch, along Oxford Street and down Regent Street and Haymarket to Trafalgar Square. After the Australian heat, London felt bone-chillingly cold. We met up at the Intercontinental Hotel at Hyde Park Corner to board the bus named 'Sweet Chariot' and were told not to worry about coats, just to wear our England suits. We were given red roses to wear in our button holes. It was flipping freezing! But the message went round that it would be a pretty quick drive. No one was prepared for one million people, for crying out loud. We got up to Marble Arch at regular bus pace with cars hooting and cabbies pulling over to applaud us. Wow! And then the message got back that something big was happening around the corner. We turned right into Oxford Street and I will never forget that sight:

people cramming the pavements, crowding every window space, squashed on ledges, roofs, anywhere that afforded a view. It was a red-and-white sea of people from pavement level right up to the rooftops that stretched back a mile, with banners waving. 'Marry me Jonny', 'Welcome home Woody's Warriors', 'Jedi Jonny, the Empire Strikes Back', 'I bunked off school to C U'. Department stores had personalised tributes – Allders blew white balloons across the convoy's path, Debenhams had congratulatory posters in the windows, Marks & Spencer had machines billowing out red and white ticker tape, John Lewis released more balloons.

Ahead of the convoy, the police parted the fans to allow the buses to crawl forward. The side streets were jammed too. People had camped all night to guarantee a vantage point. Office workers were raising glasses of champagne to us. It was nuts; it could not be for real. The buses turned right down Regent Street, also decorated with Christmas lights, and even a Santa had abandoned his store grotto to applaud us. The imaginative lengths everyone had gone to were amazing. Offices had made DIY confetti with their shredders. Crane operators hung flags of St George from their cabins. An entire façade of one building under renovation had been covered in a giant flag. For me, seeing the crowds and celebrations in central London from the top of our bus was an incredible and perfect way to round off our World Cup experience.

The bus had been provided with copious amounts of beer and Bollinger. Everyone was waving to the crowds, videoing the scene, drinking and enjoying themselves, lost in the moment. Pictures show us grinning from ear to ear or looking at each other with a mix of utter bewilderment and joy in registering the impact we'd made on the mood of the nation. Progress was very slow, and what no one could see was that the bottom of the top of the bus became a sea of wee. If you're drinking, something needs to happen at some point ... The boys were bursting. I'll never forget Lewis Moody holding the trophy up with everyone waving at him while Jason Leonard was down on one knee weeing into this Bollinger bottle. This was happening a lot – but, because of the crowds, the driver kept having to brake, the bus would lurch and the wee would miss the bottle. In Jason Leonard's case it went right the way up Lewis Moody's leg. Lewis wasn't happy but he was holding the trophy up and his grin became a grimace for a minute. We went on to Downing Street to have tea with the Prime Minister and to Buckingham Palace to meet the Queen, and Lewis's suit trousers had distinct 'water' marks on the legs – which we found hilarious.

It was a mad, mad, magical month, accepting the congratulations, knowing it was also the end of a special era of that particular England squad. We'd gone from being players known to rugby fans to household names; Wally had a whole feature devoted to him in *Hello!* The last tribute to the 22 November victory came at BBC TV's *Sports Personality of the Year* programme. Jonny won the individual award, which was well deserved, and it was great for us as a squad to win 'Team of the Year'. I have a lovely photo from that night of Jonny, Gary Lineker, Bobby Robson, Uncle George and me – with the two Cohens holding the Webb Ellis Cup between us.

The inevitable return to reality had come as soon as I was back with Northampton. In between our reception at Heathrow and the Victory Parade, I had run out at Stradey Park in Llanelli in the Heineken Cup. A few weeks after winning the World Cup, I was on a sloping pitch in Wales on a freezing cold night, not a blade of grass in sight, taking abuse from four pissed-up Llanelli fans in Santa costumes. 'Fuck off, you wanker,' they shouted at me. Not just that, but I recall thinking, 'Shit, it's only the beginning of December and I'm knackered.' I was mentally and physically exhausted, drained by the intensity of how we had been training and playing with England, having to be on the top of our game. We'd been so alert, reading the game so much better, our intensity on another level. Now the Saints were losing in Llanelli, and I'll never forget walking off the pitch, getting slagged off by Welsh Santa Clauses, out of their tree, singing Christmas songs.

At least my first home game was special. There could be no better return than hearing welcoming voices ring round the ground. Before the match against the French side Agen, I was treated to the most amazing reception from the Saints fans, who'd supported me through every up and down on and off the pitch since I was 17, and their greeting meant so much. Having spent more time during the World Cup on defensive duties than bursting through defences, I was ready to score – and duly picked up a hat-trick against Agen. Soon, weariness crept in, and injury. My old groin injury flared up after the England last-show game against the New Zealand Barbarians in late December, a hugely enjoyable game which we won 42–17, with Jason Robinson and me on deadly form. From then on I had a fitness fight to keep going throughout the rest of the season.

After seven weeks in hotels, returning home and having to cook for yourself, wash your kit and iron your clothes again was a bit weird, but it was good to be with my family again. The year ended with a notification that all the England World Cup squad were on the New Year's Honours List. George was amazed – he'd only got his MBE in 2000, thirty-four years after they'd won the Jules Rimet Trophy. It goes down as another surreal episode, sitting at Buckingham Palace with your mates, receiving an MBE from the Queen. We went up to her in positional order, so I was with Jason Robinson, Josh Lewsey and Dan Luger. The protocol was read to us: you bow and go forward. I couldn't hear the instructions that well and ended up going forward too early, then realised I was meant to bow, and bowed at the wrong time, and thought 'Oh no! I've royally messed up!'

It was a hugely levelling experience. Other people were collecting MBEs, OBEs, CBEs, knighthoods and damehoods. There were guys who'd fought in Iraq, risking life and limb, and a postman being rewarded for 30 years' service to the community, and then you've got a bunch of guys who play a game they love for a living, getting an MBE for their achievement in sport.

The frustrating thing was that we didn't have time to take stock of the past few months and enjoy our achievement. As a northern hemisphere side, England's World Cup winning players didn't get a rest. For the southern hemisphere sides, the World Cup falls at the end of their domestic season so they get the 'summer' off, enjoy their achievement and put the experience to bed. We never celebrated except in the public forum. People don't see you go back to training, absorbing game plans for the next club game, adopting a different mindset. The England coaches went away for six or seven weeks, but the players were straight back on the treadmill. Quite rightly so in some ways, because our clubs pay our salaries and in return we are their assets, star players to help put bums on seats. The Saints put on dinners and events where fans could pay to meet us. We eventually started saying no to being wheeled out as heroes for money. As a professional sportsman, you are supersensitive to what your body is telling you. If you think what the World Cup final was like – incredible pressure given all that was at stake, one hell of a game, extra time, nail-biting down to the last remaining seconds – and we went from that straight back into the domestic rugby season. It was frustrating not having the space to take stock, enjoy the moment and rest body and mind. When we returned from the World Cup, you saw players falling short through injuries and having operations. A number had played through injuries to keep their place in a team they knew was destined for greatness. With bodies now breaking down, some people retired, while others struggled on – and then before you knew it you were into the Six Nations again and then a summer tour. The England management had meticulously planned for a World Cup victory, but no one had thought through the consequences for the well-being of the players afterwards. We were knackered.

Two years previously, I'd set my goals to be the best winger in the world and to win the World Cup. Wayne Smith helped me see that I needed an all-consuming focus to distract me from the anger and pain that traumatised me following Dad's death, and I couldn't think of any greater, more ambitious goals to set myself than those. Clive Woodward's mantra – 'Greatness is achieved by the discipline of attending to detail' – enabled me to pursue those goals with purpose. I welcomed the chance to occupy myself with extra training, more practice, endless work on my game and pushing myself to the limit. In my view, I over-achieved massively in my career thanks to the emotional octane that fuelled my insatiable desire to improve. It amazes me to this day that I achieved my ambitions to reach the pinnacle of my sport. On any level, it is a sustained emotional involvement to be part of a World Cup campaign, and particularly so for a wounded guy of 21 who joined that special group of players that were galvanised under Clive and Johnno in 2000 and loved every minute of sharing a unique camaraderie and collective effort. In taking our rugby adventure to the ultimate level, I like to think I gave the biggest tribute humanly possible for my dad. Had he not died under such circumstances, I think I'd have won 15 caps or so, coming off the bench a bit, but the desire that possessed me to do him proud was almost supernatural.

There's not a day when I don't think of Dad, and I like to think he's watching me from up there, having a quiet chuckle over his cup of tea, saying, 'All right, Benny boy. All right, son.' As Geech said, 'Look, somewhere, your father knows what you've achieved. And you're sat there with a World Cup medal around your neck.'

EPILOGUE

STAND UP

England won the World Cup in the same autumn in which I turned 25. As a professional sportsman I had come to a point where I needed to re-define my aims – but I didn't have the space or the perspective or, frankly, the energy to strategise my future again so immediately. How do you identity new ambitions when you've achieved all you've ever dreamt of at such a young age? I was too emotionally and physically spent to start afresh from square one; and I was stuck on a treadmill. I needed a rest and a break, but I also had to earn money. If I missed out on the 2004 Six Nations, I would miss out on £60,000 and my endorsements. If I didn't go on the summer tour, that would cost me £30,000 plus endorsements. To 'have a rest', I would be turning my back on a ballpark figure of £100,000 – and I might not get my England place back again. So it was a no-brainer. Onwards, on autopilot, I went. It was tough. You go back in without a proper rest, you're into the first game and into a vicious cycle of catch-up. You don't get enough recovery time to maintain top condition. You become match fit, but don't do rehab or prehab properly. You suffer from persistent under-recovery. And so it goes on. Players in the northern hemisphere are not very well protected. The structure of the sport means that you are penalised for being successful in the World Cup, and it shouldn't be like that. I think we should have a world league, so that seasons are synchronised.

Before I renewed my contract with Northampton, my agent had suggested I take six months off after the World Cup and then join a club for the following season. It seemed a maverick idea at the time but, I have to say, in retrospect, he was spot on. If I'd had from December 2003 to the summer off, I could have properly recharged. Not to have done that is one of the few regrets I have in my career. In 2012 Richie McCaw, the All Blacks captain, took a six-month sabbatical to prolong his career and I should have done that nine years earlier. I was absolutely cream-crackered, and it showed – in all of us really – in that first Six Nations and the summer tour to New Zealand and Australia when we were thumped. England had never planned beyond winning the World Cup. At the beginning of September 2004, Clive Woodward stepped down as England head coach saying, 'It was clear to me that when we came back from the World

Cup I felt totally out of control'; he went on to lead the 2005 Lions tour.

Earlier in 2004 Wayne Smith returned to New Zealand as assistant coach to the All Blacks. I was upset when he left. Wayne would always say he bled the black, gold and green of Saints colours and the joke was that he lost that gold and green pretty quickly. But that joke was me thinking selfishly; I didn't want to lose a coach who could make me better, but it was fantastic for Wayne's career to return to a role with the All Blacks. It was a double whammy. Authoritative eras ended at both my club and at country level, and the loss of those inspirational coaches felt to me like a vacuum. I'd started my rugby career on the cusp of something special with both Northampton and England, achieved remarkable rewards with them, and both teams were now sliding back down from their respective arcs of achievement.

I won 57 caps for England from 2000 to 2006, but most of the wins came up until the end of 2003. My try-to-appearance ratio is telling: six tries from 8 appearances in 2000; 11 from 13 by the end of 2001; 19 from 21 by the Autumn Internationals of 2002; and 25 tries from 35 appearances by the end of the World Cup. I was on fire in that period. After that, I only scored another six tries in a further 22 appearances.

In 2005 I was selected for the initial British and Irish Lions squad but didn't get chosen to go. I wasn't playing well and I was pretty glad to at last have a considerable chunk of time off to enjoy a proper rest and structured pre-season. The break from the treadmill worked. I came back in the autumn of 2005 and played bloody good rugby. Andy Robinson selected me for all the Six Nations in 2006 and in the Autumn Internationals against New Zealand, Argentina and South Africa (twice), I earned a Man of the Series accolade.

I never got picked again. I watched those last four games I played for England and I played exceptionally well, with a dislocated shoulder and a fractured collarbone as well. Brian Ashton took over as England head coach in late 2006 and he wasn't a fan of mine, full stop. He didn't pick me for the 2007 Six Nations, to the surprise of the media, who were the messengers conveying the news that I'd been dropped. I was disappointed to be overlooked when I thought I was playing well, but ultimately I intended to work harder and play for my spot. It felt like a stab in the belly, though, to hear the news from the press. I understand no one likes to deliver bad news and when you get treated like that you certainly get sympathy from your fellow players. The season ended with Saints relegated from the Premiership and Wally announcing his retirement from rugby, at the age of 28, due to a neck injury he incurred playing in a Heineken Cup pool game against Biarritz at Franklin's Gardens in January. A prolapsed cervical disc meant that he could be left paralysed if he continued to play.

Abby had started IVF treatment in January 2007. Then we learnt that Abby was pregnant with twins, due at the end of the summer, so I withdrew from the summer tour to South Africa and made myself unavailable for selection for the World Cup that year because I wanted to support Abby and be there for the birth of my kids. Having been through the ordeal of IVF, there was no way I could miss out on their arrival. I knew, when I made that conscious decision to pull out for the birth of my girls, that I'd never play for England again. I found it hard to watch that World Cup. When England reached the final, it felt as if I'd made a mistake, but it wasn't a mistake. Nothing could replace being home for the birth of Isabelle and Harriette.

I was granted a testimonial in the 2007/08 season. With impeccable timing, this coincided with the onset of the Global Financial Crisis, and while my testimonial events were great fun, I ended up out of pocket. On the pitch, I was unhappy with the direction the Saints had been taking for a while, settling for middle of the table. What's the point of building a flipping great stadium when the team is half cocked? Great changes had been promised. I came back for pre-season. A 'behind-the-scenes' restructuring led to the appointment of Peter Sloane (formerly the forwards coach) as Head Coach with Paul Grayson as the skills and backs coach. Then in came England Saxons coach Jim Mallinder as the new Head Coach and Director of Rugby with Dorian West as his assistant and Peter left a few days later. Jim announced a new captain – Bruce Reihana, a New Zealander, a nice guy but not one I thought would offer a challenging voice from the players. It felt like the same shit. Nothing had changed. None of the promises about big changes had been fulfilled. I was playing at centre, out of position, to cover for the team. I went to see Keith Barwell and said, 'That's it. I'm off.' It was never about the captaincy, as the press made it out to be. I've never seen myself as a leader figure in that way. I was a team player, a listener, a thinker, a chipper-in. When you play on the wing, you're not going to be a dominant personality. I didn't throw my toys out of the pram. I'd simply had enough.

I do have regrets about the way I left Northampton. I shouldn't have walked out, but I'd just reached a limit. I couldn't settle for mediocre. I felt I had to rescue the club from resigning itself to second best. I wanted to reclaim the heady days of the Heineken Cup season. I was one of the few people left from the start of the professional era at Franklin's Gardens, and I tried to do my bit to push the club's ambitions up a notch again and go out and win stuff. I needed a challenge. It's inherent in my personality. But nothing was changing at Northampton. There was no clarity in their aims. I needed a fresh start.

It took me a long time to get over the manner of my departure from Saints. Initially, I tried to get my job back. I rang Jim Mallinder. I met with Keith Barwell, but Jim said, 'You walked out on your team and you can't come back.' Quite right, too. I like Jim. I wouldn't have stood for it if I were him. I have no animosity at all. I'd made my bed and I had to lie in it. I was one of the very first professional players to enter the game and therefore one of the first who had to work out how to leave a club or evolve as an employed professional. Northampton didn't have a great track record for managing tricky scenarios. Matt Dawson, still one of our star players, promptly moved to Wasps and won the Premiership title in his first season. Gary Pearce, whose shirts now decorate the walls of the clubhouse, wouldn't come back to the club for years.

I was left with little choice over where to go next. I had offers from other Premiership sides, but I'd left in my testimonial year, which was a crazy thing to do because of the salary-cap situation. If I moved to a club on a salary, say, of £100,000 per year, I also brought my testimonial pot – meaning that a new club would have that on their books, which made me a hugely expensive player for any club in 2007/08, when there was a salary cap of £2.2 million. (The following season it nearly doubled to £4 million.) I was now labelled a 'trouble-maker' and I'd take up a good lump of the budget; signing me was not an attractive option. I challenged the situation through the Players' Association, but they squirmed. The experience showed me a very ugly side of rugby, the politics and the bullshit, and partly what I saw was my own doing. I saw a lot which dismayed me, but the experience defined me in some way. Things happen for a reason. I'd have lost everything if I'd stayed at Northampton. I regret the way I handled it, but I don't regret leaving. It changed me into the person I am today – and going to Brive in south-west France took me out of that bubble of being a local lad who'd only played for his club.

The invitation from Brive was a godsend. It had been prompted by Steve Thompson – my old pal Wally – who had gone there to take up a recruitment and coaching role after the heartbreak of having to retire through injury. The club, which was bumping around towards the bottom of the league, was bankrolled by Daniel Derichebourg, a self-made billionaire. In late November, I flew to Paris to meet him and Simon Gillham, the English vice-president of the club. I remember sitting in one of the little restaurants on the Place du Tertre near the Sacré Coeur with Abby's dad, eating snails and doing the calculations on my contract. I was lucky there was virtually exchange rate parity between sterling and the euro, which worked in my favour as the recession had affected a property development business I'd started as well as a few of my testimonial events. Playing for Brive would solve a lot of problems.

I expected a culture shock in France, but not as I found it. I couldn't believe it when I walked into the changing-room and saw a Nespresso machine centre stage. Strong coffee before a game was a ritual, and the French players would pop out of the exit door to have a cigarette on the back pitch. I was thrown by what seemed to me a lack of professionalism. Pre-match preparation for me was very different from an espresso and a fag! This was a changing-room, a place to go to get your mind set for a game.

In many ways, though, the club looked after the players well. All our kit was washed for us (this never happened at Northampton or later at Sale) and we were given our own boxes of coffee capsules, according to our preference! Early on I won a Man of the Month award. Instead of the standard magnum of champagne or a meal for two at a restaurant, my prize was a live bloody goat! Even the French guys were shocked. Tethered to the radiator next to me in the changing-room, the poor thing was scared stiff. Was I supposed to take it home as a pet? Some months players got chickens.

The club needed the injection of a big-name signing. It was easy for me to slip into my rescue hero role. I was signed because they were in a very difficult position in the league, and my arrival lifted the squad. Simon Gillham would say I saved the club that season. We avoided relegation. They paid me handsomely and it was a matter of pride for me to give back on the pitch in equal measure. My first game was away to Dax and I played in the centre because they didn't have any centres. In the course of 80 minutes I went from hero to zero and back again. I was sin-binned, scored a try and got into a fight. The Brive fans loved it – here was an English mercenary who was wearing the Brive shirt for the first time and fighting with passion. They were prouder of me for taking a hit for Brive than for scoring the try. We won the game on a last-minute penalty awarded after my altercation, and the supporters were elated because we hadn't won away from home for something like three years. And because it was close to Christmas the players were given a free turkey. It was bloody nuts.

I found the coaching style a challenge. It was totally alien to me. We'd spend an hour chipping the ball over each other, stringing passes together and jogging around the local park. There was a lack of rigour and guidance, but Brive had won the

Heineken Cup in the 1990s. They were a team that had been there, done it, and lost their way.

Away games involved long, long drives. I quickly learnt what a big and beautiful country France is. I wish now that I had bought into their culture more, but I wasn't in the right mental state. I couldn't get away from the feeling I had been irresponsible in the way I had left the Saints. It was my home-town club, the hub of all my rugby aspirations, and to have left with rancour felt shameful. I found that very hard to come to terms with. Also I was conscious that I'd dragged my wife out to south-west France with our three-month-old twins. I was the breadwinner and felt I'd made the right choice, given the limited options available – and I took her to a lovely part of the world – but it was very hard with small babies. One was sleeping; one wasn't. We weren't getting any sleep; it was brutal. It played on my mind that I'd forced this move on Abby at a time when we needed a lot of support with the babies. Neither of us spoke the language – my deafness is an issue when it comes to picking up a foreign language – and that left us isolated. Brive paid for Abby's horse to be shipped out and stabled nearby, but the horse didn't settle either. In the end Abby and the girls went home and I found myself flogging back and forth on motorways – a 1,300-mile round trip – to spend time with them between games. Otherwise I spent evenings in France with Tim Exeter and his family. Tim, the former Saints strength and conditioning coach, had joined Brive for the start of the 2008/09 season. I felt bad on a domestic level and bad about my severed relationship with Northampton. I'd left my comfort zone – an easy life, easy money at my home club where I'd grown up. I'd walked out, and it took time to come to terms with that.

Rugby again provided some solace. I enjoyed the camaraderie with the Brive team. I wanted to fulfil the spirit as well as the letter of my contract and give value for money. I felt I had to perform. I had the fans chanting my name after my third game. I broke a bone in my foot, which was painful and I couldn't change direction, but I continued playing. I wanted to be seen to be a committed club player and help them do well. One young player I helped nurture, Alexis Palisson, went on to play for France. I was happy to pass on my tips and experience. We did have some laughs. On one of my journeys back to Northampton, I was stopped by the police for speeding in my Renault Espace. The police took my licence off me there and then. I came back to find a picture pinned up on the changing-room wall titled 'Ben Cohen's new car!' It was an image Tim had found on eBay of a little *Voiture Sans Permis*, practically a lawnmower, which with typical Gallic humour had been painted with Go Faster stripes. I wish I'd been in a better place to enjoy it more but, on a daily basis, I was feeling conflicted, and emotional discomfort is draining. I was walking through a supermarket one day lost in thought about something trivial and it suddenly occurred to me to ask Dad for his advice. I recall my hand going to my phone … I must have been tired.

I learnt a lot about myself in France in every way. I wish I had been in a position where I could have embraced the cultural differences more. The move extracted me from the bubble I'd lived in at Northampton. I could have stayed and said, 'Yes sir, no sir,' but I would have been living a bullshit life. It wasn't until I left that I was appreciated for being more of a player than I was. I'd felt I was taken for granted at Northampton. I got paid ten times as much in France. At the end of my second season, Brive finished fifth. Job done for me. I needed to reunite with my family and I signed for Sale.

I liked the set-up at Sale and felt lucky to go there. They'd done well in the Heineken Cup and had great players like Charlie Hodgson and Richard Wigglesworth. I got on with my rugby, made good friends and settled into a routine, commuting between Northampton and Manchester. I stayed up there one night a week and the night before a game, and I had Wednesdays off. It was brilliant. I wanted Abby and the girls to stay rooted at home, so I drove 140 miles each way for two years. I'd leave at 5.45am to get there by 7.15am and in the car I listened to a host of audiobooks: all the Harry Potters, Stig Larsson's 'The Girl with the Dragon Tattoo' trilogy, the History of England, Ian Rankin, Dan Brown, autobiographies by Andre Agassi and Richard Branson. I loved driving along, thinking and dreaming. My dad was a dreamer too. It sounds crazy as a world champion to say I felt a loser, but I did. I've never felt life's easy and when I was leaving the Saints, I remember turning around and saying,

'I'm not going to enjoy my thirties.' I realised I find it hard to live life in the moment; I appreciate great times only when I look back at them. Is that a sportsman's mentality, I wonder? You have great moments in a game, but you don't allow yourself to enjoy them until after the final whistle?

I ended the 2010/11 season at Sale as 'Player of the Year', but had already been told I was surplus to requirements. I was playing great rugby and for weeks had been led to believe my contract would be renewed, but then, Director of Rugby Steve Diamond told me they wanted to spend money on other areas of the pitch, and I got that. I had other offers on the table, but I felt it was time for a change of direction in my life. But where do I go? What do I do? I started to think about doing something more meaningful with my life, but was this the right time to make that step? I thought perhaps I could put my status as a gay icon to good use! I'd had no idea I had such a standing until 2007, when I got a call from a guy called Laurent in Paris who had set up a Facebook fan page dedicated to me. He rang to inform me I had 37,000 followers.

'Wow,' I said. 'Are you sure? Why me, in France?'

'What you need to know about the 37,000 is that they are all men,' he said.

'Oh, why's that then? Don't any ladies like me?' I said light-heartedly.

I still hadn't clicked, and he had to spell it out. My status apparently originated from a Sloggi advertising campaign, organised by Harvey Thorneycroft back in 2001 – a job I only got because Dan Luger turned it down!

In 2010 I released a sexy calendar which featured shirtless and shower shots, as well as some more artistic poses. It brought in a huge amount of money, which I could see I could put to charitable use and so it has become an annual publication. The first thought was that I could use my status as a world champion and a straight man to help bridge the gap between the gay and straight rugby communities by launching an acceptance tour in the United States. I felt comfortable about my sexuality, so I had no problem presenting myself as a figurehead to try and make a difference in breaking down stereotypes. I flew to New York to meet a guy called Patrick Davis, from the Atlanta Bucks, a rugby club which welcomes gay and diverse communities. The plan was that I would tour the United States with the Bucks. He thought he was meeting Ben Cohen Management, but found me, and it couldn't have been a more fortuitous encounter. Patrick is a leader in the field of brand development. He chatted away for 15 minutes about ways in which I could establish my charitable foundation and build a commercial enterprise to support it. It was straightforward business advice to him, but his words cut deep. I was so emotional on realising there was something positive I could contribute to help a lot of people in pain, that I broke down. I couldn't believe it. I'd felt such a loser for so long.

To cut a long story short, the process of launching the Stand Up Foundation in Atlanta and undertaking that tour of the States with the Bucks totally overwhelmed me. I drew significant crowds, not just gay fans, but all sorts of people and families who sought me out as someone to stand up and say that bullying was wrong. My perception of myself as a retiring rugby player and gay icon shifted into something much wider. I met a bi-racial family whose kid was being horrendously bullied; I listened to the parents of an autistic child who was the victim of awful abuse. Later I'd meet the mother of a child so badly bullied at school that he bled internally from the stress he was forced to absorb. These stories struck me at a visceral level. Members of the gay, lesbian and transgender community said repeatedly, 'If only there had been someone like you when I was coming to terms with my sexuality I might still have a relationship with my mother or father.' I realised there were so many people who couldn't be open for fear of losing the love of their own parents; I was horrified to realise that so many people feel beside themselves for not being able to be true to themselves. I tried to imagine how I'd feel if my girls couldn't share something with me for fear it would break our bond. How can anything break a parent-child bond?

The stories choked me, I just came apart. 'I've got to get my head around all this,' I said to Patrick, backstage in the green room at a Nike event. I suddenly saw that the Ben Cohen Stand Up Foundation could be a new, all-consuming purpose I could channel my good energy into. I came back from that trip buzzing. And that's what I've tried to do – to turn Stand Up into a global force for good. There are plenty of foundations operating that support anti-bullying in all fields and LGBT issues, but this is the first dedicated to funding real-world work in the field. Patrick showed me that the process of setting it up and developing it was part of my mourning, and that made sense. What was drawing me to it so passionately was the opportunity to promote equality and make a stand against violent, bullying behaviour. I could draw upon the pain I still felt about my dad to tackle the elephant in the room – homophobia, transphobia, the whole gay issue. I was used to being expected to play the hero on the rugby field. Here, I could rescue people from a life of pain. It was something I could trail-blaze.

My decision to retire from rugby was quite tortured. Is now a good moment? Are the platforms aligned? I'd like to have been more prepared to make the transition from professional sport to business. It wasn't exactly how I would have wanted to do it, but, like Dad, I'm not risk-averse, I do like a challenge and I need to make things happen for myself. I started to realise that in trying to keep the show on the road – my rugby dreams, my mum, my club, my country and latterly my own little family – I'd had to grow up overnight, in public, aged 21 without the luxury of ever taking time for myself. All those years I'd been driven by something very dark and sad under the surface. I'd been mourning on the pitch, and now, in my retirement from rugby, it was time to start healing by pouring my positive energies into an honourable purpose and becoming a person of impact for good.

The sign of a good parent is the legacy they inspire their children to continue. It is impossible to quantify the impact of what happened to my dad on our family, but, in the case of me and my siblings, our chosen career paths say a lot about how deeply his death affected us and how we have chosen to keep his values alive. We are all pursuing careers we would never have considered back in 2000. Justin is now a police officer working to reduce violence on the streets who also specialises in family liaison with victims of crime. My sister Sam thought about re-training as a midwife, but has now qualified as a paramedic. My mum, who took almost ten years to regain her equanimity, is a carer for dementia patients as well as being a brilliant grandmother. She has a gift with children; my girls absolutely adore her.

For 11 years, I never allowed myself to grieve. I seldom went to Dad's grave, because it wasn't where he should be at the age of 58. Visiting the cemetery made me feel vulnerable. Instead, I poured my emotions into my rugby and never shed a tear. The process of perfecting aspects of my game created some sort of order while my mind was in turmoil. The physicality of rugby, and the satisfaction in making crucial tackles, gave me a feeling of accomplishing a noble feat, protecting my side from the menace of the opposition. Making an emotional connection between what I'd lost and what I could gain from pushing myself to the limits helped me keep the rugby journey I shared with Dad on track. But it wasn't until I'd hung up my boots and stored the shirts I respected so much that I was able to start healing inwardly. I later put my shirts up on the walls of my home gym so my girls see them and I, too, have a daily reminder of some good memories. (For the record, I had long ago returned my England shirts to the Old Scouts, where they now hang, beautifully framed.)

Every week I hear stories of bullying and violence in schools, offices and homes, on the streets, in different communities, and I am moved to make a difference. To become a rugby world champion required a strong body; to challenge bullying requires strong character, and I want to encourage everyone to stand up for what is right. Most sportsmen retire and want to carry on with one strand of their life from sport. It may be the crowd-pleasing element they crave, a lifestyle they want to uphold or the buzz of live competition they seek to replace. I don't feel I'm a typical retired world champion. Winning the World Cup was the greatest time of my life, no question. I am proud of my rugby achievements, but I don't feel they define me as a person. I don't feel like a guy who's come out top in life. I'm still a guy who is learning and trying to give my all – and I like the idea that my success in the no. 11 shirt carries a resonance which might inspire other people to find the strength to be themselves.

THANKS

Ben's Thanks

I've been lucky enough to have the support of so many people, both professionally and personally, and there really are too many to name. You've got me through some tough times, and you all know who you are.

Thank you to my family for always being there for me.

For her help writing this book I'd like to thank Sarah Edworthy. And thanks to my editors at Ebury, Liz Marvin and Andrew Goodfellow.

Sarah Edworthy's Thanks

Thanks to the following for talking through memories and sharing their insights (in alphabetical order): George Cohen, Justin Cohen, Lana Cohen, Sam Cohen, Bill Conisbee, Patrick T. Davis, Matt Dawson, Tim Exeter, Simon Gillham, Alan Hughes, Paul Larkin, Sir Ian McGeechan, David Palethorpe, Phil

Pask, Tim Rodber, Wayne Smith, Harvey Thorneycroft, Sir Clive Woodward. Thank you also to Niall Edworthy, Hugh Copping at Sport Radar for statistical info and to my agent David Luxton of David Luxton Associates.

PICTURE CREDITS

THE STANDUP
FOUNDATION

The Ben Cohen StandUp Foundation is the world's first foundation dedicated to raising awareness of the long-term, damaging effects of bullying, and funding those doing real-world work to stop it. We stand up against bullying regardless of to whom it happens. We are funded through donations and work collaboratively to help connect communities to create a world of tolerance, understanding and kindness.

To find out more, go to www.standupfoundation-uk.org